THE African Diaspora IN CANADA

THE African Diaspora IN CANADA

Negotiating Identity & Belonging

Edited by
Wisdom J. Tettey & Korbla P. Puplampu

UNIVERSITY OF
CALGARY
PRESS

©2005 by Wisdom J. Tettey and Korbla P. Puplampu
Published by the University of Calgary Press
2500 University Drive NW, Calgary, Alberta, Canada T2N 1N4
www.uofcpress.com

The University of Calgary Press acknowledges the financial support of the Government
of Canada through the Book Publishing Industry Development Program (BPIDP) for our
publishing activities. We acknowledge the support of the Canada Council for the Arts for our
publishing program. We also acknowledge the support of the Alberta Foundation of the
Arts for this published work.

Canada   Canada Council   Conseil des Arts
          for the Arts   du Canada

LIBRARY AND ARCHIVES CANADA CATALOGUING IN PUBLICATION

   The African diaspora in Canada : negotiating identity and
belonging / edited by Wisdom J. Tettey & Korbla P. Puplampu.

(Africa, missing voices series)
Includes bibliographical references and index.
ISBN-10 1-55238-175-7
ISBN-13 978-1-55238-175-5

   1. Black Canadians—Race identity.   2. Black Canadians—Social conditions.
I. Tettey, Wisdom II. Puplampu, Korbla P. III. Series.

FC106.B6A373 2005   305.896'071   C2005-906297-5

Cover design by Mieka West.
Page design & typsetting by Elizabeth Gusnoski.

*To Adiki and Makafui –
that they may grow up to
be accepted as bona fide
Canadians and Africans, and
that their socio-cultural and
racial backgrounds may not
be an encumbrance to full
participation in the multiple
spaces that they occupy.*

Contents

List of Tables

Acknowledgments

The fundamental building blocks for this volume are the stories and experiences of various African-Canadians who generously shared them with the authors. It is our hope that their voices in these pages will not only help to elucidate the quotidian realities that attend the lives of African-Canadians, but will also provide the catalyst for the necessary social, political, and policy reforms that will enable them to fully participate in the multiple spaces they occupy.

We wish to express our appreciation to the authors who responded admirably to the call to fill the gap in the literature regarding the specific circumstances of continental Africans in Canadian society. Their invaluable contributions help bring a wealth of empirical insights to the issues they address. The theoretical perspectives and analytical tools they bring to bear on those discussions have significance beyond the specificities of the African experience in Canada. For their contribution of novel ideas to intellectual inquiry and to our understanding of diasporas, we are grateful.

Other people deserve recognition for contributing in diverse ways towards making this project a reality. They include the Director of the University of Calgary Press, Walter Hildebrandt, and his staff, whose invaluable support has allowed readers to access the material contained herein. We are particularly thankful to the following: Kellie Moynihan (Grants Writer), who worked assiduously on getting funding for the publication; and John King (Senior Editor, Acquisitions) for his tireless work on the manuscript. Jo-Ann Cleaver also deserves our gratitude for her sharp editorial eyes and understanding during the copy-editing stage of the process. To the anonymous reviewers whose critiques and suggestions helped strengthen the quality of the work, we say "thank you." We are also grateful to Eunice Mahama who worked hard to ensure that the manuscript followed the publisher's guidelines.

This book has been published with the help of a grant from the Canadian Federation for the Humanities and Social Sciences, through the Aid to Scholarly Publications Programme, using funds provided by the Social Sciences and Humanities Research Council of Canada. We are thankful for this support.

Our profound appreciation goes to our spouses, Natasha and Nuerki. Your support and sacrifices throughout this project once again made the road easier to navigate. For this, we owe you yet another huge debt of gratitude.

Notes on Contributors

Ali A. Abdi is an associate professor in the Department of Educational Policy Studies at the University of Alberta. His areas of research include comparative and international education; citizenship and development education; cultural studies in education; African philosophies of education; and postcolonial studies in education. His academic articles have appeared in such scholarly journals as *Comparative Education, Compare: A Journal of Comparative Education, McGill Journal of Education, Journal of Black Studies, Journal of Educational Thought*, and *Journal of Postcolonial Education*. He is the author of *Culture, Education and Development in South Africa: Historical and Contemporary Perspectives*.

Henry M. Codjoe is the Director of Institutional Research and Planning at Dalton State College, Georgia, and an adjunct assistant professor of social science in the Division of Social Sciences. His areas of research include the education of Africans in the diaspora; race and ethnic relations; and multicultural and anti-racist education. He has published in several academic journals, including *Race, Ethnicity and Education, Review of Human Factor Studies*, and *International Journal of Curriculum and Instruction*. He has also contributed chapter essays in books, such as *Inequality in Canada: Intersections of Gender, Race, and Class, Critical Perspectives on Politics and Socio-Economic Development in Ghana, Talking about Identity: Encounters in Race, Ethnicity, and Language*, and *Portraits of Human Behaviour and Performance*.

George S. Dei is a professor and the Chair of the Department of Sociology and Equity Studies in Education of the University of Toronto (OISE/UT). His research interests are in the areas of anti-racism; minority schooling; international development; and anti-colonial thought. He has published extensively in leading academic journals, such as *British Journal of Sociology of Education, Race, Gender and Class Studies, Canadian Journal of Development Studies, Canadian Journal of Education*, and *African Development*. His most recent books are *Playing the Race Card: White Power and Privilege* (with Leeno Karumanchery and Nisha Karumanchery) and *Schooling in Africa: The Case of Ghana*. Other publications include *Anti-Racism Education: Theory and Practice, Hardships and Survival in Rural West Africa, Reconstructing 'Drop-Out': A Critical Ethnography of the Dynamics of Black Students' Disengagement from School* (with Josephine Mazzuca, Elizabeth McIsaac, and Jasmine Zine), and *Indigenous Knowledge in Global Contexts* (with Budd Hall and Dorothy Goldin-Rosenberg).

John E. Hayfron teaches economics at Coquitlam College and Douglas College in Vancouver. He is also a senior researcher at the Vancouver Centre of Excellence in Immigration at Simon Fraser University. His fields of interest are applied labour economics and the economics of immigration. He has published a number of articles in international journals, such as *Applied Economics* and *Journal of Population Economics*.

Martha K. Kumsa is an assistant professor in the Faculty of Social Work at Wilfrid Laurier University. She is a former journalist who spent ten years (1980–89) in prison in Ethiopia and was released with the help of Amnesty International and PEN International. Her research is in the area of identity, cohesion, home(land) and belonging among refugee and immigrant communities in the diaspora; globalization, global homogenization and local fragmentation; reflexive learning; libratory practice; and transformatory community practice. She has published academic articles in *Affilia: Journal of Women and Social Work* and *Journal of Oromo Studies*. Her prose and poetry have appeared in *Fiery Spirits, Let my People Go!, Qunnamtii,* and the *Canadian Centre for Victims of Torture Newsletter,* as well as autobiographical pieces in *PEN Canada Newsletter* and the *Ryerson Review of Journalism.*

Samuel A. Laryea is a senior economist with the Labour Market Policy Research Unit in the Department of Human Resources and Skills Development, Government of Canada. His publications and research interests cover a wide range of issues, including the labour market impacts of immigration; Canada's brain drain to the United States; and developmental issues pertaining to Sub-Saharan African countries. He has published in *Review of Human Factor Studies,* and his latest publication (with Don J. DeVoretz) appears in *European Migration: What Do We Know?*

Philomina Okeke-Ihejirika is an associate professor in the Department of Women's Studies at the University of Alberta. Her research interests are in gender and development (Africa); gender, race, and class in education/work and development; the political economy of feminist scholarship; international feminist debates; and feminist theorizing. She has published extensively in leading academic journals, such as *Development and Change, Journal of Postcolonial Education,* and *Africa Today.* She also has contributions in books, such as *Globalizing Africa* and *"Wicked" Women and the Reconfiguration of Gender in Africa.* She is currently working with Denise Spitzer on a SSHRC-funded research project that examines transnational identities and activism among African women in Alberta.

Korbla P. Puplampu is in the Department of Psychology and Sociology at Grant MacEwan College. His research interests are in the global restructuring of agriculture and higher education; the theoretical limitations of state and non-state institutions in social change; identity politics in multicultural societies; and the politics of knowledge production and propagation. He has published articles in academic journals, such as *Teaching in Higher Education, African Studies Review, Review of African Political Economy,* and *Canadian*

Journal of Development Studies. He co-edited *Critical Perspectives on Politics and Socio-Economic Development in Ghana* (with Wisdom Tettey and Bruce Berman), and he also has essays in several books, including *Globalization and the Human Factor: Critical Insights, The International Development Program of Activities: What Are We Doing Wrong?, Globalizing Africa,* and *Portraits of Human Behaviour and Performance.*

Denise L. Spitzer is a medical anthropologist and an assistant professor in the Department of Anthropology at the University of Alberta. She is interested in the impact of, and resistances to, marginalization of the body; gender; transnational identities; and health discourses. Her work has focussed primarily on the experiences of immigrant and refugee women in Canada. She has published numerous articles in academic journals, such as *Atlantis: A Women's Studies Journal, Gender & Society, Qualitative Health Research,* and *Western Journal of Nursing Research.* She also has chapter essays in several books, including *Care and Consequences: Women and Health Reform* and *Hot Flashes: Women Writers on the Change of Life.* She is currently working with Philomina Okeke-Ihejirika on a SSHRC-funded research project that examines transnational identities and activism among African women in Alberta.

Wisdom J. Tettey is an associate professor in the Faculty of Communication and Culture at the University of Calgary. His research interests include the state and public policy in Africa; new information and communications technologies; the mass media and democratic transitions; race, ethnicity, and citizenship; and diaspora politics. He has published extensively on these areas in academic journals, such as *Canadian Journal of Development Studies, Perspectives on Global Development and Technology, Journal of Asian and African Studies,* and *Media, Culture and Society.* He co-edited *Critical Perspectives on Politics and Socio-Economic Development in Ghana* (with Korbla Puplampu and Bruce Berman) and *Asia – Who Pays for Growth? Women, Environment, and Popular Movements* (with Jayant Lele). He also has chapter essays in several books, including *Globalization and the Human Factor: Critical Insights, African Media Cultures: Transdisciplinary Perspectives* and *A Passion for Identity: An Introduction to Canadian Studies.*

Adenike O. Yesufu is in the Department of Psychology and Sociology at Grant MacEwan College. Her research interests include international and global studies; peace studies; intercultural education and communication; ethnic and multicultural studies; and gender and native studies. Her publications have appeared in *International Journal of Curriculum and Instruction, International Journal of Humanities and Peace,* and *International Multiculturalism 1998: Preparing Together for the Twenty-First Century.*

SECTION I

Theorizing & Historicizing
the 'African-Canadian' Experience

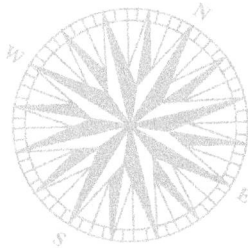

1

CONTINENTAL AFRICANS IN CANADA:
Exploring a Neglected Dimension
of the *African-Canadian* Experience

Wisdom J. Tettey & Korbla P. Puplampu

INTRODUCTION

OVER THE LAST FEW YEARS, the world has witnessed an unparalleled intensification of, and expansion in, transnational migration. It has been estimated that by the mid-1990s, more than 100 million people had taken up residence in countries different from those in which they had been born (*The Economist* 1997, 81; Wiener 1996, 128). As we enter the twenty-first century, indications are clear that the trend will continue. Figures for Canada point to the fact that, by the close of the last century, the country was recording about 200,000 immigrants annually, the highest since the early 1900s (Ley 1999).

As the processes of globalization simultaneously constrain and open up opportunities for Africans, they have responded in ways that have turned them into active participants in this phenomenon of transmigration. Economic mismanagement by governments, the structural location of the continent in the global capitalist system, and neo-liberal policy prescriptions from international financial institutions continue to peripheralize its economies to an extent that creates extensive economic hardships for a significant number of people (see Smith 2003; Amin 2002; Cheru 2002). In some countries, this situation is fused with political turmoil resulting from civil wars, political instability, ethnic conflict, and political persecution. This panoply of factors has compelled many Africans to seek better economic opportunities and/or political sanctuary abroad.

Other dimensions of globalization have enhanced their ability to realize these objectives. These include the constriction of time and space and the resulting interconnectedness made possible by innovations in air travel and in communication technologies, such as the Internet. Cultural globalization also means that it is possible for Africans to pursue professional and educational opportunities outside their countries of origin because of the increasing affinities across systems. The imperatives foisted by the push factors and the opportunities promised by the pull factors are responsible for the increasing numbers of African immigrants in the industrialized world, including Canada. Consequently, the demographics of the African diaspora in Canada reflect the varying motivations behind emigration from the continent.

The concept of *diaspora* has multiple meanings; thus its application to the African population in Canada requires further explication. In one sense, it refers to a description of movement and location in the context of globalization. It also denotes a social condition and the processes that characterize it (see Anthias 2001). In the past, the concept has been applied to a group of people who were forcibly and/or violently compelled to leave their original domiciles and settle elsewhere. The classic example of this pattern of movement is captured by the case of the Jewish people. In the contemporary meaning, the term encapsulates a group of people who have a common geographical origin, have trans-located through migratory patterns occasioned either by the forces of globalization and/or domestic stress, and share identifiable markers (e.g., ethnicity), a collective consciousness, and common experiences in their new locales. In this volume, we use the concept in its second meaning; that is,

> a people with a common origin who reside, more or less on a permanent
> basis, outside the borders of the ethnic or religious homeland – whether
> that homeland is real or symbolic, independent or under foreign control.
> Diaspora members identify themselves, or are identified by others – inside
> and outside their homeland – as part of the homeland national community,
> and as such are often called upon to participate, or are entangled, in home-
> land-related affairs. (Shain and Barth 2003, 452)

In view of this definition, the question arises as to who qualifies to be designated as part of the African diaspora in Canada. Tettey (2001) addresses the conceptual difficulties and political contestations surrounding the applicability of the term to various groups and individuals who have some connection to Africa, whether imagined or manifested in concrete and verifiable linkages. There is, however, a paucity of literature addressing the complexities implied by these contestations. Indeed, not all Africans are Black, nor do all Black people consider themselves Africans (Tettey 2001). As Mensah (2002, 60–61) correctly argues, "while most of the immigrants from Western African countries ... are likely to be Blacks, the same cannot be inferred about immigrants from Northern, Southern, and Eastern African countries. North Africans ... usually consider themselves, and are best described as, Arabs. Also, immigrants from South Africa are just as likely to be White, Indian, or Coloured as they are to be Black. The situation among Eastern Africans is equally complicated by the large number of Europeans, Arabs, and Asians, particularly East Indians, in that part of Africa." The conceptual ambiguity that results from these contestations of African identity therefore needs to be clarified for analytical and policy purposes, in order to adequately understand the specific circumstances of the continental African-Canadian population and to appropriately respond to it as a community. The next section will attempt to unravel the distinctions among the Black and African populations in Canada. The analysis will demonstrate the complexities that we are referring to here and make the case for why it is useful to engage in more nuanced analyses across the spectrum represented by those designations.

One consequence of the inflexibility of differentiation, because of the over-emphasis on race, for example, is the scant attention paid to continental Africans as an autonomous focus of academic inquiry. Unlike Asian or Caribbean immigrants in Canada about whom there is quite an appreciable amount of literature, continental Africans have generally not been the specific focus of many research endeavours. It is worth noting that this intellectual marginalization has occurred in the United States, as well. In her analysis of the literature on Black Africans in the United States, Halter (1998), for example, notes the inflexibility of census data collection patterns in differentiating among the contemporary Black American population. She contends that research on the country's Black population tends to privilege the "Americanicity of the research cohort," or it overly focuses on the in-migration patterns of people from English- and Spanish-speaking Caribbean countries. Consequently, as D'Alisera (2003, 190) observes in her critique of Matsuoka and Sorenson's *Ghosts and Shadows*,

> the complex juxtapositions that inform everyday lives in the diaspora are left unexplored, providing little insight into how these [African populations] organize meaning and action in displacement, or how complex juxtapositions of cultural forms that are shaped by the autonomous and comprehensive interplay between here and there, and everywhere play themselves out in the daily lives of the authors' informants. *Ghosts and Shadows* leaves us haunted by the past, but still wondering about the present.

The purpose of this book is to take up the challenge posed by these gaps in the literature, and to interrogate the specificities of the experiences of continental Africans in Canada. We hope, with this effort, to add to the sparse literature on this group (see, e.g.,, Mensah 2002; Leblanc 2002; Matsuoka and Sorenson 2001; Wong 2000; Konadu-Agyemang 1999; Rousseau et al. 1998; Manuh 1998). Furthermore, we hope to advance the process of engaging with this community as a worthwhile focus of intellectual discourse, quite independent of the homogenizing tendencies exemplified by writings about the Black community. It is important to point out that we recognize the affinities among members of the Black community, and indeed, among immigrant groups, as shown by the comparative analyses provided in the chapters. The undertaking that is represented by the volume is thus not an exercise in particularism or relativism, but a legitimate endeavour to highlight the specificities of the target communities, while providing critical insights into the dialectical conjunctures that allow us to understand the nuances and subtleties that differentiate immigrant groups across a variety of identity markers. These chapters also make significant contributions to the broader theoretical and conceptual literature through the critiques and novel perspectives that are brought to bear on the study of diasporas in the context of globalization and intensified transnationalism.

DEFINING *AFRICAN-CANADIAN*: INTERROGATING THE CONCEPTUAL CHALLENGES OF IDENTITY

The term *African-Canadian* is often used in everyday parlance and in the academic literature as an uncontested signifier of identity capturing all peoples of African origin in Canada. A critical effort to unpack the term, however, reveals that it is a very complex and contested concept that defies the presumed consensus of meaning implied in its usage, as well as the homogeneity of shared origin that members of the group have. Tettey (2001, 165) contends that "the lack of concurrence about interpretations of who is covered by the term results from the fact that *Africanness* as an identity is defined by several criteria that are not necessarily congruent." In order to interrogate the basis for the competing, sometimes conflicting, claims to Africanness, we adopt Tettey's (2001) framework that isolates four approaches for understanding the rationales on which avowed and ascribed notions of incorporation or exclusion are founded. These are (1) The Immigration Authorities Approach; (2) The Black equals African/African equals Black Approach; (3) The Self-Exclusion Approach; and (4) The Authentic African Approach.

The first approach derives from the nomenclature used by Canadian state institutions, such as Citizenship and Immigration Canada. It is based on formal citizenship that designates anyone who arrives in Canada with a passport issued by an African country as an African. It is also informed by a geographical construct, whereby immigrants who claim origins in an African country, such as refugees and others without official documentation, are classified as African. The classification of African-Canadians on the basis of formal citizenship and geography has, however, been criticized by those who argue that it is exclusionary. The critics content that Africanness is an innate characteristic that should not be denied because one does not fit into a territorial conception of origin, whether geographical or political. Among those who support an expanded notion of Africanness, and hence African-Canadian, are groups and individuals who avow their identity as African because of their belief in some spiritual or ancestral link to the continent, even though that connection cannot be definitively demonstrated. Descendants of African slaves in Canada who have lived in Canada for generations (since the seventeenth century) claim a legitimate right to be called African-Canadian for this reason; so do Caribbean and South American Blacks who have immigrated to Canada since the mid-twentieth century.

The need to broaden the definition of African-Canadian serves as the foundation for the second approach; Black equals African/African equals Black. This approach racializes African identity and is atavistic in terms of its assumptions about African identity. The logic in this argument is that all Black people originate from Africa and hence can claim African identity because of their genealogical origin in the continent, even if the basis for their assertion is remote or imagined. For proponents of this approach,

> [B]lack people in the diaspora should be recognized as Africans. In fact,
> some of them go as far as to argue that they are more qualified to be called
> African-Canadians than non-[B]lacks who may be recent immigrants from
> Africa but whose ancestral roots do not go as deep as those of Blacks in the
> [d]iaspora. This view ... comes from a belief in, and expression of a [B]lack
> consciousness and an identification with Africa. These internalized link-
> ages to the continent define their African-Canadian heritage. (Tettey 2001
> 165–66)

In response to this view, others have argued that, notwithstanding the historical and cultural linkages between diaspora Blacks with no immediate genealogical ties with the continent and the continental African born, it is important to acknowledge the differences that set them apart. Critiquing the notion of pan-African identity from which the Black equals African/African equals Black approach derives its inspiration, Adeleke (1998) contends that continental Africans and their non-African-born cousins in the diaspora occupy different realities in terms of their collective daily circumstances, struggles, and aspirations. Referring specifically to the relationship between African-Americans and their continental African counterparts, he opines that "[r]egardless of the degree of African cultural retentions, regardless of how far Black Americans went in changing their names and wearing African clothes, they remain, in large part, products of the American historical experience, an experience that has left its mark indelibly on Black American culture and identity" (Adeleke 1998, 187). Jones (1995) pursues a similar critique when he observes that descendants of North American, Black slaves cannot clearly identify their ethnic roots in Africa, nor can they express themselves in the cultural forms, such as language, of their African-born counterparts. Consequently, the arguments goes, their only basis for claiming an African identity is constrained to "a nebulous construct – Africa as a geographical entity, a racial origin, and a cultural imagination" (Tettey 2001, 166).

It is further argued that the different life experiences of the two groups inform their perspectives on a variety of issues in ways that sometimes conflict. Adeleke (1998) alludes to the animosity that simmers between African-Americans and recent African immigrants, as the former resent the latter for being undeserving beneficiaries of the fruits of civil rights and other socio-economic struggles, while being reluctant and/or less passionate about the causes that African-Americans consider important. In the view of these African-Americans, the lukewarm attitude of the continental African stems partly from the fact that they were not direct victims of the circumstances that underlie the kinds of passionate advocacy manifested by the former.

Another explanation that exacerbates the tension between the two groups is the reality that continental Africans in North America are generally better educated, hence more employable, than their native-born counterparts (see Djamba 1999). Competition for access to the resources of the labour market produces another wedge in the relationship between the two groups. Analysts have highlighted other distinctions between African and North American Blacks which erode the ethos of the pan-Africanist and cultural nationalist perspectives touted by the Afrocentric paradigm (see Asante 1990). Kanneh (1998, viii), for example, suggests that "modern African-American pan-Africanisms *appropriate* ideas of *Africa* for American agendas," but they tend not to engage with the African reality, and their primary loyalty is not to the continent. Beyond the debate about a shared pan-Africanism, Tettey (2001, 167) points out that

> the problem with the '[B]lack equals African/African equals [B]lack conception is that it is an exclusionary construct. It does not take cognizance of those who may not be [B]lack but whose traceable historical, culture, and cultural origins may be in Africa. Examples of these groups are East Indians and Whites from Eastern and Southern Africa who have known no other place of origin but Africa. Whilst these groups may not have originated in Africa as a racial or ethnic community, they may have no traceable origin to any other place but the continent. This may be where they call home and where they trace their roots. Out of the about 247,240 people who identified themselves as Africans in the 1996 Canadian census, about 30 percent were

Blacks, 27 percent Whites, 20 percent South Asian, and the remaining 23 percent was composed of other races ... The '[B]lack equals African/African equals [B]lack approach, therefore, effectively dismisses the African origins of [70] percent of African immigrants in Canada.

The third approach to African-Canadian identity is the self-exclusion perspective, which has two strands. The first comes from non-Blacks whose contemporary geographical origins are in Africa, while the second pertains to the children of first generation, continental African immigrants. Those incorporated into the first strand tend to contest their designation as Africans because, for them, African connotes Black. It is worth noting that even though the genotype, the invisible genetic make-up of human types, is the same across all groups, there is a tendency to emphasize the phenotype, the outwardly visible expression of the genes that varies across human types. This socially constructed emphasis on the latter is deeply ingrained because of the convenience it provides for creating hierarchies among humans, with attendant power imbalances. The contestation of the Black designation, then, stems from the socially constructed, negative connotations associated with the word. Things considered evil, for example, are associated with *Black*, while *White* denotes grace (see Mensah 2002, 20). These individuals, therefore, consider the arbitrary *colour* designations a more important marker of identity than geography, even though the fact is that colour designations and skin pigmentation do not match. Consequently, the Africans in this group assert their racial identity as the primary signifier of who they are, rather than their geographical, or even cultural, origins, because their skin pigmentation can be socially constructed as White, and that would secure certain mainstream privileges. Brodkin (2000) brilliantly captures the process in *How Jews Became White Folks and What That Says about Race in America*, and that process is quite different from the one Frantz Fanon (1968) addresses in *Black Skin, White Masks*. In the hierarchical formulation of identity, the individuals who invoke a racial category present a subtle distinction between being African and being from Africa.

The second dimension of the self-exclusion approach reveals the dialectical tensions between ascribed and avowed identities as far as children of African immigrants are concerned. Even though these children have verifiable genealogical ties to the continent through their parents, they do not see themselves, at least not wholly, as part of the socio-cultural milieux with which their progenitors identify. As far as they are concerned, they are *Canadian* and not African, since their values and worldviews are shaped by the *here and now*, rather than the environment from which their parents came. "Consequently, the definition of these individuals as African, based solely on the origins of their forebears or on the colour of their skin, may appear inaccurate to them" (Tettey 2001, 168). The following narrative (in the Irish context) captures the frustration of these children:

I was born and raised here. I am Irish. I don't know any other country. But now, everyone thinks I should know something about Nigeria. People want to know where I come from. Even African people expect me to be like them. They are surprised when they find out I'm Irish. But I don't identify with them. I've gone other places. But I always come back here. This is home. (White 2002, 257)

The fourth perspective from which to look at African-Canadian identity is the Authentic African approach. It provides an insightful basis for understanding assertions of, or challenges to, avowed Africanness within the demographic cohort that the immigration authorities designate as African. The contestations emanate from varying conceptions of authentic Africanness. While some have suggested that there is no homogeneous African worldview (see Hountundji 2002; Appiah 1992), there is the belief among a significant number of ordinary Africans, as well as some analysts, that there are, indeed, certain basic values that cut across all African societies. These values, they contend, constitute a common ethos that underlies African personality. Jahn (1961), for example, asserts that there is a spiritual and philosophical *common denominator* of Africanness which encapsulates the Bantu worldview shared by all sub-Saharan Africans. Abraham (1962, 42) corroborates this viewpoint when he argues that "there is a type of African culture ... this type finds expression in the art, the ethics and morality, the literary and the religious traditions, and also the social traditions of the people." Based on these perspectives about an intrinsic thread that all Africans share, anyone who does not manifest the tenets of that worldview is dismissed as not embodying the true essence of an African, and hence is not an authentic African. Consequently, those who subordinate the supposedly fundamental values of Africanness to mainstream Canadian values that do not dovetail with the former are, for example, considered to have adulterated their African identity. This calls into question their claim to a legitimate designation as African. What such ascription shows is that "there is a continuum of Africanness in which the most authentic form is manifested in a static preservation of cultural values and norms. Static preservation and adherence to the cultural values and social norms that characterize African societies is, therefore, a key manifestation of what it means to be a true African" (Tettey 2001, 168).

The Authentic African approach is the basis for the misgivings that some continental African immigrants have about the claim to Africanness by children born to African parents in Canada or those who, although born in Africa, have spent their formative years in Canada and have had their socio-cultural worldview informed by mainstream, Canadian values. The misgivings are premised on the belief that language and culture are both the central signifiers of identity and the "collective memory bank of a people's experience in history" (wa Thiongo 1987, 15). Therefore, from the perspective of advocates of the Authentic African approach, "those born in the diaspora [who] cannot speak [any] indigenous African languages, lack a deep understanding of the African experience, or do not express the ritual forms of the continent ... are more Canadian than African, and so [they] cannot legitimately claim an African identity" (Tettey 2001, 169). Adeleke (1998) also conceptualizes the logic in terms of the notion of the *sovereign power* of African culture, a power whose authority elicits obligatory responses from all Africans and adherence to which is a *sine qua non* for qualification as an African. He uses the example of filial responsibility to illustrate his argument. In the view of Adeleke and those who advocate the Authentic African perspective, Africans, irrespective of their age, are expected to defer to the authority of, and be reverent towards, their parents. Therefore, children who imbibe a different set of norms in mainstream Canadian society that encourages them to challenge the authority of their parents are perceived to be operating with a value system antithetical to the sovereign power described above. The foregoing discussion about the Authentic African perspective "highlights not only the importance of self-categorization, but also the reality that our self-categorization might not coincide with how others categorize us" (Kelly 1998, 9).

Advocates of the Authentic African approach have been criticized for basing their definition of African identity on conformity to an unchanging, singular worldview, adherence to a uniform set of values, and attitudes that are concordant with a predetermined standard. Such a supposition, or proposition, suggests that one can only belong to the African community in Canada if one identifies with particular backgrounds, historical experiences, and worldviews. It fails to recognize the significant diversity that characterizes Africans, a diversity based on race, region, religion, ethnicity, gender, and so on. Even in Africa, one would be hard pressed to find the concordant constructions that the proponents of this approach offer as the sole determinants of Africanness. As several chapters in this volume reveal, this is a flawed way of defining continental Africans in Canada, because it loses sight of the dialectics of identity construction that result in multiple identities, all of which can be legitimately claimed, as well as the contestations that emerge within what is definitely not a homogeneous community (See especially Kumsa, and Okeke-Ihejirika and Spitzer in this volume). It is important "when we talk about African-Canadians, to recognize these sub-identities and their impact on the definition of how people conceptualize themselves as Africans, the collaborations and contestations between various groups, and their relationship to the meta-identity of *African*" (Tettey 2001, 169).

In the preceding discussion, we highlighted the complexities ingrained in the term *African-Canadian*. The analysis emphasizes the need to understand "African diasporic and Black identities as historically textured and politically determined constructs, constructs which rely on particular understandings of time, memory, and race" (Kanneh 1998, 48). In the midst of this contested terrain, this book focuses on first generation, Black, continental Africans who have immigrated in the last forty years and who have traceable genealogical links to the continent. It is significant to note that they are the only group whose claim to an African-Canadian identity raises minimal, if any, objections. Furthermore, in view of the relational character of identity and the fact that it is not only avowed but ascribed, the analyses in this volume will show that these individuals and their children are likely to be characterized on the basis of race as Black African immigrants by the larger society, even if they choose to self-exclude. In the rest of the book, therefore, African-Canadian will be operationalized to mean continental, Black African immigrants and their children who have not explicitly and comprehensively chosen to self-exclude from that hyphenated identity. This definition is a departure from the omnibus categorization used by some academics and by various Canadian government agencies (including Statistics Canada), that tend to lump all Blacks together as though they were an undifferentiated mass. Admittedly, some of the analyses in the ensuing chapters of this volume are based on statistics derived from such a categorization. This use of the statistics should not, however, be construed as an endorsement of their validity as accurate measures of the situation of all Blacks, but rather, as the employment of the best proxy measures available. What our definition seeks to do is to initiate a rethinking, not only of the qualitative measures of African-Canadianness that take into account its nuances and heterogeneity, but also to engender a fundamental change in the current assumptions behind, and approaches to, quantitative data collection methods.

The rationale behind highlighting the experiences of the first generation of African immigrants within Canadian society is to address the empirical, conceptual, and methodological gaps in the literature. This study, as was pointed out above, seeks to highlight the peculiar, transnational characteristics of that group that may not be shared by other Blacks or non-Black Africans. The book also explores their children's circumstances as they try to negotiate a sense of self vis-à-vis their parents and the larger Canadian society. This latter focus is worth examining because it is germane to understanding the daily lives of the parents. The lifestyles, struggles, and aspirations of the children constitute an intrinsic part of the parents' reality.

This volume is long overdue because "as African immigrants become a visible part of the Canadian landscape, it is important that the rest of society understands their history in this country, the social constructions that have shaped that history, and the specific features that characterize the African-Canadian community" (Tettey 2001, 178). It is only through such an exercise that we can begin making viable efforts towards genuinely recognizing this group of immigrants as Canadians, not only in a legal sense, but also as a group worthy of scholarly investigation. Furthermore, an understanding of African-Canadians and an appreciation of their reality would help generate a feeling of belonging in Canada as they negotiate their multiple locations, and give them a conducive atmosphere within which to develop their abilities and hence enhance their contributions to the larger society. To provide a basis for this process of understanding, reflection, and belonging, this book addresses a number of issues that are categorized thematically into four sections.

SECTION ONE: THEORIZING AND HISTORICIZING THE AFRICAN-CANADIAN EXPERIENCE

This section synthesizes the fundamental theoretical tools for understanding, analyzing, and designing policies that recognize the multiple locations of Africans in Canada and provide appropriate responses to their integration into Canadian society. The authors link these theoretical insights to a wealth of empirical material that reveals how antecedent constructions of Blacks and Africa have shaped the dominant society's ideas about Africans and their place in Canada. The interrogation of the historical connections between Africans and Canada and the circumstances under which people of African descent and African-born immigrants became a legally accepted and recognized community within Canada provide an important context for examining the issues addressed in the other sections of the book. It is, for example, useful to explore how the dialectical tensions between ascribed and avowed constructions of identity and the valorizations that undergird those constructions shape the positionalities of African-Canadians in Canadian society and their relationships to other groups. The political dimensions of these tensions and the attendant power dynamics that flow from them are critical determinants of who gets what, when, and how (Lasswell 1958). The benefits and/or deprivations of distributional politics go a long way towards determining access to political resources and hence, power. They also determine how the nationality and citizenship of specific groups are defined in relation to the state, what cultural symbols, values, and practices are accorded pride of place, and who is included in, or excluded from, the socio-economic sphere.

In chapter two, Puplampu and Tettey examine the theoretical and political basis of identity. Identity is a contested concept, especially when it comes to accessing political, economic, and social resources, and it has implications for representation and integration. The concept of ethnicity can offer insights into the dynamics of identity. Drawing on Weber's conceptualization of ethnicity, Puplampu and Tettey examine the implications of identity for African-Canadians vis-à-vis government policies on immigration and multiculturalism. Their analysis shows a disjuncture between the rhetoric of government policies and the reality within which African-Canadians function. They argue that there is a disconnection between formal/legal notions of citizenship and the everyday constructions of the concept among mainstream Canadians and institutions. The discrepancy leads to a questioning of the authenticity of African-Canadians' claim to citizenship and stymies their full participation in their new locales. According to Puplampu and Tettey, these queries and the difficulties they generate for African-Canadians are, for example, manifested in the devaluation of knowledge and skills from Africa, as well as in the subordination of merit to the reality of political and social networking in employment situations. They also argue that policies designed to celebrate cultural differences have had unintended consequences, such as perpetuating the status of African-Canadians as *outsiders*, and hence *eternal immigrants*, despite the fact that some African-Canadians have acquired legal citizenship.

In chapter three, Abdi reflects on the historical and contemporary relationships that have structured the position of Blacks, including African-Canadians, vis-à-vis mainstream society. He argues that Blacks are currently positioned at a level within the social structure that peripheralizes them and constrains their capacity for structural transformation. He arrives at this conclusion by tracing the historical background to the contemporary circumstances of Blacks in Canada, including the political and social processes that defined their place and the resistances that they engendered. This analysis helps us to understand antecedents of interaction within which the *third wave* of Black immigration since the 1960s, including continental Black African immigration, was inserted and how they inform the contemporary location of Africans in Canada. He concludes that, although "legal racism or socially sanctioned, forced exclusion" has been neutralized, African-Canadians continue to face systemic and institutional discrimination that is subtle in form, but nonetheless constraining in effect.

SECTION TWO: LOCATION, THE POLITICS OF KNOWLEDGE CONSTRUCTION, AND THE CANADIAN EDUCATION SYSTEM

Location is a critical determinant of the perspective from which individuals and groups see themselves and others, and how they are seen in return. It also informs the value and power that they wield, or that is accorded to them, in the context of their relationships with others in the polity. Codjoe, in chapter four, addresses the politics of knowledge construction and validation in an empirical study of African students' experiences in Edmonton, Alberta. Findings from his sample population of pre-tertiary education students indicate that there has been "little effort to systematically interrogate issues and questions about the nature of knowledge, positionality, and knowledge construction." He argues that curricula in the school system reproduce structures of domination, and both marginalize and denigrate Africa, its people, its knowledge systems, and the contributions of African-Canadians. The consequence of these hegemonic curricula alienates African-Canadian students who cannot see themselves, their communities, or their histories reflected in what is supposedly a pan-Canadian body of knowledge. The chapter contends that the absence of African knowledge in the school system is a deliberate case of institutional racism. In view of the relationship between knowledge and power, Codjoe argues that knowledge has historically been constructed by the powerful to perpetuate their control over the subaltern and to prevent the emergence of ideas in the public sphere that challenge their power base. Another debilitating impact of the skewed curricula and the invisibilization of Africans is the stultification of social capital formation among the youth. This then erodes the incentive for learning and achievement engendered by seeing oneself in the curricula, as well as the social mobilization that involvement in the educational system fosters among peers and other role models within one's immediate community.

In chapter five, Dei relates some of Codjoe's arguments to an analysis of knowledge construction and validation and to authoritative voice in the Canadian academy. He employs an anti-racist theoretical framework and personal narrative to interrogate how race, class, and gender are implicated in our ways of knowing and of knowledge itself (see James 1994; Williams 1991). He shares the view that "we all speak from a particular place, out of a particular history, out of a particular experience" (Hall 1996, 447). Consequently, the knowledges that are upheld and propagated reflect specific experiences that cannot be generalized to all members of society. Unfortunately, however, knowledges that emanate from the specific experiences of the dominant *White* society are held up as indisputable facts, valid for all. Alternative ways of knowing and the experiences that shape them are denigrated, and their legitimacy as authoritative perspectives is questioned. The chapter thus advances the concept of *minoritization* and how it has been used to deny access to power and to structurally constrain the exercise of agency by minority faculty. To address these barriers, Dei advocates what he calls *structural hegemonic rupturing*. This involves resistance to the dominant power structures and forms of knowledge through concerted processes that challenge dominant discourses, advance alternative knowledges, and appropriate an authoritative voice for hitherto marginalized members of the academy.

SECTION THREE: THE SOCIO-ECONOMIC CONTEXT AND CONTESTS OF THE AFRICAN-CANADIAN EXPERIENCE

There is significant literature reinforcing the argument that ethnic minorities suffer workplace discrimination in Canada. Discrimination in this setting takes a variety of forms, including less pay than racially-dominant counterparts for commensurate work with comparable qualifications, as well as more constrained access to upward mobility (see Stodolska 1998, 545; Croucher 1997, 328; Torczyner 1997; Henry and Tator 1995, 92–96). Bloom et al. (1995), while suggesting that discrimination may not fully explain the declining absorption of recent immigrants into the Canadian labour market, acknowledge that it could provide at least part of the reason. What is striking about the situation of recent independent-class immigrants is the fact that a significant number tend to be highly qualified because of the value placed on education in the point system under which potential independent immigrants are assessed (Hou and Balakrishnan 1996). Tettey (2001, 175) suggests that

> For a lot of these highly qualified individuals, however, the prospects of se-
> curing jobs commensurate with their qualifications remain very bleak. There
> is widespread perception among African-Canadians that their continent of
> origin and the racist stereotypes that it engenders in Canada constrains their
> employment opportunities. It is true that graduates from outside Canada
> are generally not accorded the same recognition as their Canadian-educated
> counterparts. But it must be pointed out that African certificates tend to be
> on the bottom rungs of the accreditation hierarchy.

As a result of these attitudes, African immigrants, like most minority immi-grants, suffer significant earnings penalties (see Pendakur and Pendakur 1998, 531; Stelcner and Kyriazis 1995).

In chapter six, Laryea and Hayfron seek to ascertain the validity of the assertions made by the above-mentioned studies regarding the presence of a *vertical mosaic* in Canada (Porter 1965), with particular reference to the African community. They employ an econometric analysis to measure labour market performance by African-Canadians, comparing their earning differentials, ca-reer opportunities, and job satisfaction with their Canadian-born counterparts. The findings corroborate earlier work about workplace discrimination against African immigrants, as they reveal significant earnings gaps between the two groups. Laryea and Hayfron note that this earning differential exists, even though the available data show that African-born immigrants tend to have a higher level of education than their Canadian-born counterparts. Another significant finding from the study is that African-Canadians, despite their levels of educa-tion, are less likely to be employed in a highly skilled occupation, implying an underutilization of their skills. This conclusion is theoretically relevant because it calls into question the explanatory power of human capital theory. The authors argue that the theory only partially explains the employment circumstances of African-Canadians. They contend that, whilst the evidence confirms the theory's prescription that higher education is positively correlated with higher earnings, it also provides insights that reveal the limitations of the theory, that is, its in-ability to explain the earning differentials between Africans and native-born Canadians with comparable levels of education.

Yesufu continues the labour market theme in chapter seven, where she documents the daily struggle of African-Canadian women in Edmonton, a struggle complicated by structural inequalities, such as inadequate access to information, lack of social support services, and non-recognition of previous work experiences from Africa. She suggests that, in addition to facing labour market discrimination because their qualifications were earned in Africa, the women's race also seems to affect their ability to secure jobs commensurate with their qualifications. The argument is based on the fact that, even in situations where the women have pursued further training in Canada and received accreditation from recognized institutions, their chances in the labour market have not necessarily been enhanced. Most of them are therefore compelled to accept low-paying menial and/or part-time jobs. This situation puts severe pressure on these women, some of whom serve as sole breadwinners for their families. This is certainly the case where they have student husbands who are not allowed to work more than twelve hours a week on campus and are restricted from seeking employment outside their academic institutions. The limited earning capabilities of the husbands, coupled with the pressure of their academic work, leads to dependence on the women to sustain the family. With such an obligation, the women, even those with tertiary educational qualifications, are compelled to put their career aspirations on hold and take any available job in order to take care of their families.

SECTION FOUR: PLACE, *IN-BETWEEN* SPACES, AND THE NEGOTIATION OF IDENTITIES

In response to the literature on immigration espousing a zero-sum model of acculturation among trans-migrants (see Faist 2000), other authors have argued that the time-space compression that has accompanied globalization and the embodied nature of cultural practices tend to generate hybrid cultures and identities among immigrant communities. Tettey (2004, 137), for example, observes that "geographical mobility does not translate into an inevitable replacement of home cultures by host cultures ... [Transnationalism] has made it even easier for diaspora communities to maintain attachments to, and retain, their cultures and communities of origin." Faist (2000), for his part, critiques both the canonical assimilation and cultural pluralist views of cultural adjustment among immigrants, arguing that they both fail to take cognizance of processes of diffusion and syncretism that characterize contemporary migration. These include mixed languages, hybrid practices, and hyphenated, collective identities.

As a corollary to this line of argument, Lyons (2004) notes that we are seeing a world where political, social, and economic actions are not confined to the specific territories of the sovereign state in which immigrants reside, but are straddling borders as transnationals engage with their home countries in those spheres. Shami (1998, 617) sums up the reality of the contemporary world when he points out that "[d]iasporas are an increasingly important phenomenon in the *era of globalization*. Transitional networks structure and restructure economic linkages, familial bonds, cultural identities, and political mobilization." The spatio-psychological fluidity that accompanies these interactions suggests that, far from being dissociated from their places of origin, diaspora communities need to be seen as constantly evolving communities that are products of "a sociopolitical process involving negotiation of *who we are* and what it means to be *who we are* during particular performative moments," not only in the context of their host societies, but in relation to their societies of origin, as well (Tettey 2004, 137). The authors in this section provide critical analyses of the complexities of attachment, social networks, identity, and the attendant contestations that define the lives of African-Canadians as they navigate the spatio-pyschological fluidity of their deterritorialized environments.

In chapter eight, Tettey and Puplampu use *translocational positionality* as a framework for examining the connections between African-Canadians and their societies of origin. They argue that African-Canadians maintain significant linkages with home countries that cover a wide gamut of interactions, including cultural transfers, transnationalization of civil society, and the re-enactment of traditional differences in the diaspora setting. These linkages are manifested in the replication of traditions, attitudes, and rites that confirm the diaspora's avowed identity with their home communities, even as they adapt to the locales in which they are domiciled. The authors also explore the moral economy and the reciprocal obligations that come with it as a basis for the mobilization of social capital in the diaspora for developmental purposes at home. They contend, however, that despite the affinities that characterize the home-diaspora linkage, there are also areas of tension between the two milieux. These derive from the differences between the essentialized ideal of home that people in the diaspora imagine and the realities brought on by the socio-economic changes of globalization. The irony of this situation is that the more the home communities look like the world in which diasporan Africans live, the more they seem to clash in terms of expectations and perceptions of each other. Tettey and Puplampu also interrogate the discursive political spaces that African-Canadians occupy. These take the form of internal conflicts within the diaspora itself, which are largely importations of political differences from their home countries. Further evidence of the deterritorialization of domestic politics is seen in advocacy work by diaspora civil society groups against individuals and host and home governments, as well as multinational corporations whose activities are perceived to be inimical to the interests of particular groups in the home countries.

Kumsa, in chapter nine, provides a context for understanding how the interplay of local and global forces creates nation-states through processes of exclusion and inclusion, a process that then results in the production of refugees. Situating this analysis vis-à-vis the Ethiopian state, she argues that Western powers helped disenfranchise Oromos while simultaneously offering them *safe passage* into exile. She then shifts the focus to an interrogation of the lives of exiled Oromo youth in Toronto, concluding that the binary perspectives put forward by both constructionist and nativist/essentialist notions of identity fail to capture the "creative possibilities of the in-between spaces of marginality in which refugee lives are embodied and embedded" (Kumsa in this volume). She contends that Oromo youth are located in the interstices of three spheres of belonging – Canadian, Black, and Oromo – characterized by different forms of mutual tension and resulting in conflicts of identity for these youth. Their *Canadianness* is constantly questioned by those who think that their origin in another place, a place constantly denigrated by media images of poverty and war, makes their Canadian citizenship inauthentic. They share an affinity with other Black youth because of their common experience of racism vis-à-vis other groups in Canada and the racialization of identity that homogenizes all Black people. At the same time, however, they also have to contend with criticism from their Black peers who consider them not to be *Black enough*. The dialectical tensions surrounding identity for these youth are further complicated by the fragmented spaces within the diasporic Oromo community. This is manifested in Internet chat rooms, where fractures in Oromo identity are revealed through clashes in perspectives on a variety of issues based on differences in religion, region of origin in Oromia, and current location in the diaspora.

Drawing on rich narrative data from interviews and focus group discussions with the youth, Kumsa advances an alternative framework for analyzing the situation of exile communities – what she calls *dispersal affinity*. That framework allows us to capture how continuities and discontinuities of Oromia nationality and slavery affect the sense of belonging among the youth, as well as the impact of the simultaneous processes of global homogenization and local fragmentation on identity. Finally, it provides an appreciation of the dialectical processes of negotiation between the self and the community that create possibilities for multiple assertions of identity – at once conflictual and concordant with the group.

In chapter ten, Okeke-Ihejirika and Spitzer address the intergenerational experiences of African-Canadian youth, specifically young women. The authors situate their work in critical feminist scholarship and find considerable tension and conflict in the relationship between African parents and their children, whether born elsewhere or in Canada. In either case, the authors show that the young women take their parents as a frame of reference to shape their behaviour, values, expectations, and aspirations. Nevertheless, there are significant differences in expectations between parents and the children. These differences stem mainly from the different contexts in which the two generations were socialized and developed.

The authors analyze the multiple ways in which young, African-Canadian women negotiate their identity and sense of belonging. They not only retain some of their parents' expectations, they also contest some of the values their parents hold, and in the process, create their own sense of self – a self that challenges the dichotomization of *African* and *Canadian* identities, *à la* the Authentic African approach referred to earlier, and imbibes a perspective that involves a synthesis of those worlds. In the final analysis, "they must fluidly meander through the *homeland* identity they occupy with their parents, the multicultural identity still under construction, and the racist (and sometimes ignorant) perceptions of Euro-Canadian society they must continually reject" (Okeke-Ihejirika and Spitzer in this volume).

Overall, this collection makes an important contribution to an understanding of continental Black Africans and their children in Canada. It goes beyond the implicit homogenization of Canadians of African descent and shows how the unique characteristics and circumstances of continental Black Africans inform their place – not only in their new locales, but also in relation to their places of origin – as they negotiate their existence within both worlds. The specific negotiations, contestations, and collaborations that define these communities provide unique insights that are not only empirically illuminating, but theoretically engaging, as well. The chapters advance imaginative theoretical perspectives for understanding diasporas and immigrant communities in addition to offering useful conceptual frameworks for analyzing important issues in our increasingly globalized, yet asymmetrical, world; issues such as hybridity, transnationalism, identity, and belonging. The volume's value for guiding public policy is also immense. The chapters not only provide a critical examination of the Canadian state's role in determining the conditions of entry and the subsequent experiences of continental Black Africans and other immigrant groups; they offer ideas on how to make that role enabling, rather than constraining, for these groups. The analyses suggest that, while the state's power may be eroding with globalization, it nonetheless still has the capacity and the responsibility to provide an equitable, inclusive, and truly democratic polity in which citizenship is not just an abstract construct, but has positive meaning for all members of this diverse society (see Castells 1997, 243).

REFERENCES

Abraham, Willie E. 1962. *The mind of Africa*. Chicago, IL: University of Chicago Press.
Adeleke, Tunde. 1998. Black Americans, Africa, and history: A reassessment of the pan-African and identity paradigms. *Western Journal of Black Studies* 22, no. 3: 182–94.
Amin, Samir. 2002. The African crisis. *Monthly Review* 53, no. 10: 41–50.
Anthias, Floya. 2001. New hybridities, old concepts: The limits of "culture." *Ethnic and Racial Studies* 24, no. 4: 619–41.
Appiah, Kwame. 1992. *In My Father's House: Africa in the Philosophy of Culture*. Oxford: Oxford University Press.
Asante, Molefi K. 1990. *Kemet, afrocentricity and knowledge*. Trenton, N.J.: Africa World Press
Bloom, David E., G. Grenier, and M. Gunderson. 1995. The changing labour market position of Canadian immigrants. *Canadian Journal of Economics* 28, no. 4b: 987–1001.

Brodkin, Karen. 2000. *How Jews Became White Folks and What That Says about Race in America*. New Brunswick, NJ: Rutgers University Press.

Castells, Manuel. 1997. *The Power of Identity*. Oxford: Blackwell.

Cheru, Fantu. 2002. *African Renaissance: Roadmaps to the Challenge of Globalization*. London/New York: Zed Books.

Croucher, Shiela L. 1997. Constructing the image of ethnic harmony in Toronto, Canada: The politics of problem definition and nondefinition. *Urban Affairs Review* 32, no. 3: 319–34.

D'Alisera, JoAnn. 2003. Review of *Ghosts and shadows,* by Atsuko Matsuoka and John Sorenson. *Journal of the Royal Anthropology Institute* 9, no. 1: 189–90.

Djamba, Yanyi. 1999. African immigrants in the United States: A socio-demographic profile in comparison to native Blacks. *Journal of Asian and African Studies* 34, no. 2: 210–15.

Faist, Thomas. 2000. Transnationalization in international migration: Implications for the study of citizenship and culture. *Ethnic and Racial Studies* 23, no. 2: 189–224.

Fanon, Frantz. 1968. *Black Skin, White Masks*. New York: Grove.

Hall, Stuart. 1996. New ethnicities. In *Stuart Hall: Critical Dialogues in Cultural Studies,* ed. D. Morley and K. Chen, 441–49. London: Blackwell.

Halter, Marilyn. 1998. Studying immigrants of African descent in the twentieth century. *Immigration History Newsletter*. Philadelphia: Balch Institute for Ethnic Studies.

Henry, Frances, and Carol Tator. 1995. *The Colour of Democracy: Racism in Canadian Society*. Toronto: Harcourt Brace.

Hou, Feng and T.R. Balakrishnan. 1996. The integration of visible minorities in contemporary Canadian society. *Canadian Journal of Sociology* 21, no. 3: 307–26.

Hountondji, Pauline. 2002. *The Struggle for Meaning: Reflections on Philosophy, Culture and Democracy in Africa*. Translated by John Conteh-Morgan. Athens, OH: Ohio University Centre for International Studies.

Jahn, Janheinz. 1961. *Muntu: An outline of neo-African culture*. London: Faber and Faber.

James, Carl. E. 1994. I've never had a Black teacher before. In *Talking about Difference: Encounters in Culture, Language and Identity,* ed. C. E. James and A. Shadd, 125–40. Toronto: Between the Lines.

Jones, Rhett. 1995. Why pan-Africanism failed: Blackness and international relations. *The Griot* 14, no. 1: 54–61.

Kanneh, Kadiatu. 1998. *African identities: Race, nation and culture in ethnography, pan-Africanisms and black literatures*. London and New York: Routledge.

Kelly, Jennifer. 1998. *Under the Gaze: Learning to Be Black in White Society*. Halifax: Fernwood.

Konadu-Agyemang, Kwadwo. 1999. Characteristics and migration experience of Africans in Canada with specific reference to Ghanaians in Greater Toronto. *Canadian Geographer* 43, no. 4: 400–416.

Lasswell, Harold D. 1958. *Politics: Who Gets What, When, and How*. Cleveland: Meridian.

Leblanc, Marie Nathalie. 2002. Processes of identification among French-speaking West African migrants in Montreal. *Canadian Ethnic Studies/Études ethniques au Canada* 34, no. 3: 121–41.

Ley, David. 1999. Myths and meanings of immigration and the metropolis. *Canadian Geographer* 43, no. 1: 2–19.

Lyons Terrence. 2004. [online] *Globalization, Diasporas, and Conflict.* [cited 4 May 2005] (http://www.intlstudies.ucsd.edu/iicas_research_papers/Globalization,%20Ter ritoriality,%20and%20Conflict%20Conference/GlobalDiaCon.pdf).

Manuh, Takyiwah. 1998. Ghanaians, Ghanaian Canadians, and Asantes: Citizenship and identity among migrants in Toronto. *Africa Today* 45, nos. 3–4: 481–94.

Matsuoka, Atsuko, and John Sorenson. 2001. *Ghosts and Shadows: Construction of Identity and Community in an African Diaspora.* Toronto: University of Toronto Press.

Mensah, Joseph. 2002. *Black Canadians: History, Experiences, Social Conditions.* Halifax: Fernwood.

Pendakur, Krishna, and Ravi Pendakur. 1998. The colour of money: Earning differentials among ethnic groups in Canada. *Canadian Journal of Economics* 31, no. 3: 518–48.

Porter, John A. 1965. *The Vertical Mosaic: An Analysis of Social Class and Power in Canada.* Toronto: University of Toronto Press.

Rousseau, Cécile, Taher M. Said, Marie-Josée Gagné and Gilles Bibeau. 1998. Between myth and madness: The premigration dream of leaving among young Somali refugees. *Culture, Medicine & Psychiatry* 22, no. 4: 385–411.

Shain, Yossi, and Aharon Barth. 2003. Diasporic and international relations theory. *International Organization* 57: 449–79.

Shami, Seteney. 1998. Circassian encounters: The self as other and the production of the homeland in the North Caucasus. *Development and Change* 29: 617–46.

Smith, Malinda, ed. 2003. *Globalizing Africa.* Trenton, NJ: Africa World Press.

Stelcner, Morton, and Nota Kyriazis. 1995. An empirical analysis of earnings among ethnic groups in Canada. *International Journal of Contemporary Sociology* 32, no. 1: 41–79.

Stodolska, Monika. 1998. Assimilation and leisure constraints: Dynamics of constraints on leisure in immigrant popuplations. *Journal of Leisure Research* 30, no. 4: 521–51.

The Economist. 1997. Workers of the world. Nov. 1, 81–82.

Tettey, Wisdom J. 2001. What does it mean to be African-Canadian? Identity, integration, and community. In *A Passion for Identity: An Introduction to Canadian Studies,* 4th ed., ed. D. Taras and B. Rasporich, 161–82. Toronto: ITP Nelson.

———. 2004. Globalization, diasporization and cyber-communities: Exploring African trans-nationalisms. In *Globalization and the Human Factor: Critical Insights,* ed. E. Osei-Prempeh, J. Mensah, and S. B-S. K Adjibolosoo, 121–42. London: Ashgate.

Torczyner, James. 1997. *Diversity, mobility, and change: The dynamics of Black communities in Canada.* Montreal: McGill Consortium for Ethnicity and Strategic Social Planning.

wa Thiongo, Ngugi. 1987. *Decolonising the Mind: The Politics of Language in African Literature.* London: James Currey.

Weiner, Myron. 1996. Nations without borders: The gifts of folk gone abroad. *Foreign Affairs* 75, no. 2: 128–34.

White, Elisa J. 2002. Forging African diaspora places in Dublin's retro-global spaces: Minority making in a new global city. *City* 6, no. 2: 251–70.

Williams, Patricia. 1991. *The Alchemy of Race and Rights: Diary of a Law Professor.* Cambridge: Harvard University Press.

Wong, Madeleine. 2000. Ghanaian women in Toronto's labour market: Negotiating gendered roles and transnational household strategies. *Canadian Ethnic Studies/Études ethniques au Canada* 32, no. 2: 45–78.

2

ETHNICITY & THE IDENTITY OF AFRICAN-CANADIANS:
A Theoretical & Political Analysis

Korbla P. Puplampu & Wisdom J. Tettey

INTRODUCTION

CANADA'S EFFORTS to build an inclusive and democratic society are marked by many policies. The *Immigration Act* in 1967 and subsequent changes, for example, were to create a somewhat level playing field for those seeking to immigrate into Canada. The 1982 *Charter of Rights and Freedoms* guarantees equality and freedom from discrimination on the basis of ethnicity, race, gender, and other ascribed characteristics. Beginning in 1971 with official multiculturalism, the passage of the 1988 *Multicultural Act* made Canada the first official multicultural country in the world. In principle, the act provides the policy platform for celebrating cultural differences.

Overall, these policies provide the context and the space for legal membership and, hopefully, optimum participation in the Canadian political and socio-cultural family. It is important to note that their enactment was controversial at the time. However, the very fact that national leaders implemented them can be taken as an indication of their desire to address some historically embarrassing episodes in the treatment of certain groups of people. These policies support Canada's official multiculturalism policy and offer a guide to the future trajectories of the country's journey towards building an inclusive and truly democratic society.

As a country built by immigrants from different generations, Western Europeans dominated the early history of Canadian immigration, leaving the Aboriginal population, the original inhabitants of the land, in a subordinate position. As far as Western Europeans were concerned, the English and French were the major players, with the English in a relatively dominant position. It is therefore not surprising that Western Europeans constituted the majority of the earlier waves of immigrants, hence Canada's self-image – religion, language, and values – were inherently European (Samuel and Schachhuber 2000, 16). However, the traditional source of immigration to Canada, Western Europe, started to dry up in the 1960s following a period of political stability. Meanwhile, with the formal end of the colonial era in many developing societies, especially in Africa, new sources of immigration were emerging. These new sources could only be engaged if changes were made to the previously exclusionary and racist immigration policies. Canada was also eager to keep pace with global changes to eliminate discriminatory laws, especially when Lester Pearson won the Nobel Peace Prize in 1957 and later served as prime minister (1963–68). These were some of the antecedent factors for revising Canadian immigration policies in order to woo immigrants from previously *non-preferred* regions.

The changes in immigration policies since 1967 gave rise to the arrival of immigrants to Canada from previously non-preferred sources, basically non-Western European countries. From the latter part of the 1990s to the early part of the 2000s, significant waves of immigration came from the People's Republic of China, India, Sri Lanka, and the Philippines (Citizenship and Immigration Canada 2002). One particular source or group of people who also benefited from the changes in the immigration policy were Africans. Even though Canadians of African descent have been in Canada since the seventeenth century, this study examines the life experiences of Africans who migrated to Canada since the 1960s. The figures for African immigrants to Canada have increased considerably over the last two decades. While 64,265 Africans immigrated to Canada during the whole of the 1980s, the number between 1991 and 1996 alone was 76,260 (Statistics Canada 1996). The number of African immigrants in Canada jumped to 282,600 in 2001 (Statistics Canada 2003).

With the arrival of various ethnic and racial groups, it became imperative to have a "public policy which is inclusive" (Samuel and Schachhuber 2000, 15). Multiculturalism was the policy position designed to engage diversity within the framework of equality (Fleras 2001). "From afar, Canada strikes many as a paragon of racial tranquility" (Fleras and Elliott 2003, 55). However, ethnicity and race feature, whether intentionally or unintentionally, in human interactions. They shape access to political, economic, and social resources in Canada, even though Canadians, compared to Americans, tend to hold on to a mythical refrain that "race doesn't matter here" (James 1994, 7). The historical account shows the salience of race in social policies in Canada. National policies on immigration, from head taxes to the outright refusal of entry of *undesirables* or *non-preferred* groups, are illustrations of race-based policies. In the pecking order that has ensued, the English and the French have been at the top, several other groups are in-between, while African-Canadians and Aboriginal Canadians compete for the bottom rungs (see Boyko 1995). The status and power differentials that go with this pecking order create dilemmas, tensions, and frustrations for African-Canadians as they attempt to define their identity, control their representation, and forge their integration within Canada.

An understanding of how African-Canadians deal with the issues of identity, representation, and integration, and how the larger society responds to it, is extremely significant if the goals of liberal multiculturalism, for example, are to be attained (Rickard 1994). After all, the aspirations of foreign-born Canadians are not drastically different from their native-born counterparts – that is, the desire "to build a prosperous, secure, peaceful life for themselves and their families" (Samuel and Schachhuber 2000, 21), as well as contribute to the well-being of their new home or country. A major challenge to the realization of these aspirations, however, is the prerogative that the French and the English have arrogated to themselves, as the two charter groups (or *founding nations),* to decide "what other groups … [were] to be let in and what they … [would] be permitted to do" (Porter 1965, 62). Pertinent to an understanding of identity and to the implications for representation and integration, therefore, is how particular groups fit into, and respond to, the structures and processes established by the founding nations.

Group dynamics over access to resources are contingent in nature. Contingency presupposes that these dynamics be situated within the social, cultural, economic, and political nuances of inter-group relations and the construction of meanings that comes with them. As Cornell and Hartmann (1998, 12) observe, there is an "unanticipated and often dramatic staying power of ethnic and racial identities … [in] significant parts of the modern world." Consequently, these factors constitute an intrinsic part of the dynamics that shape access to resources and can engender bitter struggles within social systems (Giddens 1984).

This chapter addresses the theoretical and political difficulties posed by the location of African-Canadians as they explore the problematics of identity, representation, and integration. It specifically examines how government policies, particularly those on immigration and multiculturalism, shape those problematics. The chapter argues that there are considerable inconsistencies between the official discourse on African-Canadians and the reality of African-Canadian experiences. These inconsistencies are reflected in systematic, systemic, and interpersonal structures of interaction. It is argued that the nature of those structures account, in part, for the difficulties that confront African-Canadians.

ETHNICITY AND IDENTITY: A SOCIOLOGICAL FRAMEWORK

In Canada and in other multi-ethnic societies, the question of identity relates to how several ascribed and socially determined factors interact to define people's sense of self and their treatment, or place, in the larger society. Two significant factors in the definition of identity are ethnicity and citizenship. The terms *ethnicity, ethnic,* and *ethnic groups* have a flexibility or elasticity about them that has made it difficult to arrive at a common definition. In many cases, they are used according to the whims and caprices of the source(s) employing them and their motivations.

Fleras and Elliott (2003, 86) identify several ways, both positive and negative, in which ethnicity is used. First, it is presented as a blight on modernity because of its tendency to revert to *tribalism* and *groupthink*. Ethnicity, in this context, is used in a negative sense. In the second usage, ethnicity refers to the way in which individuals and groups experience the world and relate to others. Here, it is seen as a positive force, because it shows the remarkable variations of human differences, differences that add to the diversity of the world (see also Kallen 1995, 61). Third, ethnicity, depending on the context and the rationale for invoking it, can have both positive and negative connotations. Finally, ethnicity is a political tool used in framing and setting the basis for the competition over scarce political, economic, and socio-cultural resources (Fleras and Elliot 2003, 86). Irrespective of how ethnicity is used, it does have socio-political import. In this chapter, we examine the significance of the concept in terms of how it shapes identity and opportunities for integration in Canadian society within a multicultural policy framework.

Ethnicity forms the basis for social struggle among groups. However, few social theorists have paid attention to the role of ethnicity in competitive political and socio-economic relationships, even though several social theorists have addressed broader questions regarding the nature of group solidarity and conflict and of social inequalities (Driedger 1996, 4). In modern societies, ethnicity, either intentionally or unintentionally, looms large in the dynamics of group solidarity and the processes that give rise to, or sustain, social conflict and inequalities. Max Weber devoted a chapter to ethnic groups in his massive, three-volume study, *Economy and Society,* and provides what is perhaps the most insightful definition of ethnicity. According to him (1996, 35), ethnic groups are

> those human groups that entertain a subjective belief in their common
> descent because of similarities of physical type or of customs or both, or
> because of memories of colonization and migration; this belief must be

important for the propagation of group formation; conversely, it does not matter whether or not an objective blood relationship exists. Ethnic membership (*Gemeinsamkeit*) differs from the kinship group precisely by being a presumed identity, not a group with concrete social action, like the latter ... ethnic membership does not constitute a group; it only facilities group formation of any kind, particularly in the political sphere. On the other hand, it is primarily the political community, no matter how artificially organized, that inspires the belief in common identity.

Weber's conceptualization of ethnic groups contains several important elements that have informed various sociological discussions of ethnicity (see Puplampu and Codjoe 2001, 88–89; Cornell and Hartmann 1998, 35; Schermerhorn 1978). First, ethnic groups identify themselves on the basis of a subjective belief tied to a real or assumed common descent. This common descent may be based on claims of a common genealogy, shared history or heritage, and/or attachment to a real or imagined territory or homeland. In addition to being an avowed basis for ethnic identification, others may ascribe ethnic labels to groups of people, a process which subsequently generates a degree of collective consciousness among those so designated. A second element implicit in the relational nature of ethnic group formation is power. How it is distributed and employed among various groups has significant implications for inter- and intra-group relations.

Many sociological studies tend to discuss ethnicity and race as separate concepts. In Canada, however, ethnicity and race tend to be used interchangeably (Kendall et al. 2004, 49; James 2003, 50–53). Generally, the criteria employed in ethnic classification vary with changing social conditions (Kallen 1995, 64). Weber's conceptualization of ethnic groups has a clear reference to similarities of physical type, a biological criterion. Indeed, if the biological criterion is employed in human classification and identity, what "we may speak of is [a] *racially defined* ethnic category" (Kallen 1995, 64; emphasis in original).

From a Weberian perspective, this study would consider race within the broader context of ethnicity. As Richmond (1994, 23) argues, ethnicity "combines different dimensions of cultural identity into a relatively coherent whole." Weber's outline on ethnic groups contains variables that "define ethnic identity" (Driedger 1996, 5). The variables that are important for this study are race, kinship affiliation, and peoplehood, or nationality (see Driedger 1996, 5–9). Ethnicity is based on a subjective belief attached to similarities in physical type and cultural practices. Physical type constitutes the basis for the discourse on race. For that matter, height and the shape and texture of hair, eyes, and nose could all form the basis for theorizing ethnicity and race. However, skin colour has been the most consistently used criterion, and this has given rise to the crude formulations of *White* and *non-White* human types.

The former serves as the *gold standard*, and the latter includes all other colours. This typology has significant theoretical problems.

First, the characterization between White and non-White has given rise to the equally unsophisticated and erroneous belief of equating White to a *superior* status and non-White to an *inferior* one (see Fleras and Elliott 2003). Second, there are inconsistencies in the genotypical and phenotypical colour designations. The former, largely invisible, is the genetic basis of human types, and despite the attempts to classify human beings and impute differences in worth, the genetic basis of human beings is the same. For example, one cannot tell whether an unlabeled blood sample belongs to a White or non-White person. The phenotype is the visible expression of the genotype. These expressions are different as demonstrated by the variety of human beings. However, the labels given to the expressions are not consistent with the colour types. For example, the phenotypical expression labeled as White is not the same as snow, which is also called white. Third, even though white is also a colour, non-White human types are those referred to in the literature and everyday discourse as *people of colour*, implying a normality of *Whiteness*. This practice, in part, sustains the process of *othering* and the view that Whites are *colourless* and do not constitute an ethnic group, hence Sollors' (1995) classic question, Who is ethnic?

However, if Weber's conceptualization of ethnicity is taken to its logical conclusion, there is no doubt that every single soul in Canada is an ethnic. Hence the view of Hughes and Hughes (1952, 7) that "we are all ethnic." In reality, ethnicity is often used in a pejorative sense to give the impression that some, and not all, are ethnic. The process of othering makes it possible to blame the ethnics for undesirable social outcomes, and encourages the questioning of any claims they might make on the larger society in terms of political, economic, and socio-cultural goods and services. That is why, for example, Jacques Parizeau, the former Premier of Quebec, contended that the *Yes* side lost the 1995 Quebec referendum because of "the power of money and the *ethnic vote*" (Seguin 1995, A1; italics ours).

The idea of race and the physical features often used to delimit it are creations of human beings, and the processes involve never-ending political and social struggles over meanings and the social construction of reality. As Thomas and Thomas (1932, 572) argue, "If men (*sic*) define situations as real, they are real in their consequences." These consequences are germane in the conceptualization, operationalization, and reality of ethnicity on the basis of racialized constructions (Codjoe 1998; Allahar 1993).

Beyond race, kinship also looms large in Weber's concept of ethnic groups. Kinship derives from blood or marriage (affinal) ties or relations. Tracing blood ties to earlier generations in the absence of written records can, however, be challenging with regard to the accuracy of memories. Given that memories can fail, it goes without saying that to base ethnicity, and for that matter, identity, on such ties would be a highly subjective process. As Weber (1996, 35) clearly maintains, "it does not matter whether or not an objective blood relationship exists." Consequently, "the fact of the common descent is less important than the belief in it" (Puplampu and Codjoe 2001, 89). The belief in blood ties, or what Barber (1995) calls *blood brotherhood*, contributes greatly to peoples' attempt to create a sense of belonging, especially in times of rapid social change. Kinship ties integrate individuals and collectives, and are socially constructed and recognized in human relations (Wellman 1983; Granovetter 1995, 1983). Individuals and collectives "may have differential access to valued resources (wealth, power, information). The result is that structured systems tend to be stratified, with some components dependent on others" (Ritzer 2000, 430; see also Turner 1998, 520–21). The dynamics that emerge from these systems determine the nature of social exchanges and access to opportunities. It is on the basis of these dynamics that somebody might *drop a word* in the right place for an acquaintance (Wallace and Wolf 1999, 348). Thus, contrary to the assumption that

> the advent of *modernization* leads to a widespread use of formal and *universalistic* procedures, liberating individuals from the limitations once imposed by particular social milieus ... empirical sociological studies continually demonstrate the crucial importance of informal interaction in systems that are formally rationalized. (Granovetter 1995, 4)

Peoplehood, or nationality, is another key feature in Weber's conceptualization of ethnic identity. The historical antecedents of nationality, as part of the broader national question, can be situated in the aftermath of the French Revolution and the consequent forging of the imaginary concept of the nation-state (Breuilly 1994; Anderson 1991; Hobsbawm 1991; Gellner 1983; Hobsbawm and Ranger 1997). Peoplehood, or nationalism has been expressed in terms of belonging or community, territorial integrity, language, race, and ethnicity. The sense of belonging is the backdrop for various forms of nationalism (see Ignatieff 1993), and the mark of nationalism in modern, large-scale societies is the imagination of a community (Anderson 1991).

This imagination is fostered by several symbols provided by the nation-state. The nation-state had to devise strategies to operationalize the imaginary concept of the nation. The operationalization called for, among other things, cultural institutions (e.g., the Canadian Broadcasting Corporation) that would produce and give legitimacy to existing social beliefs, norms, myths, and symbols (e.g., the national flag) in order to enhance social reproduction (Morrow and Torres 1995). These institutions and symbols give members or residents in the community the conviction of their togetherness and belonging, even though they have no real knowledge of the living circumstances of members residing in distant communities. Again, it is evident that perception is the key galvanizing force, as subjective notions of the imaginary construct of the nation frame peoplehood, as do discussions on nationalism and citizenship. It is therefore not surprising that these concepts are contested.

The link between nationalism and citizenship deserves some further remarks. In its classical form, "citizenship … [is] the status of the individual in relation to the land, the state, and to each other. It reflected the emergence of liberal individualism, and a growing democratic emphasis on liberty and equality. As a formal-legal construct, it means that citizens enjoy rights and have obligations within the territorial boundaries of their nation-states" (Gibbins, Youngman, and Stewart-Toth 1996, 270). The formal construct of citizenship has evolved and can now be conferred on the basis of "place of birth or length of residence. For instance, an individual is a Canadian citizen because [he or] she was born in Canada, or immigrated to Canada, remained in the country and … applied for legal membership in the national community" (Gibbins, Youngman, and Stewart-Toth 1996, 271). Formal recognition, however, does not guarantee one's social acceptance in the community. The discrepancies between formal citizenship and informal citizenship, as discussed later in the chapter, have significant implications for identity formation and community attachment. Indeed, the question of "who does and does not belong – is where the politics of citizenship begins" (Hall and Held 1989, 175; see also Isajiw 1999).

The foregoing discussion highlights two related aspects of identity – subjectivity and power. Subjectivity has several components. One component is how individuals and groups "contribute to the integration of society as a whole in their intentions and their consequences" (Isajiw 1999, 29). Another aspect is the extent to which individuals, and subsequently group behaviour, can be understood with respect to their sense of self. The idea of the self, as used here, is an active entity, and so it is capable of deriving meanings from a given social situation. These meanings are drawn from state-sanctioned symbols and rituals. However, the meanings are interpreted according to the position (ascribed or achieved, real or imagined) of the individual or group and constitute the social construction of reality. Ethnic background, for example, plays a role in determining the extent to which people feel a sense of belonging and identify with particular symbols and rituals, thus creating "their meanings and their identity" (Isajiw 1999, 30). The impact of power on identity becomes obvious when individuals and groups compete for scarce resources. Powerful groups tend to legitimize their identity in relation to the nation-state, while labeling others as not belonging and therefore not qualified to be considered authentic members of the polity. It is in this context that identity and belonging are contested, a contest that could give rise to social conflict (Puplampu and Codjoe 2001).

Having used Weber's framework to theoretically situate ethnicity and identity, in the next section we examine how the subjective construction of these concepts shapes government policies on immigration and multiculturalism, and creates a discrepancy between their professed intent and their practical manifestations vis-à-vis African-Canadians. We also discuss the role of ethnicity in identity construction among African-Canadians and argue that that process is, in part, a response to government policies.

IMMIGRATION POLICIES AND AFRICAN-CANADIANS: THE POLITICS OF GETTING IN AND CREDENTIALIZATION

The Canadian government, like many others, offers the structure and mechanism with which to address the identity, representation, and integration of the various ethnic groups. After all, the government has historically been the sole authority for setting the terms under which groups have entered and stayed in the country, even though, in many cases, it left the actual process to market forces and private institutions (Whitaker 1991). Therefore, government actions or inactions set the stage for the treatment of respective ethnic groups, and for that matter, their engagement with the dynamics of identity construction. As Bibby (1990, 21) notes, government "historically was the direct or indirect agency of minority misfortunes. Discrimination was either perpetrated or tolerated by the government well into the latter half of the twentieth century." Policies from the latter half of the twentieth century to date have also not been without implicit discriminatory undertones.

The nature of the relationship between government policies and the identity of African-Canadians can be analyzed at two related levels: first, at the level of policy, and second, the impact of such policies. At the policy level, a racial dimension underpins immigration and multicultural policies and subsequently informs how government authorities (e.g., immigration authorities) deal with Africans. The 1967 immigration policies abandoned the notion of preferred and non-preferred countries as a determinant in the immigration process. In its place, the emphasis (in addition to other considerations) has been on age, education, and potential contribution to Canadian society. These indicators, under the points system, are supposed to create a level playing field for potential immigrants, including Africans. The steady increase in the number of immigrants from continental Africa might give the impression that this goal is being achieved. Such an impression would, however, be naïve. Simmons (1998) identifies an important policy variant in Canadian immigration and calls it neo-racist. Such a policy reveals "significant racist influences and outcomes within a framework that claims to be entirely non-racist" (Simmons 1998, 91). A neo-racist immigration policy has several features: rationalization of immigration outcomes on economic and other legitimate grounds; constrained access to immigration officers and difficulties with application procedures in certain countries; an attempt to link crime with immigration, and by extension, an entire ethnic group; and labour market segmentation in which the

Table 2.1 Location of Canadian Immigration Officers Worldwide – 1980

Geographical Location	Immigration Officers
Europe	46
Australia	2
Japan	2
South East Asia	26
South Asia	10
West Asia	5
Caribbean	11
Latin America	8
Africa	8
Worldwide	118

Source: Simmons 1998, 104.

ethnics occupy the bottom rungs in terms of wages and benefits, despite their qualifications and skills (Simmons 1998, 91–92).

Canadian embassies and consulates are the first point of contact for potential immigrants. Thus, the distribution of such offices and the resources they have to work with in different regions of the world would be a good indicator of the desire of the Canadian government to encourage immigration from a particular region. Simmons (1998, 104) shows that, before the cost-cutting programs began about two decades ago, specifically in 1980, the location of the 118 Canadian immigration officers worldwide were distributed as shown in Table 2.1.

Currently, six African countries (Morocco, Côte d'Ivoire, Ghana, Egypt, Kenya, and South Africa) have Canadian missions that deal with immigration issues (Citizenship and Immigration Canada 2004). Based on the number of countries served by each of these offices, the crowded spectacle of prospective applicants at these locations, and the delays that potential immigrants have to endure to get processed relative to applicants in other locations, it can be safely speculated that the facilities have resource constraints (both human and physical) in dealing with the demands of growing numbers of Africans intent on coming to Canada.

It can be argued that the increase in immigration offices between 1980 and 2004 does not necessarily remove barriers for African immigrants. They still have to contend with the ingrained default mindset among immigration officials, not only from Canada but from other industrialized countries, that they are economic refugees and potential burdens on their countries' social systems. These mindsets influence the attitudes of officials towards applicants, the kind of scrutiny they undergo, the rates of success among applicants, and the services they receive at Canadian immigration offices in their countries (see Olarinam and Williams 1995). Complaints by many Africans in Canada suggest, at least anecdotally, that there is a high rate of rejection of visitor visa applications by their parents and other immediate relatives who want to visit them.

Those who are fortunate enough to be granted visas find out that their African origin does not make the situation any easier when they arrive at a Canadian port of entry. The case of Tinoula Akintade, a British citizen who was not allowed to enter Canada, is an example of how an encounter with Canadian immigration officers can be mediated by unstated assumptions. According to the Canadian immigration officer, she "did not sound British" and had "an accent." In this particular case, the supporting documents of her British citizenship, including being born in London, were of no value because, according to the immigration officer's logic, sounding British was of greater significance than having documents showing British citizenship. The British, according to the same logic, are not supposed to have an *accent*, and so, for failing to sound British while having British documents, she had to spend a night in jail while her Britishness was being verified (Canadian Broadcasting Corporation [hereafter CBC] 2001a). It seems that some immigration officials have a static notion of linguistic systems, fail to recognize variations within them, and equate accents to citizenship. Thus, if someone claims to come from a particular country but does not have the expected accent, he or she must be an imposter!!

The stereotypical connection between Africa and disease also features in the immigration experiences of Africans as they attempt to enter Canada. They are therefore required to undergo extensive medical examinations that are strictly enforced. The disease-carrying image of Africans was in full force when a woman from Congo arrived in Canada and fell ill a day later. The media headline was "Deadly Ebola Virus May Be in Canada," because the woman was from Congo and had symptoms common to Ebola and other hemorrhagic fevers prevalent in Central Africa (CBC 2001b). Given the fact that there is no cure for Ebola, the health authorities took unprecedented steps, including allowing experimental drugs to be administered to the woman until test results ruled out the Ebola virus (CBC 2001c). The issue here is not the duty consciousness of the health authorities, which must be commended, in theorizing that the woman might have the Ebola virus. It is the idea that anyone from Congo who arrives in Canada and falls ill within a short period of time must have the Ebola virus. The processes followed in declaring the woman a likely carrier of the Ebola virus suggest nothing less than unwarranted stereotyping. It is this stereotyping that eventually leads to racism.

It is worth contrasting this case with the experience of Kosovar refugees who arrived in Canada in 1999 to show how race and ethnicity are implicated in immigration decisions. Perhaps based on the image of Europeans as being *clean* and not being health hazards, the immigration authorities did not require the refugees to undergo any of the extensive medical examinations required of African immigrants. Unfortunately, however, some flight attendants on the planes that brought the Kosovars to Canada and a woman who worked as a Salvation Army volunteer at Camp Borden, a large military training establishment near Toronto, contracted tuberculosis (CBC 1999). The two cases clearly show the limitations posed by stereotyping whole groups and communities.

While the economic- and public health-based stereotypes about Africa continue to influence how African immigrants are treated, the emphasis on skills, language, and other aspects of the immigration process is proffered as evidence to debunk any claims of racism against these immigrants once they arrive in Canada. It is argued that the point system offers equal chances to all prospective immigrants, irrespective of their countries of origin (see Laryea and Hayfron in this volume). However, a question that has not been critically engaged is how the educational credentials and skills of immigrants are evaluated and valued in Canada (Harding 2003; Dixon 2003; Reitz 2003, 2001; Li 2001; Dabrowski 2000).

Though immigration policies encourage the migration of highly skilled labour, the system of credentializing and legitimizing the knowledge of immigrants involves multiple agencies – the federal government, provincial governments, post-secondary institutions, professional bodies, and employers. The legitimation process brings, once again, racialized ethnicity to the fore. There is an implicit hierarchization of knowledge embedded in the process that tends to devalue and/or delegitimize certain kinds of knowledge.

The correlation between the value assigned the skills of specific professionals and their country of origin can best be illustrated with medical doctors. The province of Manitoba, until February 2003, had preferred and non-preferred International Medical Graduates (IMGs). Graduates from the United Kingdom, the Republic of Ireland, Australia, New Zealand, and South Africa were preferred, and their licensing requirements were different from those of their counterparts from non-preferred countries. For example, Dr. Dumatol-Sanchez, a family doctor in the Philippines, took almost eight years to secure the accreditation needed to practice in Canada (Dixon 2003).

South Africa's inclusion in the preferred category needs to be put in perspective. The official apartheid system in that country gave Whites preferential access to medical training. Consequently, the vast majority of South African medical doctors in Canada are Whites, thereby raising questions about the extent to which the racial history of medical training in that country informed its inclusion in the preferred category. The government of Manitoba, in abandoning the preferred and non-preferred categories, argued that the changes were aimed at ensuring all IMGs went through the same licensing requirements. However, it is also obvious that the basis for the earlier categories, like Canada's pre-1967 immigration policies, was based on an implicit notion of superior and inferior countries and knowledge systems.

Beyond foreign-trained medical doctors, the market chances for other skilled immigrants from Africa have been disappointing, to say the least (Toneguzzi 2003; D'Aliesio 2003; also see Laryea and Hayfron in this volume). These trends are consistent with findings from Henry and Ginzberg's (1985) classic study of racial discrimination in employment practices in Toronto. One aspect of the disappointment, discussed shortly, is how political- and social-networking are becoming unstated factors in one's ability to secure a job. This is a trend that undermines notions of merit and equity, values that are supposed to be at the heart of a diverse and democratic society.

The categorization of preferred and non-preferred countries and the implicit questioning of the competence of graduates from the latter set of countries are not justified by the evidence. Indeed, there is no evidence to suggest that the rate of competence among immigrant professionals from the non-preferred countries who have been given the opportunity to prove themselves have, as a group, been any worse than their Canadian-trained counterparts. Thus, while the shortage of skilled labour continues to make national headlines, there is a significant brain waste due to the complexities of evaluating foreign degrees (see Stromquist 2002; Finnie 2001; Bloom 2001; Hayhoe 1993). The conservative attitude to accreditation in Canada has led Jim Gurnett, executive director of the Edmonton Mennonite Centre for Newcomers, to conclude that "some of the European countries that have a more progressive approach [to the accreditation process] will increasingly pick off the best educated, the brightest, and the people who have a lot to contribute" (cited in D'Aliesio 2003, A2).

We are not calling for an uncritical acceptance of knowledge systems. Rather, the emphasis should be on being open-minded enough to acknowledge the value of training systems based on objectively ascertained merit, rather than arbitrarily drawn distinctions of preferred and non-preferred countries, thereby shielding the accreditation system from bureaucratic or professional interests. These interests sometimes masquerade as protectors of the public interest when, in fact, what they are protecting is their own political and economic agendas.

As pointed out in the previous section, ethnicity serves as a basis for social networks of privilege or exclusion. The configuration of ethnicity and race in Canadian society places African-Canadians and their social networks in a subaltern position. Thus, beyond the problems of credentialization, they are further disadvantaged by a lack of access to powerful social networks within organizations as they seek employment opportunities. Job advertisements in Canada stress the principle of merit in addition to encouraging visible minorities or under-represented groups to apply. It seems, however, that instead of enhancing their chances, these designations instead constrain opportunities for members of these groups as they navigate their way through the social structures and connections that characterize institutions whose meritocratic credentials have been questioned.

Miller (2001), for example, documents how, even though he had the requisite qualifications, it was his connections (social capital and networking) that opened several job opportunities for him in his career. He indicates that, in most cases, there was no point of comparison or competition because the job was not advertised, and so there was no one to compete against. In essence, no other search was conducted, and his powerful insiders simply handed the job over to him. He also notes that "it is not easy to build and maintain procedures that are truly meritocratic," arguing further that "[e]ven the simple open posting (what currently is termed *transparency*) of job openings is easily subverted" (Miller 2001). Several years ago, he found a "position which asked for a most unusual combination of experience and interests. [He] learned that the job description was written to fit the individual whom the [organization] wanted to hire." Based on his experiences and analysis, Miller (2001) poses a critical question. "If decisions [for example, hiring] will always come, in part, through social capital and networks, how do we ensure that the poor, the minority, the disadvantaged, get into the loop of the privileged?"

The revelations made by this personal narrative were confirmed in a September 2002 study on the hiring practices of Canada's Public Service Commission (Curry 2004). The report found that there was nothing like merit-based hiring in about 51 percent of placements (out of 1,000 hirings analyzed) across the public service. There were instances where job advertisements were *tailor-made* for specific persons, and some managers prepared lists of potential candidates even when no competition was ever held to select them. The inevitable result is that nepotism and cronyism have become the norm with respect to hiring practices in the public service, giving rise to instances were some managers offered jobs to their kinsfolk, turning the departments into the exclusive preserve of families – husbands, wives, sisters, brothers, cousins, and so on. This constrains opportunities for applicants who do not have the *proper* political and social networks.

MULTICULTURALISM AND THE
IDENTITY OF AFRICAN-CANADIANS

Since 1971, official multiculturalism has been the policy platform to manage diversity in Canada, a platform that also derives its legal and constitutional undertones (equality guarantees) from the 1982 *Charter of Rights and Freedoms*. The arrival of a large pool of immigrants from previously non-preferred regions of the world, among other reasons, account for the multicultural policy. As a policy, multiculturalism evolved from a folkloric orientation, through an institutional focus, to a civic focus in the 1970s, 1980s, and 1990s, respectively (Fleras 2001, 340–41).

The folkloric orientation to multiculturalism emphasizes the *celebration of differences* as a means of eradicating prejudice and racism. Institutional multiculturalism focuses on *managing diversity* by establishing relevant organizations and adjusting the modus operandi of others, with a view to addressing systemic and systematic barriers to access and hence *equalizing the playing field* for all actors in the political, economic, and socio-cultural spheres. The principal focus of civic multiculturalism is to forge a sense of citizenship and belonging as a way of deepening loyalty and allegiance to Canada (Fleras 2001, 341). Multiculturalism, in practice, has been the subject of critical reviews (see Henry and Tator 2000; Bissoondath 2002; Bibby 1990). For African-Canadians, the practical implications of multiculturalism are similar to the problems they encounter in their interaction with immigration policies.

One major tenet of multiculturalism is to promote the equality of all cultures. However, the reality is that certain cultures are accorded a pride of place in Canadian society, while the values and practices of other cultures, which are not concordant with those of the dominant groups, are rejected and/or denigrated as *backward* and likely to contaminate the *civilized* ethos of the dominant culture. Minorities are thus put in a situation where they have to reject certain parts of their culture if they want to gain acceptance in mainstream society. The equality that is expected from multiculturalism is, therefore, a mirage, as minority cultures are, at best, subordinated, or at worst, derided, even criminalized.

This is illustrated by the protocols set out for naming children in Canada. In African matrilineal societies, for example, children are not necessarily given the surname of their father, and siblings may have different last names. This is because the practice is to name them after a maternal uncle or uncles from whom they will inherit. There is, however, little understanding of this tradition by state institutions. Thus, when an African-Canadian invites a sibling to visit him or her, immigration officials question the veracity of their relationship and refuse to grant the relative a visa, using the Eurocentric lens of a common last name for siblings. Canadian hospitals also manifest this Eurocentric practice when they insist that birth certificates of newly born children should definitely bear the last name of one parent or the other. Consequently, they have denied African-Canadian parents the desire, indeed the right, to give their children a last name other than their own.

State policies dealing with child care and discipline constitute one area of major conflict between Africans and mainstream institutions, such as schools and law enforcement agencies. There is no question that children, as the most vulnerable members of any society, must be adequately protected. In fact, the protection of children is recognized by African societies as much as any other, and appropriate social sanctions are brought to bear on parents who step beyond the bounds of acceptable behaviour, whether physical, verbal, or otherwise. We therefore want to sound a caveat that the critique below is not an endorsement of child abuse, but a caution against universalizing what constitutes abuse based on subjective predispositions and values. It seems that, in Canada, various African strategies of child rearing are questioned and criminalized. Stern rebukes from parents and spanking are said to constitute verbal and physical abuse. Many African-Canadian families complain about the fact that they are sanctioned for bringing up their children the *African way* which, in the uni-dimensional system defined by mainstream society, is construed as *backward* and abusive. These differences in perceptions about the right way to bring up children have led to a clash of values between Africans and Canadian state institutions. What makes the situation even more contentious is the fact that there is no incontrovertible evidence to support the subjective notions of abuse that the latter are accused of. The only basis for designating their child raising strategies as such is the fact that it does not conform to the practices of the mainstream society. It must be pointed out that, even within mainstream society, there is no consensus about the right way, as shown by the recent controversy surrounding the Supreme Court's ruling on spanking (CBC 2004).

The following narrative about cases involving social agencies further illustrates the uni-dimensionality of knowledge and values, and the attendant assumptions that characterize some Canadian institutions. Bissoondath (2002, 82) cites the case of two young children in Surrey, British Columbia, and three toddlers in New Brunswick who were detained by daycare personnel on suspicion of abuse. The evidence for the *abuse* in both cases was the *Mongolian blue spot* – a light birthmark common to children of Asian and African descent. The duty consciousness of the daycare workers, while commendable, exposes the nature of their training, as well as the broader issue of the nature and quality of knowledge about the *other* at various levels of the Canadian educational system. The liberal-technocratic paradigm of education that has sustained the Canadian educational system is excellent at promoting a "cultural understanding which is fragmented into superficialities and trivialities" (Toh 1993, 10). Consequently, "we are cognizant of the differences – the shape of the eyes, the colour of the skin – that do not count, but we remain uninformed of the ones that do" (Bissoondath 2002, 82). Canadians, in the face of stereotypes, do not really know each other as well as they think they do (Bibby 1990, 171).

Hyphenated identities are a celebrated part of Canadian multiculturalism. However, while policy makers use hyphenation to showcase the diversity of Canadians, it is applied inconsistently, leaving some, but not all, Canadians hyphenated. For example, one rarely hears about *European-Canadians*. The inconsistency leads, either intentionally or unintentionally, to distinguishing *real* Canadians from *mere* Canadians. The ethnicized and racialized character of identity in Canada, in a context where White is normalized and considered the non-ethnic standard, leads inevitably to a situation where only non-Whites are hyphenated in both official and unofficial discourse. Hyphenation then presupposes an adulteration of the *standard*. This implicit meaning of hyphenation is what makes non-Whites, including African-Canadians, the most likely candidates for the question, 'Where are you originally from?' The issue, as Tettey (2001, 172–73) argues, is not the fact of the question being raised, since the question could be asked without malice; it is the persistent probing "even when they identify themselves as Canadian." There appears to be an unstated assumption that "to be Black [in Canada, and unlike the others], you have to come from somewhere else [outside the country]" (Shadd 1994, 10). It is the frequency and persistence of such questions, based on the assumptions stated above, that cast African-Canadians as perpetual outsiders and eternal immigrants, no matter how long they have been legal citizens.

One consequence of the dichotomization of citizenship, in terms of the *authentic* and the *adulterated*, is that those who are categorized as the latter become targets of derision and disdain in times of economic difficulties in particular, and social or political difficulties in general. They are seen as the undeserving intruders sponging off what the *real Canadians* have achieved, or held responsible for society's woes and told to "go home." This reality is a persistent aspect of social relationships in Canada at the same time as official multicultural policies trumpet the virtues of equality and tolerance. The outsider status of the hyphenated Canadian is brought into bold relief, particularly when those who are not considered Canadian enough engage in anti-social behaviour. This is exemplified by the shooting death of a man at the hands of a Calgary police officer in October 2003. The deceased's Sudanese origin was trumpeted in the media – which begs the question, 'Why?' What was the relevance of his birthplace to the issue at hand? Does his Sudanese status help us understand what happened? The only impact that his identification as Sudanese had, as far as *mainstream* society was concerned, was to introduce an *us* versus *them* mentality that pitted "our civilized police officer" with "their innately aggressive and culpable other." He is not the only one who has had a deadly confrontation with the police. Indeed, there are examples of incidents involving White people, as well, but we almost never hear about their place of origin or birth. The media are not the only institution to construct these inconsistent and binary classifications of citizenship. Police authorities have also been known to racialize their strategies and patterns of law enforcement (see James 1998; Henry and Tator 2000).

The process of otherness is not unique to African-Canadians. Indeed, otherness (whether based on race, place of origin, or something else), as a general pattern, comes in handy when the mainstream wants to dissociate itself from a situation. Take the cases of Ben Johnson and Valery Fabrikant. Ben Johnson was the Canadian who won the gold medal in the 1988 Seoul Olympic Games, until the results of his drug tests were announced. When the results indicated that he had tested positive for banned substances, he quickly became the Jamaican-Canadian – the cheating outsider and immigrant. Johnson was a *Canadian* when his fame as an Olympic champion made him worth embracing, and an *immigrant* when his positive test made him a pariah (see Bissoondath 2002, 107). Valery Fabrikant, a research professor in the Faculty of Engineering and Computer Science at Concordia University in Montreal, shot and killed four of his colleagues and seriously wounded an administrative staff member (Pocklington and Tupper 2002, 121–37). Born elsewhere, Valery Fabrikant was referred to as the *Russian émigré* murderer (see Bissoondath 2002, 107; italics in the original).

It is fascinating to note that the prefix of the hyphenated identity tends to be dropped altogether when immigrants are involved in major positive achievements, and they are accepted simply as Canadians. For example, John Polanyi, born elsewhere, is the *Canadian* Nobel Prize winner in chemistry; Michael Ondaatje, also born elsewhere, is the *Canadian* Booker Prize winner (Bissoondath 2002, 107; italics in the original). What the foregoing discussion about the selective use of Canadian vis-à-vis immigrants shows are the connotations implicit in ethnic identifiers and the fact that they are only applied to those who are not members of the country's *founding peoples*, especially when they are involved in negative cases or situations.

Apart from hyphenation, simplification of culture is another problem in multicultural Canada. Culture is simplified when the supposed exotic features of the *ethnics* are put on display without any context or intention to learn anything of value, let alone challenge existing stereotypes. Simplification of culture is best seen in the so-called *ethnic festivals* that are part of the summer rituals in several Canadian cities. Policy makers present these festivals and related cultural differences as mechanisms "towards intercultural sharing [and] ... a means of demolishing barriers" (Fleras 2001, 344). However, sharing cultural foods and music, which seem to be the main practices at such festivals, would not, by themselves, contribute to demolishing intercultural barriers. To put it bluntly, ethnic festivals cannot engender acceptance of the equality of cultures and respect for differences unless they are anchored in critical learning and interrogation of culture that promotes intercultural learning and understanding. African groups have organized festivals and other events, such as Independence Day celebrations, to showcase their cultures and histories to the larger society. By and large, however, these events only tend to reinforce their otherness, as those who attend only focus on the *strange* and *exotic* performances and cuisines.

CONCLUSION

Government acts, whether consciously or unconsciously, play a major role in the consistencies or inconsistencies in the theoretical and practical implications of identity construction. With implicit and explicit barriers to belonging in Canada, it is no wonder that African-Canadians seem marginal in terms of their social location. This outcome is both the result of, and the response to, structural and attitudinal constraints.

The foregoing analysis invites some policy recommendations. It is reasonable to argue that, of all the groups that are most likely to be hyphenated, Africans in Canada would be at the very top. Hyphenation shows the simple fact that government policies cannot, therefore, promote equality and celebration of difference, because the implicit "separate but equal" tone in the call would not guarantee equality of outcomes for all and sundry. This is because, for the vast majority of Africans in Canada, there is no way for them to change their physical attributes of colour to a colourless one, and they therefore remain the most visible of the so-called visible minorities.

Government policies on classification of Canadians combine physical features (read, colour) and geographical categories. It is important to clarify the basis for the classifications and the context in which features and geographical categories would hold sway. If the goal of classification is to showcase the diversity of the Canadian population, it would be necessary to be consistent in the classification. Otherwise, some Canadians, irrespective of the length of their stay in the country, would continue to be perpetual immigrants who, because of that, could easily be invited to go home in times of political and economic difficulties or upheavals.

Government immigration policies should begin to alert potential immigrants, in no uncertain terms, about the reality of the Canadian job market. The problem is the inconsistency of encouraging and approving the application of highly skilled immigrants to come to the country, only to find that their qualifications and skills are not valued. The result is a complete waste of talent, and the Canadian society at large is the ultimate loser. It is also important to confront the rhetoric and reality of merit in hiring vis-à-vis the job market. The use of political and social capital to secure jobs as documented in the Public Service Commission study might reflect a general, but reluctant, admission that, in Canada, a good job is reserved for a chosen few. Meanwhile, the aspirations, hopes, and dreams of the broader society are limited to the recitation of feel good multiracial and multi-ethnic (cultural) slogans. Underlying the inconsistencies in immigration and multicultural practices are beliefs and values that inform social attitude, behaviour, and practices from the individual to the institutional levels.

Education is often cited as one viable option to address some of the stereotypical and prejudicial origins of values and beliefs. The question is: What kind of education? Perhaps that education should include an understanding of political, socio-cultural formations that have affected, and continue to shape, the experiences of several ethnic groups in Canada. It should be a transformative education that "empowers learners, not only to critically understand the world's realities in a holistic framework, but also to move learners and teachers [and the larger society] to act towards a more peaceful, just, and liberating world" (Toh 1993, 11).

While enacting policies to ensure successful integration, the ability of the Canadian government to implement its policies is hostage to the complex interaction between internal domestic, socio-political forces and external structures of the global, political economy. Indeed, the broader context of belonging, treatment, and participation of citizens is the ability of the nation-state to forge the collective sense of identity. In Canada, as in other countries, that ability is mediated by forces of globalization (Abu-Laban and Gabriel 2002; Laxer 2000). At the same time, there is nothing inevitable about policy choices. Hence, if the goal of an inclusive and democratic society is still a policy objective in Canada, policy makers need to better address the theoretical and political barriers in the identity, representation, and integration of Canadians, not only of African descent, but of all descents.

REFERENCES

Abu-Laban, Yasmeen, and Christina Gabriel. 2002. *Selling Diversity: Immigration, Multiculturalism, Employment Equity, and Globalization.* Peterborough, ON: Broadview.

Allahar, Anton L. 1993. When Black first became worth less. *International Journal of Comparative Sociology* 34, nos. 1–2: 39–55.

Anderson, Benedict. 1991. *Imagined Communities*, 2nd ed. London: Verso.

Barber, Benjamin. 1995. *Jihad vs. McWorld.* Toronto: Random.

Bibby, Reginald. 1990. *Mosaic Madness.* Toronto: Stoddart.

Bissoondath, Neil. 2002. *Selling Illusions: The Cult of Multiculturalism in Canada.* Rev. ed. Toronto: Penguin.

Bloom, Michael. 2001. *Brain Gain: The Economic Benefits of Recognizing Learning and Learning Credentials in Canada.* Ottawa: Conference Board of Canada.

Bolaria, Singh B., and Peter S. Li. 1988. *Racial Oppression in Canada.* Toronto: Garamond.

Boyko, John. 1995. *Last Steps to Freedom: The Evolution of Canadian Racism.* Winnipeg: Watson and Dwyer.

Brueilly, John. 1994. *Nationalism and the State.* Chicago: University of Chicago Press.

Canadian Broadcasting Corporation (CBC). 1999 [online]. *Volunteer angry after contracting TB in Kosovar refugee camps* [cited 15 March 2004]. (www.cbc. ca/stories/print/1999/09/28/canada/tb990928).

———. 2001a [online]. *Immigration minister wants to know why British tourist detained* [cited 15 March 2004]. (www.cbc.ca/stories/2001/06/04/canada/akintade_ immig010604).

———. 2001b [online]. *Deadly ebola virus may be in Canada* [cited 15 March 2004]. (www.cbc.ca/stories/print/2001/02/06/canada/virus_reax010206).

———. 2001c [online]. *Congolese woman cleared of deadly type of virus* [cited 15 March 2004]. (www.cbc.ca/stories/2001/02/08/canada/ebola_010208).

———. 2004 [online]. *Supreme Court upholds spanking law* [cited 15 March 2004]. (www. cbc.ca/stories/2004/01/30/canada/spanking040130).

Citizenship and Immigration Canada. 2002. *Pursuing Canada's Commitment to Immigration*. Ottawa: Department of Citizenship and Immigration Canada.

———. 2004 [online]. *Visa offices* [cited 15 March 2004]. (www.cic.gc.ca).

Codjoe, Henry M. 1998. Race and economic development: Some historical and contemporary perspectives. *Review of Human Factor Studies* 4, no. 2: 88–113.

Cornell, Stephen, and Douglas Hartmann. 1998. *Ethnicity and Race: Making Identities in a Changing World*. Thousand Oaks, CA: Pine Forge.

Curry, Bill. 2004 [online]. *Family connections key to civil-service job, review finds* [cited 6 January 2004]. (www.canada.com).

Dabrowski, Wojtek. 2000. Educated immigrants find it hard to get jobs in their field in Canada. *Canadian Press Newswire*, 28 September.

D'Aliesio, Renata. 2003. Immigrants find Canada less likely to pay for their skills. *Edmonton Journal*, 12 March, A2.

Dixon, Guy. 2003 [online]. *License to cure is a long time coming* [cited 15 January 2004]. (www.workopolis.com).

Driedger, Leo. 1996. *Multi-Ethnic Canada: Identities and Inequalities*. Toronto: Oxford University Press.

Finnie, Ross. 2001. *The Brain Drain: Myth and Reality: What It Is and What Should Be Done*. Montreal: IRPP.

Fleras, Augie. 2001. *Social Problems in Canada: Conditions, Constructions, and Challenges*. 3rd ed. Toronto: Prentice Hall.

Fleras, Augie, and Jean L. Elliott. 2003. *Unequal Relations: An Introduction to Race and Ethnic Dynamics in Canada*. 4th ed. Toronto: Prentice Hall.

Gellner, Ernest. 1983. *Nations and Nationalism*. Oxford: Blackwell.

Gibbins, Roger, Loleen Youngman, and Jennifer Stewart-Toth. 1996. Ideologies, identity, and citizenship. In *Mindscapes: Political Ideologies towards the Twenty-First Century*, ed. R. Gibbins and L. Youngman, 266–92. Toronto: McGraw-Hill Ryerson.

Giddens, Anthony. 1984. *The Constitution of Society*. Cambridge: Polity.

Granovetter, Mark. 1983. The strength of weak ties: A network theory revisited. In *Sociological Theory*, ed. R. Collins, 201–33. San Francisco: Jossey-Bass.

———. 1995. *Getting a Job: A Study of Contacts and Careers*. 2nd ed. Chicago: University of Chicago Press.

Hall, Stuart, and David Held. 1989. Citizens and citizenship. In *New Times: Changing Face of Politics in the 1990s*, ed. S. Hall and M. Jacques, 173–90. London/New York: Lawrence & Wishart.

Harding, Katherine. 2003 [online]. *A leap of faith* [cited 15 January 2004]. (www. workopolis.com).

Hayhoe, Ruth, ed. 1993. *Knowledge across Cultures: Universities East and West*. Hubei/ Toronto: Hubei Education and Ontario Institute for Studies in Education Presses.

Henry, Frances, and Carol Tator. 2000. *The Colour of Democracy: Racism in Canadian Society*. 2nd ed. Toronto: Harcourt Brace.

Henry, Frances, and Effie Ginzberg. 1985. *Who Gets the Job?: A Test of Racial Discrimination in Employment*. Toronto: Social Planning Council of Metropolitan Toronto and Urban Alliance on Race Relations.

Hobsbawm, Eric J. 1991. *Nations and Nationalism since 1780: Programme, Myth, Reality.* Cambridge: Cambridge University Press.

Hobsbawm, Eric, and Terrence Ranger, eds. 1997. *The Invention of Tradition.* Cambridge: Cambridge University Press.

Hughes, Everett C., and Helen M. Hughes. 1952. *Where Peoples Meet: Racial and Ethnic Frontiers.* Glencoe, IL: Free Press.

Ignatieff, Michael. 1993. *Blood and Belonging: Journeys into the New Nationalism.* Toronto: Viking.

Isajiw, Wsevolod W. 1999. *Understanding Diversity.* Toronto: Thompson.

James, Carl E. 1994. The paradoxes of power and privilege: Race, gender, and occupational position. *Canadian Women Studies* 14, no. 2: 47–51.

———. 1998. "Up to no good": Black on the streets and encountering police. In *Racism and Social Inequality in Canada,* ed. V. Satzewich, 157–76. Toronto: Thompson Educational.

———. 2003. *Seeing Ourselves: Exploring Race, Ethnicity, and Culture.* 3rd ed. Toronto: Thompson Educational.

Kallen, Ellen. 1995. *Ethnicity and Human Rights in Canada.* 2nd ed. Toronto: Oxford University Press.

Kendall, Diana, Vicki Nygaard, and Edward Thompson. 2004. *Social Problems in a Diverse Society.* Canadian ed. Toronto: Pearson.

Laxer, Gordon. 2000. Surviving the Americanizing new right. *Canadian Review of Sociology and Anthropology* 37, no. 1: 55–75.

Li, Peter. 2001. The market worth of immigrants' educational credentials. *Canadian Public Policy* 26 (March): 23–38.

Miller, Seymour M. 2001 [online]. *My meritocratic rise* Tikkun, March/April. [cited 30 May 2002]. (www.tikkun.org).

Morrow, Raymond A., and Carlos A. Torres. 1995. *Social Theory and Education: A Critique of Theories of Social and Cultural Reproduction.* Albany: State University of New York Press.

Olaniram, Bolanle, and David Williams. 1995. Communication distortion: An intercultural lesson from the visa application process. *Communication Quarterly* 43, no. 2: 225–40.

Pocklington, Tom, and Alan Tupper. 2002. *No Place to Learn: Why Universities Aren't Working.* Vancouver: UBC Press.

Porter, John. 1965. *The Vertical Mosaic.* Toronto: University of Toronto Press.

Puplampu, Korbla P., and Henry M. Codjoe. 2001. Human factor studies and social conflict: A socio-historical and comparative analysis of racial and ethnic dimensions. In *Portraits of Human Behavior and Performance: The Human Factor in Action,* ed. S. Adjibolosoo, 79–108. Lanham, MD: University Press of America.

Reitz, Jeffrey. 2001. Immigrant skill utilization in the Canadian labour market: Implications for human capital research. *Journal of International Migration and Integration* 2, no. 3: 347–78.

Reitz, Jeffrey, ed. 2003. *Host Societies and the Reception of Immigrants*. San Diego: Center
    for Comparative Immigration Research, University of California Press.
Richmond, Anthony H. 1994. *Global apartheid: Refugees, racism, and the new world
    order*. Toronto: Oxford University Press.
Rickard, Maurice. 1994. Liberalism, multiculturalism, and minority protection. *Social
    Theory and Practice* 20, no. 2: 143–70.
Ritzer, George. 2000. *Sociological Theory*. 5th ed. New York: McGraw-Hill.
Samuel, John, and Dieter Schachhuber. 2000. Perspectives on Canadian diversity. In
    Twenty-First Century Canadian Diversity, ed. S. E. Nancoo, 14–35. Mississauga:
    Canadian Educators'.
Schermerhorn, Richard A. 1978. *Comparative Ethnic Relations: A Framework for Theory
    and Research*. Chicago: University of Chicago Press.
Séguin, Rhéal. 1995. Firm rejection of the status quo is only clear result. *Globe and Mail*,
    31 October, A1, A10.
Shadd, Adrienne. 1994. Where are you *really* from?: Notes of an "immigrant" from
    North Buxton, Ontario. In *Talking about Difference: Encounters in Culture,
    Language, and Identity*, ed. C. E. James and A. Shadd, 9–15. Toronto: Between
    the Lines.
Simmons, Alan. 1998. Racism and immigration policy. In *Racism and Social Inequality in
    Canada: Concepts, Controversies, and Strategies of Resistance*, ed. V. Satzewich,
    87–114. Toronto: Thompson Educational.
Sollors, Werner. 1995. Who is ethnic? In *The Postcolonial Studies Reader*, ed. B. Ashcroft,
    G. Griffiths, and H. Tiffin, 219–22. London: Routledge.
Statistics Canada. 1996. *1996 Census*. Ottawa: Statistics Canada.
———. 2003. Catalogue No. 97F0009XCB011002.
Stromquist, Nelly P. 2002. *Education in a Globalized World: The Connectivity of Economic
    Power, Technology, and Knowledge*. Lanham, MD: Rowman & Littlefield.
Tettey, Wisdom J. 2001. What does it mean to be African-Canadian? Conflicts in
    representation, identity, and community. In *A Passion for Identity: Canadian
    Studies for the Twenty-First Century*, ed. D. Taras and B. Rasporich, 161–82.
    Toronto: Nelson.
Thomas, William I., and Dorothy S. Thomas. 1932. *The Child in America: Behaviour
    Problems and Programs*. New York: Alfred A. Knopf.
Toh, Swee H. 1993. Bringing the world into the classroom: Global literacy and a question
    of paradigms. *Global Education* 1: 9–17.
Toneguzzi, Mario. 2003. Time to recognize credentials, feds told. *Calgary Herald*. 27
    August, B1.
Turner, Jonathan. 1998. *The Structure of Sociological Theory*. 6th ed. Belmont, CA:
    Wadsworth.
Wallace, Ruth A., and Alison Wolf. 1999. *Contemporary Sociological Theory: Expanding
    the Classical Tradition*. Upper Saddle River, NJ: Prentice Hall.
Weber, Max. 1996. The origin of ethnic groups. In *Ethnicity*, ed. J. Hutchinson and A. D.
    Smith, 35–40. Oxford/New York: Oxford University Press.

Wellman, Barry. 1983. Network analysis: Some basic principles. In *Sociological Theory*, ed. R. Collins, 155–200. San Francisco: Jossey-Bass.

Whitaker, Reginald. 1991. *Double Standard: The Secret Story of Canadian Immigration*. Toronto: Lester and Orpen Dennys.

3

REFLECTIONS ON THE LONG STRUGGLE FOR INCLUSION:
The Experiences of People of African Origin

Ali A. Abdi

INTRODUCTION

WITH THE NUMBER of African-Canadians now residing in this country approaching the half-million mark, it would be very useful to increase the number, as well as the breadth, of scholarly treatments that investigate the social, political, economic, educational, and cultural situations of these Canadians. African-Canadians expect and strive for full participation in all these arenas, especially in a highly developed nation that is consistently ranked among the *best* places to live in the world. However, as we shall see, the historical marginalization of Blacks has not been completely overcome, even though there has been some limited progress, including an increasing number of people who are using all available economic institutions and, where necessary, legal avenues to better their lives. Hence, it is clear that while legal racism and/or socially sanctioned exclusion from viable sectors of economic, political, and educational development have been neutralized, institutional forms of exclusion have not yet been completely overcome.

In order to discuss and analyze these and related issues, this chapter combines a historical focus with a quasi-subjective interrogation of current realities to account for the problems and prospects of the socio-economic situation of Blacks. Let me state that, while the overall focus of the book is on the experiences and social conditions of those from continental Africa, this generalist chapter provides observations and analyses that thematically speak about the case of all Blacks, including those from the Caribbean region and possibly from elsewhere. Such an overview will set the context for understanding the socially constructed *racial* and historico-cultural positioning of continental Africans in Canada.

CRITICAL HISTORICAL AND SOCIO-POLITICAL POINTERS

History, it is often said, tends to be unkind to people who neglect it. Historical accounts of a society, whether accurately recorded or not, play a major role in our interpretation of the contemporary social world. Therefore, the historical context of African-Canadians, to a large extent, is the appropriate starting point for understanding their contemporary experiences (Bolaria and Li 1988). Blacks were among the first non-Indigenous residents of Canada. As Robin Winks (1997 [1971]) notes in his authoritative book *The Blacks in Canada: A History*, Blacks were here before the middle of the seventeenth century. This early presence is partly related to slavery. But beyond slavery, Blacks have also been here as free, educated, and skilled people earning a decent living and contributing greatly to society over the past 350 years.

Broadly speaking, the Black experience can be categorized into three major historical periods. The first spans the early part of the sixteenth century to the end of the eighteenth century, followed by the second period, dating from the early 1800s to the mid-twentieth century. The last extends from the mid-twentieth century to the present (Mensah 2002; Winks 1997; Lampkin 1985; Boyko 1995). The first wave of Blacks was comprised of people who arrived as servants, slaves, or indentured labourers. Olivier le Jeune, from Mozambique, is the first African "to have been transported directly from Africa, to have been sold as a slave in New France, and apparently to have died a free man" (Winks 1997, 1–2). However, Matthew da Costa (or Mathieu da Coste), the Negro servant of Governor Sieur Du Gua de Monts, is generally considered to be the first known Black settler in Canada (Saney 1998; Winks 1997; Lampkin 1985). He worked in Nova Scotia, then later with Champlain as an interpreter in other Canadian communities.

Labour shortages towards the end of the seventeenth century prompted a concerted effort to import Blacks, mostly slaves, in significant numbers, an exercise that continued well into the early nineteenth century (Mensah 2002, 44; Walker 1980). This labour infusion was critical for the economic well-being of Ontario and Quebec, as well as the Atlantic Provinces (New Brunswick and Nova Scotia). Black slaves "were used to build Halifax, which later became a leading centre for the public auction of Black slaves" (Mensah 2002, 45).

Typical immigrants, in the sense of free people, did not arrive in Canada until the early 1800s. The initial group was composed of Black fugitives from the United States of America who arrived via the Underground Railroad. The Underground Railroad, which has become a legendary part of the Black experience in Canada, "was unquestionably the highly effective means by which a number – an exaggerated and indefinite number – of fugitive slaves reached British North America" (Winks 1997, 233). The Underground Railroad was possible because the *Abolition Act of 1793* in Upper Canada made runaway slaves who entered Canada theoretically free. The number of Black fugitives who actually came to Canada this way remains a mystery, and that adds to the legendary nature of the Railroad. What is known is that some fugitives did come into Canada through the activities of various organizations and individuals. With reference to the former, the Pennsylvania Society for Promoting the Abolition of Slavery, the Quakers, and the American Baptist Free Mission Society deserve some attention (Winks 1997). On an individual level, Harriet Tubman was instrumental, not only in arranging for the movement of people, but also in providing accommodation to some of the refugees (Mensah 2002). Estimates place the number of Black fugitives who entered Canada between 1850 and 1860 at about twenty thousand (Mensah 2002, 50).

Among those who came to Canada during the era of slavery in the United States were hundreds of freedom seekers who saw Canada as a place where they could exercise their full humanity. Many of the so-called "fugitive" African slaves saw Canada "as the promised land, the land of freedom. Canada was romanticized as being a utopia" (McClain 1979, 1). Indeed, a popular song during those times was "I am on my way to Canada ... That cold and distant land ... Farewell old master ... I am on my way to Canada. Where coloured men are free" (Hill 1981, 25).

There was undoubtedly some physical freedom that accompanied the escape to Canada, but the rest of the *story*, that is, definable and reliable notions of equity, full socio-economic and political rights, and the support and open mechanisms required to earn a decent living, were never a reality. It is indeed the case that this country has always been organized around a complex web of, if not legal, at least institutional, racism and its attendant modes of socio-economic and political exclusion. As Tulloch (1975, 140) noted, Blacks "in Canada, as in the United States, [have been continuously] victims of an excruciatingly destructive system of oppression, [not only via] the economic and social legacy of slavery but also [through] its ideological heritage, institutional racism."

Despite these impediments, Hill (1981) observes that early arrivals from the United States in the mid-1800s, were, as was the case with other immigrant groups, hardworking and determined men and women. They cleared the land, built their own homes with their own hands, and successfully raised large, families under trying and, by all accounts, fundamentally racist surroundings and circumstances (see also Winks 1997). Some became successful and prosperous. Winks (1997, 247–48) documents the case of John Long who, in the Toronto of the 1830s, acquired property in the Niagara district, as well as that of the "276 Negroes in London [who] owned real estate valued at $13,504" in 1853. But the hard work and self-reliant ethic of Blacks did not diminish their socio-economic marginalization. Theoretically, the fugitive slaves were free in Upper Canada. In practice, their conditions were unstable. The fortunes of even the successful ones would change with the economic panic of 1857 to reflect the lot of those who had to contend with prejudice and racism in accessing resources and rewards. The point is that, whether successful or not, the cultural marker of being labeled Black held sway in their relationship with the larger society.

The relationship between Blacks and the dominant segments of Canadian society is demonstrated by the case of Africville. Established in 1842, Africville, near Halifax, was an important community of Black slaves until the City of Halifax, under circumstances still being contested, decided to relocate it in the 1960s (Clairmont and Magill 1999). A major contention is that the City of Halifax withheld basic social services (water and sewer) from the community, located undesirable services (a garbage dump) nearby, and then cited the lack of water and sewer services as reasons to demolish the community. Perhaps it is the contested nature of the relocation, which some contend smacked of racism, that prompted the Federal Government, in 2002, to declare Africville a national historic site (CBC 2002). Africville highlights, directly or indirectly, how race influences social policies and the implications for those judged "inferior" and undeserving of social goods and resources. It is instructive to note that the Roman Catholic Church presented the relationship between slaves and their masters as "inherent in man [*sic*] but was a temporary condition arising from the accident of events" (Winks 1997, 12). In essence, slaves should be morally upright, because spiritual life should be their priority and not their status as slaves! This case lends some theoretical significance to Karl Marx's famous dictum of how religion "is the sigh of the oppressed creature [but also] the *opium* of the people" (Sayer 1989, 137, italics in the original).

The experiences of Blacks who fanned out to Western Canada were, by and large, not different from those of their counterparts in other parts of Canada. They encountered official obstacles by way of policies that, in turn, encouraged the larger society to harass or deny services to the "unwanted." In effect, it was an atmosphere characterized by a collective conspiracy to denigrate and exclude. In Manitoba, J. S. Woodsworth, Superintendent of the Peoples' Mission of Winnipeg and co-founder of the Co-operative Commonwealth Federation (CCF), referring to John R. Commons' comments in the *Chautauquan* (November 1903) regarding American Blacks, stated, as follows: "All travelers speak of their impulsiveness, strong sexual passion, and lack of will power. The very qualities of intelligence and manliness which are essential for citizenship in a democracy were systematically expunged from the [N]egro race through two hundred years of slavery" (Woodsworth 1972, 158). Woodsworth, writing on behalf of a religious organization interested in ensuring the smooth assimilation of immigrants in Canada, noted that Canada did not have a "Negro problem" (Woodsworth 1972, 158). One cannot help but notice how Woodsworth, without any critical analysis, sanitized the experiences of Blacks in Canada with the self-congratulatory remark that the country had no "[N]egro" problem. Whether the lack of analysis of the [N]egro problem in Canada was an act of commission or omission, the comment fits a general pattern (see Winks 1997, 233).

Gwyn (1995, 174), for example, maintains that "only a relatively small number of native-born [B]lacks have had to endure historical discrimination" in Canada, and the experiences of those few, while horrible, were not "comparable to the slavery and legalized segregation suffered by their counterparts in the United States." The implicit suggestion of slaves in Canada having a *better* life than those in the United States is distasteful, minimizes the human indignities of slavery in general, and fails to acknowledge that their particular experiences in Canada included legalized segregation (see Mensah 2002; Boyko 1995).

While Woodsworth was announcing the absence of a Negro problem in Canada, "Prairie governments, business establishments, and many ordinary citizens did all they could to frustrate the existing Black communities and also to prevent the influx of additional Blacks into the region" (Mensah 2002, 52). In Woodsworth's own Winnipeg, Bruce Walker, the Dominion's Commissioner of Immigration in the city, admitted that the Canadian government "was doing all in its power through a policy of persuasion, to keep [N]egroes out of Western Canada" (cited in Winks 1997, 311). The policy of persuasion had several components. The Commissioner expected the American Consul-General in Winnipeg "to bar [Blacks] from Canada, upon the broad ground of being undesirables" (cited in Winks 1997, 311), and remind them that the climate was unsuitable for them. The Dominion Commissioner of Immigration also built an incentive into the work of agencies that dealt with American Blacks by, for example, rewarding the medical examiner for every Negro rejected (Boyko 1995, 166; Winks 1997, 310–11; see also Lampkin 1985).

In order not to be perceived as soft on the settlement of American Blacks or outdone in the efforts to halt their migration, the cities of Calgary, Edmonton, and Winnipeg passed resolutions between 1910 and 1911 that called for the immigration of Blacks to be stopped. Not content with the resolution alone, the Edmonton City Council, in April 1911, went ahead and "passed a resolution completely banning Blacks from the city" (Boyko 1995, 155; see also Thompson 1979). Besides the resolution of the city councils, organizations like the Edmonton Board of Trade, the Athabasca Landing Board of Trade, and the Imperial Order of the Daughters of the Empire registered their opposition to the settlement of Blacks in the province through petitions to the Federal government. These petitions were, in many cases, based on stereotyping and outright lies designed to engender a hostile reception towards Blacks (Kelly 1998, 38–39). The Great Northern Railway was also instrumental in preventing the settlement of Blacks on the Prairies by refusing to sell tickets to would-be travelers (Winks 1997, 312). Yet Blacks refused to succumb to discrimination and other difficulties. Some of them single-handedly cleared the wilderness and created, in the process, new cultivable lands, which led to their relative prosperity in areas such as the Amber Valley (Thompson 1979).

The reception of Blacks in British Columbia can be placed on a continuum from warm to hostile. On the warm end of the continuum, the leadership offered by Governor James Douglas is noteworthy. Perhaps he offered that kind of leadership on pragmatic and personal grounds. As a critical voice among the established elite in Victoria, he articulated the general impression that the island needed as many settlers as possible to serve as a bulwark against the Native Indians. On a personal note, Douglas' approach was also influenced by the "knowledge that his mother was either a West Indian mulatto or a Creole" (Winks 1997, 275).

Once a member of the establishment had set the tone, some media outlets, notably the *British Colonist*, reminded the larger society about the "sobriety, honesty, industry, intelligence, and enterprise" the Black settlers would bring with them (cited in Winks 1997, 275). Indeed, as Krauter and Davis (1978) note, the Black settlers went into various businesses (e.g., carpentry and trading), mainly as sole proprietors, but sometimes in competition with the Hudson's Bay Company, which also employed Blacks (Winks 1997, 275; see also Lampkin 1985). On the hostile end of the continuum were the activities of some religious organizations. The "church," as Mensah (2002, 51) notes, "was one of the first major sources of racial division on Vancouver Island." However, because Blacks in British Columbia "were not barred from the common schools, public office, or the churches, as they were in Ontario and Nova Scotia" (Winks 1997, 286), Krauter and Davis (1978, 45) conclude that that was the "closest approximation to equality for Canadian Blacks in the nineteenth century."

Until the middle of the twentieth century, Blacks were generally less forthcoming in demanding their rights. This was due to their vulnerable status vis-à-vis the larger society and their relatively small numbers. They therefore sought more accommodating ways to achieve their objectives. This approach, which conformed more to the development ideology of Booker T. Washington in the United States (see Winks 1997 [1971]), set the context for the failed and fundamentally flawed philosophy of separate and essentially unequal development between dominant and subordinate groups.

Up to the 1960s, the best a Black could hope for in the world of work, regardless of level of education and skills, was to become a domestic servant, a porter, a shoe shine boy, or other cleaning jobs. The pay for such jobs, not surprisingly, was pathetic, benefits were unheard of, and job security and employee rights were technically oxymoronic. Indeed, this was the case of Earle Swift, an African-Canadian who graduated from McGill University with a bachelor's degree in economics in the mid-1920s. The only job Earle Swift could find was to work as a sleeping car porter for the Canadian National (CN) railways (Holas 2000).

The tendency of Blacks to approach relationships with dominant groups with a sense of docility showed long-term continuities that were remarkably visible up to the 1960s. It was only in the post-1960s era that Blacks in Canada, mainly emulating the civil rights movement in the United States, became more vociferous in their demands for political and economic rights. The inter-generational difference in approach was evident in the fact that the post-1960s group was more willing to take risks in achieving livelihood possibilities in a country where they were, for all practical purposes, third or even fourth class citizens. The new demands by Blacks for a more meaningful place in Canadian society shattered long-held and pathetically false perceptions about their capacity to achieve much beyond childish excitement, generally triggered by satisfied physical needs. An example of these perceptions was expressed in the following racist comment by none other than Adams Archibald, the former Lieutenant Governor of Nova Scotia. The Governor was *sure* at the beginning of the twentieth century that "a [N]egro with plenty to eat and drink, with clothes and a shelter, had little care for anything else, has no other ambition, [and] to him, labour is a last resort" (in Walker 1985, 4). In other words, the overwhelming majority of Blacks were, until recently and in terms of earning a living, at the mercy of widespread and exclusively racist practices.

The above discussion of the broad historical experiences of Black-Canadians provides the background for understanding the situation of Africans who have come to Canada since the latter part of the 1960s as part of the third major wave of Black migration to Canada. The major stimuli for this wave, as noted in the introductory chapter, were the changes in immigration policy, the declining number of immigrants from traditional sources, and deteriorating economic conditions in several African countries during the latter part of the 1970s. With these changes, tens of thousands of Blacks arrived, initially from Caribbean countries, later from continental Africa. It was mainly as a result of these changing demographic realities that new and more forceful demands for political and general human rights for Blacks, including continental African immigrants, became a more visible feature of Canada's public space. It must be acknowledged, nevertheless, that while the numbers were important, they cannot, by themselves, empower people. Those who hold economic power, even if their numbers are small, can control the economically weak. Another significant dimension of the post-1960 era is the fact that a large number of new Black immigrants were professionals seeking better economic and educational opportunities. These immigrants were first class citizens in their countries of origin and were culturally and socially endowed, even if socio-economically deprived. As such, many in this new group of immigrants did not see themselves as inferior vis-à-vis anybody. These dynamics arguably contributed significantly towards elevating the influence of African-Canadian voices beyond where they had hitherto been.

SOME CURRENT SOCIO-ECONOMIC AND POLITICAL REALITIES

Despite the more *noisy* struggles of the post-1960 period, Blacks continued to be marginalized, especially in terms of job opportunities as they tried to earn a decent living in urban centers. The extent of their economic participation was constrained by painful but hard-to-prove practices of institutional prejudice. Mensah (2002) notes that, by and large, African-Canadians are predominantly marginalized in terms of income, employment, and occupational status. Indeed, as promulgated in John Porter's (1965) classic work *The Vertical Mosaic* (1965) and as re-affirmed by Helmes-Hayes and Curtis (1998) in *The Vertical Mosaic Revisited*, the Canadian terrain is still, overall, rife with situations where ethnic and racial considerations determine employment and the concomitant advancements that result from it. It must be acknowledged that some highly determined and enterprising African-Canadians have made progress in the business and professional realms. By and large, however, African-Canadians with qualifications similar to their non-African compatriots are less likely to be employed and more likely to be concentrated in jobs with less prestige and lower income (Mensah 2002; Torczyner et al. 1997; also see Laryea and Hayfron in this volume). Their marginalization in this regard is aptly captured by Cecil Foster (1996, 84), as follows:

> How vulnerable the [African-Canadian] community is can be seen in the daily hardships of the thousands of professional people who have spent the last while walking the streets of major Canadian cities looking for jobs. None of them seem to have a resume good enough to get the job they deserve. Most of them protest about how they always manage to come up short because of someone with connections who jumps ahead of them because of a special relationship with the person hiring, *including, of course, good old ethnicity and colour affiliations, and, therefore, psycho-cultural and emotional (some would call this trust and dependability assumptions)* relationships, because of a special position in the network (emphases are mine).

These challenges have not subsided, even with their increasing numbers in the Canadian population. In fact, the multi-layered racism that African-Canadians have to contend with is so entrenched within institutions and in the collective psyche of mainstream society that "striving to be twice or three times as good to have a chance" is usually not enough (see Alexander and Glaze 1996;

Ruggles and Rovinescu 1996; and Thompson 1979). As Walker (1985, 24) correctly points out,

> [t]he [African-Canadian] experience demonstrates that racial discrimination has not been directly linked to numbers, cultural differences, economic depression, or prosperity. [While] legal reforms have restrained openly hostile behaviour, these have not affected the essential factors leading to discrimination.

In the midst of continuing complaints by both public and private enterprises and their managers about the shortage of engineers and other technical professionals in Canada, one cannot help but share the bewilderment of many African-Canadians trained in those professions, some of whom received their training in Canada. Anecdotal evidence suggests that a good number of them cannot find gainful employment.

The preceding points are not intended to indicate that others in Canada, especially members of so-called visible minority groups, are not subjected to these exclusionary practices. The realities of the *colour* coded considerations so prevalent in Canada, complemented by the harsh legacies of history and by the current conditions that African-Canadians endure, suggest their marginalization is exacerbated by the fact that they are the darkest *parcel* of *The Dark Side of the Nation* (see Bannerji 2000). They bear the brunt of the crime of racism and its enduring derivatives more than other visible minorities, as evidenced by the 1992 Stephen Lewis *Report on Racism in Ontario*.

The preceding observations represent the overall situation of African-Canadians in Canada. It is important to note, however, that the situation varies across the country, albeit not significantly. Mensah (2002), for example, notes that Blacks are socio-economically better off in the Prairie provinces (Alberta, Manitoba, and Saskatchewan). This observation is surprising, because one would have expected that the province of Ontario, due to the high concentration of Blacks there, would provide a better socio-economic environment. Blacks tend to be major targets of racial profiling, unlike Whites and other non-White groups. They are more likely to be stopped, questioned, searched, and generally harassed by the police. The connotations (as well as the realities) of the situation here are that some Canadian police departments are willfully criminalizing a person's skin colour by violating the legal rights of Black Canadians.

A problematic, possible by-product of this encounter is a situation wherein young Black men, especially, react negatively to this abominable violation of their rights and risk incriminating themselves due to the counter-persecution behaviour that might be expected after suffering such persecution. The criminal records that result from such incidents then stunt their employment and economic prospects, and hence, any potential for socio-economic development.

Worse still, the cycle becomes inter-generational, not only in terms of socio-economic mobility, but also, and more destructively, in the continuities of the labeling *game* which casts Blacks as troublemakers and underachievers, while positive contributions and accomplishments by members of that community are ignored (see Codjoe 2001).

The foregoing discussion depicts a situation where Blacks, especially, are hardly the agents of their lives and are simply falling into predetermined traps. Centuries of subjugation continue to be sustained by current oppressive practices by police and other powerful authorities from the dominant society. The following words by Paul Laurence Dunbar (in Thompson 1979, 93) reflect the situation of a large number of African-Canadians:

> We wear the mask that grins and lies
> It hides our cheeks and shades our eyes
> This debt we pay to human guile
> With torn and bleeding hearts we smile
> And mouth with myriad subtleties.

The reality is that racism is alive and well in multicultural and multiethnic Canada, whether it is structured through the mechanics of modernity or sustains itself in the more nuanced framework of postmodernism. Indeed, this was the finding in a nation-wide survey conducted by *Maclean's Magazine* at the end of 1993, which dubbed so-called mainstream Canadians as *polite bigots* (read, discursively promulgated and cleverly implemented institutional racism).

CONCLUSIONS

In this chapter, I have engaged in a general discussion on certain historical points of African-Canadian life, with more systematic pointers to the current socio-economic situation of this specifically marginalized group of the Canadian population. From re-visiting some of the perspectives propagated in the preceding pages, it should be clear that the contemporary case of African-Canadians is not as bleak as it used to be. However, an examination of Canadian reality, especially those segments of life that represent the *sine qua non* for meaningful and inclusive social development, suggests the country is still not adequately responding to the needs (employment, social mobility, and overall cultural liquidity) of its African-Canadian population. Symbolic gatherings and so-called cultural celebrations, such as *Caribana* in Toronto, *Carifête* in Montreal, and *Cariwest* in Edmonton, will not lead to concrete improvements in the lives of rank-and-file African-Canadians. Let me end with these eloquent, but above all else, existentially powerful lines from the contemporary African-Canadian poet George E. Clarke (2000, 258) who, in his poem "Casualties," writes:

> Our minds chill; we weather
> the storm, huddle in dreams.
> Exposed, though, a woman
> lashed by lightening, repents
> of her flesh becomes a living
> X-ray, "collateral damage."
> The first casualty of war
> is language.

Clarke's poetic perspectives are analytically highly relevant for the topics I have been treating in the context of this chapter. That is, for far too long, Blacks have been fighting institutional racism and have suffered the most conspicuous collateral damage from the subtle and infinitely stealthy forms that it assumes. As Cornel West (1994) noted in the African-American case, the language of liberation must become the basis for embarking on viable projects of horizontally inclusive, social development.

REFERENCES

Alexander, Ken, and Avis Glaze. 1996. *Towards Freedom: The African-Canadian Experience*. Toronto: Umbrella.

Bannerji, Himani. 2000. *The Dark Side of the Nation*. Toronto: Canadian Scholars'.

Bolaria, Singh B., and Peter S. Li. 1988. *Racial Oppression in Canada*. Toronto: Garamond.

Boyko, John. 1995. *Last Steps to Freedom: The Evolution of Canadian Racism*. Winnipeg: Watson and Dwyer.

Canadian Broadcasting Corporation (CBC). 2002 [online]. *Africville named historic site in Halifax* [cited 14 January 2004]. (www.cbc.ca/cgi-bin/templates/2002/07/05/Africville020705).

Clairmont, Donald H., and Dennis W. Magill. 1999. *Africville: The Life and Death of a Canadian Black Community*, 3rd ed. Toronto: Canadian Scholars'.

Clarke, George E. 2000. Casualties. In *Fiery Spirits and Voices: Canadian Writers of African Descent*, ed. A. Black, 257–58. Toronto: Harper Perennial.

Codjoe, Henry M. 2001. Fighting a "public enemy" of Black academic achievement – The persistence of racism and the schooling experiences of Black students in Canada. *Race, Ethnicity, and Education* 4: 343–75.

Foster, Cecil. 1996. *A Place Called Hope: The Meaning of Being Black in Canada*. Toronto: HarperCollins.

Gwyn, Richard. 1995. *Nationalism without Walls: The Unbearable Lightness of Being Canadian*. Toronto: McClelland & Stewart.

Helms-Hayes, Rick, and James Curtis. 1998. *The Vertical Mosaic Revisited*. Toronto: University of Toronto Press.

Hill, Daniel. 1981. *The Freedom Seekers: Blacks in Early Canada*. Agincourt, ON: Book Society of Canada.

Holas, Wilma, P. 2000. *Millennium Minds: 100 Black Canadians*. Ottawa: Pan-African.

Kelly, Jennifer. 1998. *Under the Gaze: Learning to Be Black in White Society*. Halifax: Fernwood.

Krauter, Joseph, and Morris Davis. 1978. *Minority Canadians: Ethnic Groups*. Toronto: Methuen.

Lampkin, Lorna. 1985. Visible minorities in Canada. In *Research Studies of the Commission on Equality in Employment*, ed. R. S. Abella, 651–83. Ottawa: Supply and Services Canada.

Lewis, Stephen. 1992. [online] Stephen Lewis report on racism in Ontario to the Premier. [cited 3 May 2005] (www.geocities.com/CapitolHill/6174/lewis.html).

Maclean's Magazine. 1993. A nation of polite bigots. 27 December.

McClain, Paula D. 1979. *Alienation and Resistance: The Political Behavior of Afro-Canadians*. Palo Alto, CA: R & E Research Associates.

Mensah, Joseph. 2002. *Black Canadians: History, Experiences, Social Conditions*. Halifax: Fernwood.

Porter, John. 1965. *The Vertical Mosaic: An Analysis of Social Class and Power in Canada*. Toronto: University of Toronto Press.

Ruggles, Clifton, and Olivia Rovinescu. 1996. *Outsider Blues: A Voice from the Shadows*. Halifax: Fernwood.

Saney, Isaac. 1998. The Black Nova Scotian odyssey: A chronology. *Race and Class* 40, no. 1: 78–91.

Sayer, Derek. 1989. *Readings from Karl Marx*. London: Routledge.

Thompson, Colin. 1979. *Blacks in Deep Snow: Black Pioneers in Canada*. Don Mills, ON: J. M. Dent & Sons.

Torczyner, James, et al. 1997. *Diversity, Mobility, and Change: The Dynamics of Black Communities in Canada*. Montreal: McGill School of Social Work Press.

Tulloch, Headley. 1975. *Black Canadians: A Long Line of Fighters*. Toronto: NC.

Walker, James W. 1980. *A History of Blacks in Canada*. Ottawa: Minister of State and Multiculturalism.

———. 1985. *Racial Discrimination: The Black Experience*. Ottawa: Canadian Historical Association.

West, Cornel. 1994. *Race Matters*. New York: Oxford University Press.

Winks, Robin. 1997 [1971]. *The Blacks in Canada: A History*. Montreal/Kingston: McGill-Queen's University Press.

Woodsworth, James S. 1972 [1909]. *Strangers within Our Gates: Or Coming Canadians*. Toronto: F. C. Stephenson.

SECTION II

Location, the Politics of Knowledge Construction,
& the Canadian Educational System

4

AFRICA(NS) IN THE CANADIAN EDUCATIONAL SYSTEM:
An Analysis of Positionality & Knowledge Construction

Henry M. Codjoe

INTRODUCTION

WHEN IT COMES TO THE EDUCATION of Africans in the diaspora, multicultural societies like Canada have made very little effort to systematically interrogate issues and questions about the nature of knowledge, positionality, and knowledge construction. Nowhere is this more central than in the schooling experiences of African-Canadian students. In fact, as Dei and James have observed, "many African-Canadian youths are experiencing alienation from the dominant school system" and, as a consequence, "have to deal with unfortunate attacks by some educational professionals on African cultures, histories, and identities" (Dei and James 1998, 103). An unmistakable manifestation of this modus operandum is the role of curricula in reproducing a structure of domination embedded in Canada's social relations, institutions, and practices. For example, concerning education, it is noted that

> Education in Canada is based on and fundamentally reflects the culture, values, and

experiences of a White, middle-class, largely urban population of northern European origins. The society most curricula present to students – indeed, the society personified by most teachers – is one with which non-Whites from poorer, non-urban, or immigrant backgrounds seldom can identify. Compared to their classmates, therefore, visible minority students find little in education that speaks directly to them. There is little that reflects the cultures or heroes of their heritage, that evokes their interest, or strengthens their self-image. Their respect for education dries up; they drop out. (cited in Kilgour 1994)

This lends credence to the notion that "curriculum and teaching are political matters" (Apple and Beyer 1998, 13b) and that "we need see it as being integrally connected to the cultural, political, and economic institutions of the larger society, institutions that may be strikingly unequal by race, gender, and class" (Apple and Beyer 1998, 4b). Canadian schools naturally are but a part of the larger societal dynamic, and their functions perpetuate these structural and cultural inequalities; in this context, the content and structure of schooling are not neutral, but actively reproduce this societal inequality through the knowledge and cultural forms which have been designated as *high status* and through ways by which groups are sorted and treated differentially (Apple 1990; Cheng et al. 1979; Ghosh 1995; Morrow and Torres 1995; Ogbu 1991). From this perspective, there is considerable importance to schooling and the curriculum as a major vehicle for hegemony by the dominant class in society (Aronowitz and Giroux 1985). In other words, "how a society selects, classifies, distributes, transmits, and evaluates the educational knowledge it considers to be public, reflects both the distribution of power and the principles of social control" (quoted in Bullivant 1983, 22).

There is no doubt that this distribution of power in Canada is skewed "towards a White, majority population [that] operates at many levels within the educational hierarchy, from teaching to research about teaching and schooling. Critical pedagogical discourse derives, in part, from an academic tradition created and shaped by Western European and Anglo-[Canadian] thinkers." For instance, "the language in which we discuss our issues is a language permeated with ideas, beliefs, values, and positionings that have been formulated by the dominant majority. Terms such as *multiculturalism, diversity, ethnicity, race,* and more, have been defined and discussed by White, upper-middle-class, male academicians and politicians. Women and minorities who engage in this discourse must do so using a language formed by those who, historically and currently, occupy power positions in our society" (Estrada and McLaren 1993, 28). Minnich puts it this way:

There is a *root problem* underlying the dominant meaning system that informs our curricula. It is visible in the false universalization that has taken a very few privileged men from a particular tradition to be the inclusive term, the norm, and the ideal for all. The faultiness, or partiality, of that universalization has been hidden from us, in part, because we too often tend to express ourselves in singular terms (especially *man* and *mankind*, but also, for example, the *citizen*, the *philosopher*, the *poet*, the *student*). Singular universals, even adequate ones, make thinking of plurality, let alone diversity, very difficult. (1990, 2–3; emphasis in the original)

This embodies what has been called the *selective tradition*: "Someone's selection, someone's vision of legitimate knowledge and culture, one that in the process of enfranchising one group's cultural capital disenfranchises another's" (Apple 1992, 5). The point here is that, all too often, *legitimate* knowledge does not include the historical experiences and cultural expressions of labour, people of colour, and others who have been less powerful (Roman and Christian-Smith with Ellsworth 1988). The absence of Black knowledge in many Canadian school curricula is not a simple oversight. Its absence represents an academic instance of racism, or what has been described as "willful ignorance and aggression towards Blacks" (Pinar 1993, 62). Indeed, Apple (1990) has argued that the selection and organization of knowledge for schools is an ideological process, one that serves the interests of particular classes and social groups, dynamic in nature and associated with continuities and contradictions. This important point is also echoed by Ghosh when she writes that

> [c]ontemporary theories have uncovered the relationship between knowledge and power. They point to the highly political and subjective nature of knowledge because it serves the interests of the group in power and represents a world-view which is predominantly Eurocentric, Judeo-Christian, middle-class, White, and male-oriented. Knowledge is now seen increasingly as being historically located and socially constructed. The recognition that school knowledge is far from neutral provides a significant explanation as to how it serves students of different groups unequally. If knowledge is politically based, historically embedded, and socially constructed, and therefore, subjective, then questions arise as to what constitutes acceptable *knowledge*. (1995, 234)

For African-Canadian students, then, the structural and ideological reference points here are that "being educated in the Western canon not only perpetuates social exclusion but continues the fiction that Blacks have been marginal to the history and growth of [Canada]" (Sardar and Davies 2002, 141). The implication is obviously racist, and despite persistent denial by Canadians, race continues to be a problem in the nation (Mensah 2002; Barrett 1987; Cannon 1995; Campbell 1989; Lewis 1992; McKague 1991). In fact, the concept of race in Canada persists, and its permanent feature is shown by "the presence of a system of racial meanings and stereotypes, of racial ideology" (Omi and Winant, in Rothenberg 2001, 15). This form of modern racism, as Flecha calls it, "occurs when the rules of the dominant culture are imposed on diverse peoples in the name of integration ... and presumes that different races have unequal levels of intellectual, cultural, economic, and political progress, rather than simply different ones" (Flecha 1999, 154). Within current educational practices in Canada, the image of the African student is thus viewed in this context, and it is "manifested in discriminatory treatment by teachers, counsellors, and administrators, and in curriculum and school practices that excluded Black students" (James and Brathwaite 1996, 18–19; Head 1975; D'Oyley and Silverman 1976).

In this chapter, I shall attempt to show "the role school curricula played in the creation and recreation of the ideological hegemony of the dominant classes" in the name of "legitimate knowledge, and how it is used to denigrate and *stigmatize* African peoples" (Apple 1995, 17; see also Rosenblum and Travis 2000, 26). In fact, I argue that the Canadian curriculum does not merely teach Western ideas and culture, it teaches the *superiority* of Western ideas and culture; it equates Western ways and thought with *Civilization* itself (Levine 1996, 20). This would explain why William Thorsell, the editor of the Toronto *Globe and Mail*, writing about why the "United States is clearly fragmented," will opine that "Blacks and Hispanics constitute significant, visible, urbanized minorities that are largely unreconciled to the U.S. mainstream. They do not easily share some of its most treasured values, or virtues (such as, perhaps, love of education)" (1996, D6). It would also explain why the theoretical knowledge about the education of African-Canadian children advanced by such Black theorists as Carl James (1990), Enid Lee (1992), and Patrick Solomon (1992), to name a few, are rarely read or cited by Euro/Anglo-Canadian scholars in critical ways that challenge the status quo. In fact, there is minimal educational literature about Black students in Canada (Henry 1993). Pertinent to this discussion, then, is the failure of Canadian schools to effectively address the cultural, social, psychological, and educational needs of African students (Brathwaite and James 1996). Takaki puts it better when he observes, "What happens when someone with the authority of a teacher describes our society, and you are not in it? Such an experience can be disorienting – a moment of psychic disequilibrium, as if you looked into a mirror and saw nothing" (Takaki 1993, 16). Indeed, growing numbers of minority students are being socialized in an institutional context which does not reflect their experiences, values, and beliefs. As Banks has argued, "the assumption that all children can learn equally well from teaching materials that only reflect the cultural experiences of the majority group is questionable and possibly detrimental to those minority group children who have strong ethnic identities and attachment" (Banks 1981, 64). This begs the following questions:

Rather than asking how we could get a student to acquire more curricular knowledge, I asked a more political set of questions. "Why and how are particular aspects of a collective culture represented in schools as objective, factual knowledge? How, concretely, may official knowledge represent the ideological configurations of the dominant interests in a society? How do schools legitimate these limited and partial standards of knowing as unquestioned truths?" (Apple 1995, 17)

The foregoing analyses lead us to the following additional, neglected questions: What should count as knowledge? Who shall control the selection and distribution of knowledge? Through what institutions? What knowledge is of most worth? Whose knowledge is it? How has certain knowledge come to be more appropriate for school curriculum content than other knowledge? By what mechanisms have certain realms of knowledge been given higher status than others? Whose class and social interests have been served by the form and content of schools? Why are the views and concerns of African people so often ignored in the school curriculum? (Beyer and Apple 1998a; Apple 1978; Noffke 1998; Minnich 1990; Sarup 1991)

In what follows, I briefly review the concepts and theories of knowledge, knowledge construction, and positionality. For the purposes of this chapter, I pay particular attention to the so-called *Western Canon* and how it has (mis)informed the debate on multiculturalism and the professed *culture wars* or *canon debate* in North America. And in a section I call "Knowledge Construction and the African World Experience," I show how the historical reconstruction about race has been used in Western thought and ideas to advance an *essentialist* view that African peoples' "unchangeable physical characteristics [are] linked in a direct, causal way to psychological or intellectual characteristics, and that on this basis distinguishes between superior and inferior racial groups" (Feagin and Feagin, in Codjoe 2001a, 281). Finally, I concretize these theoretical perspectives with research I carried out with African-Canadian students in Alberta (Codjoe 1997, 1998, 1999, 2001a and b), as well as other research findings on the schooling experiences of Black students in Canada (e.g., Dei 1996; Hoo Kong 1996; Solomon 1992; Brathwaite and James 1996; Spencer 1995). My empirical research is an effort to highlight certain aspects of the African-Canadian educational experience not commonly known to the general public. It seeks to speak "about the silences that often are registered but not so often highlighted and analyzed" (Sultana 1995, 113). With this in mind, my study focused on the successful secondary school experiences of African-Canadian students in Alberta. The primary purpose was to examine the experiences and narratives of these students in order to learn about and document some of the significant factors that influence and contribute to their educational achievement, with a particular focus on the biases in school curriculum and textbooks.

Study Methodology

The sample for the study was drawn from a population of Black students in the metropolitan area of greater Edmonton. It was not a random sample, but rather, I sought – with the help of Black youth and community and student groups – Black students for this purpose. I did this because, unlike cities like Toronto, Halifax, or perhaps Montreal, there is no concentration of Black students in specific areas of Edmonton. I chose the students from an extensive list of individuals supplied to me by a Black community group. There were thirty students on the list, and more responded later to requests to take part in the project. Since I couldn't involve all thirty and more students, my first task was to select the required number of students needed. After some discussions with a number of the students and advice from my dissertation supervisor, I selected twelve students from the pool. The major reason or rationale for choosing these students is that they showed more awareness of the issues concerning Black education and could articulate more clearly their feelings, experiences, and thoughts as compared to the other students. Although I chose participants mainly on the basis of race, academic success, and urban experience (Edmonton), there were other important criteria. Chief among them were (1) successful graduation from an Alberta high school and entry into one of Alberta's colleges or universities; (2) gender; (3) place of birth or country of origin; (4) student availability and willingness to participate in the study; and (5) conversance with Black educational and other social issues. My primary aim here was to ensure a wide range of the Black student experience in Edmonton, as well as to keep the study size manageable in order to facilitate in-depth inquiry.

The sample included young men and women who had a variety of experiences in schools in Canada and, in some cases, in other countries as well. About half graduated from high school in the last two years of my study, the other half graduating in the last three or more years. Thus, at the time I interviewed these students, they were between twenty-two and twenty-six years of age and represented a number of linguistic and social class groups, as well as both sexes. In fact, there are an equal number of men and women. They are also first, second, or third generation Canadians coming from a variety of socio-economic backgrounds. Some of the students were from single-parent families, although the majority were from two-parent families. I can thus argue that my sample represents important dimensions of the diversity within the African-Canadian community.

The one common characteristic of my student sample (something which may not be true of many of their peers) was this: they could be considered *successful* students. As Nieto (1992, 1994) points out in a similar study, although there may be disagreements about what it means to be successful, the students in my sample have been able to develop both academic skills and positive attitudes about themselves and about the value of education. They generally had excellent grades, and they enrolled in and graduated from Alberta's post-secondary institutions. In fact, all but two were enrolled at the University of Alberta. Two have actually completed a first degree. In retrospect, I agree with Nieto's observation that "it seemed logical that students who are successful in school are more likely to want to talk about their experiences than those who are not" (Nieto 1992, 11).

To seek answers to the questions posed by the research, I utilized a qualitative research method. With the help of an interview guide, I conducted in-depth personal interviews with the twelve informants. My questions were not necessarily structured as interview questions, as I permitted questions to emerge from my discussions and interactions with the participants. Indeed, I gave informants the opportunity to introduce new themes that would throw light on the African-Canadian experience in Alberta schools. There were both individual and focus group interviews. In the former, each student participated in about an hour-long, semi-structured interview. In the latter, I used the interviews to encourage students to build on and react to comments of their peers, creating a dialogue around each question. I used open-ended questions in both the individual and focus group interviews because they are "important when you want to determine the salience or importance of opinions to people, since people tend to mention those matters that are important to them" (cited in Spencer 1995, 17). Data from the individual and focus group interviews were further supplemented and corroborated by secondary data to give a holistic picture of the African-Canadian school experience in Canada. There was so much interest in the subject matter that it led to many hours of non-structured, informal conversations and discussions after the structured interviews. Because some of these informal conversations contained important information that was not recorded during the structured interviews, I wrote and kept a notebook for later use. In the end, the study used four distinct sources of data: (1) twelve individual interviews with students; (2) two focus group interviews with students; (3) personal notes based on informal conversations and discussions; and (4) summary and reading notes from a variety of secondary published, written material. All these personal memos, observer comments, conversations, and interview transcripts make up what has been referred to as the case study data base (Yin 1984). The student interviews generated perceptions about ethnic and racial identity, self-esteem, personal academic expectations and achievements, home-cultural expectations, multiculturalism, racism, stereotypes, parental influence, knowledge of African-Canadian culture and history, school experiences, peer groups, extracurricular activities, and more.

My overall data analysis drew on the student narratives, as well as relevant secondary sources and my own experiences. The theoretical and empirical support for my study came from the broader theoretical framework of schooling, education and social reproduction theories, multicultural/anti-racist education, race/class and social conflict, sociology of education, international and global education, Black sociology, and sociological/political analysis of the experiences of racial and cultural minorities in the West.

Finally, a note about terminology is necessary. The term preferred by the students in this study and that many used to describe themselves is *African-Canadian*. For them, "the African-Canadian construct serves as a powerful internal redefinition of racial and ethnic pride – a statement of pride in being both Canadian and African" (Dei 1994, 4).

Before using the student narratives as supporting evidence for my thesis, an overview of some theoretical perspectives is in order.

KNOWLEDGE, KNOWLEDGE CONSTRUCTION, AND POSITIONALITY

I rely primarily on works by Banks (1993, 1995, 1996, 2002) to present the concepts of knowledge, positionality, and how knowledge is constructed. Like Banks, I define knowledge to mean a way a person explains or interprets reality. In this conceptualization, "knowledge is ... used the way in which it is usually used in the sociology of knowledge literature to include ideas, values, and interpretations" (Banks 1993, 5). Consequently, I share his view and those of other social scientists (e.g., Code 1991; Ladner 1973) that knowledge is socially constructed and reflects human interests, values, and action. Banks further explains that

> Although many complex factors influence the knowledge that is created by an individual or group, including the actuality of what occurred, the knowledge that people create is heavily influenced by their interpretations of their experiences and their positions within particular social, economic, and political systems and structures of a society. (1993, 5)

However, when viewed within Western social and political thought, knowledge and knowledge construction have often been presented as *neutral* and *objective*, and therefore, *universal*. This has meant, for example, that "the ideal within each academic discipline is the formulation of knowledge without the influence of the researcher's personal or cultural characteristics," and that "the effects of values, frames, or references, and the normative positions of researchers and scholars are infrequently discussed within the traditional empirical paradigm that has dominated scholarship and teaching in [North] American colleges and universities since the turn of the century" (Banks 1993, 5). Although this type of *hegemonic knowledge* promotes the interests of the powerful, elite groups have often and successfully obscured its value premises by promoting knowledge as totally objective. It has taken on the form of an *ideological* process that has come to serve the interests of particular classes and social groups and come to constitute the context for power and domination in society (Apple 1990; Dei and James 1998). In fact, Banks (2002, 12) notes that "knowledge is viewed as most influential when it reinforces the beliefs, ideologies, and assumptions of the people who exercise the most political and economic power within a society." Knowledge, then, "does not transcend, but is rooted in, and shaped by, specific interests and social arrangements" (Code, cited in Banks 2002, 11). Bank's analysis is compelling, particularly in linking the conception of power/knowledge found in the work of Foucault (1980) and others. In this analysis, it is noted "how power is expressed in boundaries and positions, between the *thinkable* and the *unthinkable*, and how, at its most general, *power* is to silence as *control* is to communication" (Morrow and Torres 1995, 197).

It is no wonder, then, that there has been "the requestioning of entrenched subjective positions/reasonings and assumptions about power" (Dei and James 1998, 92) as it relates to knowledge and knowledge construction. Critical and postmodern theorists have developed important critiques of empirical knowledge and pointed out that personal, cultural, and social factors influence the formulation of knowledge, even when objective knowledge is the ideal within a discipline. Despite its claims, they argue that "modern science is not value-free but contains important human interests and normative assumptions that should be identified, discussed, and examined" (cited in Banks 1993, 5). Myrdal, for example, has stated that valuations are not just attached to research, but permeate it: "There is no device for excluding biases in social sciences other than to face the valuations and to introduce them as explicitly stated, specific, and sufficiently concretized value premises" (cited in Banks 1993, 5). Code, a feminist epistemologist, also states that academic knowledge is both subjective and objective, and that both aspects should be recognized and discussed. She argues that we need to ask questions, such as, "Out of whose subjectivity has this ideal [of objectivity] grown? Whose standpoint, whose values does it represent?... The point of the questions is to discover how subjective and objective conditions together produce knowledge, values, and epistemology. It is neither to reject objectivity nor to glorify subjectivity in its stead. Knowledge is neither value-free nor value-neutral; the processes that produce it are themselves value-laden; and these values are open to evaluation" (cited in Banks 1993, 5).

In sum, knowledge is both subjective and objective, and the knowledge constructed "by the knower reflects both her[his] subjectivity and the objective phenomena perceived" (cited in Banks 1995, 15). Indeed, objective and subjective factors influence knowledge construction, and so "people perceive and understand the world based on their experiences and previous knowledge; they construct their understandings of the world by interpreting new information based on what they already know and believe. Two basic assumptions underlie knowledge construction: (1) there is no single truth, and (2) reality is defined by positionality" (Ovando and Gourd 1996, 298). The theme of *positionality* is relevant here, as it points to the concept that knowledge is only "valid when it takes into account the knower's specific position in any context, a position that is always defined by gender, race, class, and other socially significant dimensions" (Maher and Tetreault 1994, 22). Put another way, "one's location in the social structure is based partially on the relations of race, social class, and gender," and "race, gender, sexuality, and class differences influence how knowledge is constructed, interpreted, and institutionalized.... Knowledge is valid when it is contextualized in the knower's subject position and location" (Dei and James 1998, 92). Finke further explains that

> [w]hat is perceived as marginal at any given time depends on the position one occupies ... In other words, you have to see centrality and marginality, oppression, oppressor, and oppressed as relational concepts. And so what you have to do is keep the whole thing moving ... keep seeing it as relational, keep seeing it as position. (Maher and Tetreault 1994, 22)

When it comes to positionality and knowledge construction, then, I share Banks' (1993, 5) point of view that "positionality means that important aspects of our identity, for example, our gender, our race, our class, our age ... are markers of relational positions rather than essential qualities. Their effects and implications change according to context ... [P]ositionality reveals the importance of identifying the positions and frames of reference from which scholars and writers present their data, interpretations, analyses, and instruction." This means that to understand how knowledge is constructed, "we must not only be aware of the knowledge produced, but must also understand that the knowledge producer is located within a particular social, economic, and political context of society" (Banks 1995, 15). This would explain why,

> [f]or many years, and not so long ago, the voices of the majority of people in our society were missing from the books in libraries and on our course reading lists. The experiences of women from all racial and ethnic groups, regardless of their class position, were missing, as was the history, culture, and experience of many men. In their place were the writings and teachings of a relatively small group – predominantly privileged, White, and male – who offered their experience and their perspective as if it were universal ... White sociologists, psychologists, and anthropologists set themselves up as experts on American Indian, Hispanic, Black, and Asian experience and culture ... Novels chronicling the growth of manhood of young White males from upper or middle classes were routinely assigned in high schools and college English courses and examined for *universal themes*, while novels about the experiences of men of colour, working people, and women of all groups were relegated to *special interest* courses and treated as marginal ... In short, by definition, serious scholarship, *real* science, and *great* literature was what had been produced by well-to-do, White males

and often focused exclusively on their experiences; accounts of the lives of other groups, if available at all, were rarely written by members of those groups. (Rothenberg 2004, 333–34)

We can conclude that, in this regard, Canadian society is fundamentally un-equal, and this inequality is perpetuated by limiting the access of subordinate groups to political, economic, and social power. It explains and answers the following questions: What counts as knowledge? What knowledge is of most worth? Whose knowledge is it? This will be an appropriate way to segue into my discussion on the *Western Canon*. It is, in my view, a concrete example of *official knowledge* representing the ideological configurations of the dominant group. It is relevant to the thesis of this chapter and goes to the heart of the debate about multiculturalism in societies like Canada.

Knowledge Construction and the Western Canon

In recent times, conservative commentators in North America have attacked attempts by peoples of colour, for example, in the case of people of African de-scent, to "develop a new, empowered sense of self-worth, new curricula [that] are needed [to] reflect Black experience and incorporate learning about African roots and African cultural achievement" (Sardar and Davies 2002, 141). It is a demand for a system of social justice and the redistribution of power that is more inclusive, especially regarding what is taught in schools, especially as it pertains to "a redefinition of self, an assertion of power, and a rejection of oth-ers' ability to impose an identity" (Rosenblum and Travis 2000, 6). It is a debate about what knowledge related to ethnic and cultural diversity should be taught in the school and university curriculum.

Multicultural education and neo-conservative critics like Ravitch and Finn (1987), Hirsch (1987), Bloom (1987), D'Souza (1991), and Schlesinger (1991) have argued that this attempt to make curricula more inclusive "dilutes *real* civilization". For these authors,

> Western civilization constructed not only terrestrial empires and colonies but also an intellectual empire in which it alone exemplified the proper meaning and use of reason, objectivity, and adherence to universal con-cepts and principles, the routine procedures of its disciplines of knowledge. Therefore, Western civilization has always known the reality, history, and ideas of other civilizations better than they have known themselves. By definition, then, other societies and their cultural manifestations are not universal, and to make them the basis of modern education is to depart from the path of human progress and debase the currency of education. (Sardar and Davies 2002, 141)

Others, like Williams are so unabashed that they have boldly claimed that "Western values are superior to all others" and that "Western values of reason and individual rights have produced unprecedented health, life expectancy, wealth, and comfort for the ordinary person" (Williams 2002, 4A). Therefore, knowledge, or what Banks has called "mainstream academic knowledge," *must* "reflect the established, Western-oriented canon that has historically dominated university research and teaching in [North America]" (Banks 1993, 7). In fact, these critics have initiated a concerted effort to defend the dominance of Western civilization in the school and university curricula and have "chastised professors who fail to teach the *truth* that civilization itself is best exemplified in the West, and indeed, in [North] America" (Foner 2002). They believe that "Western history, literature, and culture are endangered in the school and university curriculum because of the push by feminists, ethnic minority scholars, and other multiculturalists for curriculum reform and transformation" (Banks 1993, 4). Couched in Flecha's (1999) concept of *modern racism*, it legitimizes a global order in which White supremacy and European domination are prevalent. This is why, historically, *Canadian* has meant White, as many of us African-Canadians learn when we are asked, "Where do we come from?", or "When will we be going back to where we came from?", and when we are complimented on our English- or French-speaking abilities.

Knowledge Construction and the African World Experience

From the above discussion, by implication, African peoples "have not contributed to the rise of civilization," and "there was nothing in Africa except Egypt, and Egypt was White, not Black" (Farrell 1991, 20). In the history of Western thought, the idea of Africa and Africans as *uncivilized, primitive*, and *savage* has permeated the fabric of Western society (Eze 1997). In fact, there is a general neglect and disparagement of Africans. Writings by European philosophers, such as Voltaire, Hume, Kant, Hegel, and Locke, "played a strong role in articulating Europe's sense not only of its cultural but also racial superiority. In their writings ... *reason* and *civilization* became almost synonymous with *White* people and northern-Europe, while *unreason* and *savagery* were conveniently located among non-Whites, the *Black*, the *Red*, and the *Yellow*, outside Europe" (Dei 1999, 20). This "enlightenment philosophy," as Eze (1997) has argued, "was instrumental in codifying and institutionalizing both the scientific and popular European perceptions of the human race" (Eze 1997, 5) and defined *valid* knowledge and normalcy. Thus, as Hexham pointed out, "while it is usual to regard the Enlightenment as a period of reform and progress, it was anything but progressive for Blacks. A good case can be made that modern racism originates in the Enlightenment" (Hexham 2002).

In his short essay *The Negro*, the French philosopher Voltaire set the general tone in that age of enlightenment with this position towards Africans:

The Negro race is a species of men as different from ours as the breed of spaniels is from that of greyhounds ... if their understanding is not of a different nature from ours, it is at least greatly inferior. They are not capable of any great application or association of ideas, and seem formed neither of the advantages nor abuses of our philosophy. (cited in Hexham 2002)

English philosopher David Hume agreed when he wrote that "I suspect that Negroes ... [are] naturally inferior to Whites. There never was a civilized nation of any other complexion than Whites" (cited in Goldberg 1993, 31–32). And the German philosopher Hegel probably did not hesitate to write that

[t]he peculiarly African character is difficult to comprehend ... In Negro life, the characteristic point is the fact that consciousness has not yet attained to the realization of any substantial objective existence ... The Negro, as already observed, exhibits the natural man in his completely wild, untamed state. We must lay aside all thought of reverence and morality. Among Negroes, moral sentiments are quite weak, or more strictly speaking, non-existent ... At this point we leave Africa to mention it no more. For it is no Historical part of the World. (Hexham 2002)

These racist ideas led to the lack of recognition and identification of the biases, assumptions, perspectives, and points of view that have frequently victimized Africans because of the stereotypes and misconceptions that were perpetuated about them in the historical and social science literature. An example of this bias became evident when, in the autumn of 1990, the Encyclopedia Britannica published the *Great Books of the Western World*, its selection of Western civilization's sixty best works. Commentators hailed the selection as an affirmation of Western culture. Indeed, a scholarly symposium at the United States Library of Congress celebrated the collection's publication. Amid the celebration, some critics pointed out that the series contained no books by authors of colour. An obvious omission, it was suggested, were the writings of W.E.B. DuBois, which should have been included in the selection. In response, Mortimer Adler, a self-proclaimed interpreter of the Western canon, opined that no Black had ever written a great book. Specifically addressing DuBois' exclusion, Adler argued that DuBois' best book was his autobiography "which simply failed to meet the inclusion criteria in the series" (Farrell 1991, 20). This is why "in canonical literature, [Africans] have always been spoken for. Or have been spoken to. Or have appeared as jokes or as flat figures suggesting sensuality" (Chavanu 1996, 1). It explains, for example, why there is a major Holocaust museum in Washington, DC, but no such memorial exists for African-Americans anywhere in North America. And it explains why *The Bell Curve*, a book by Herrnstein and Murray (1994) that is riddled with racism and argues that African-Americans have less intellectual ability than Whites was on the *New York Times* best-seller list for several weeks. It echoed and gave academic legitimacy to many of the institutionalized beliefs about African peoples within North American society. Against this background, I would like now to present one part of the results of a research study chronicling the experiences of African students in Canadian secondary schools. It provides a concrete example of the distortions purposely done to create the illusion that Africans have been of little consequence in world history. For Africans in Canada, it seems like a fight for survival in a society that continuously constructs them as *the other*.

AFRICAN-CANADIANS, POSITIONALITY, AND BIASES IN KNOWLEDGE CONSTRUCTION

> African-Canadian culture is often relegated to an inferior status by schools, thus hiding our group's true, historic struggle for survival, liberation, and enhancement. On the one hand, the suppression, destruction, distortion of a group's history and culture by others, and the surrender of one's own culture results in low self-esteem. On the other hand, ignorance and disrespect for African-Canadian history and culture breed low expectations and unhealthy educator assessments of African [Canadian] students, personalities, and potential. (Black Learners Advisory Committee [BLAC] 1994)

As my opening quotation demonstrates, perhaps no other area in the education of Black students in Canada attracts more concern than does attention on the curriculum. As James and Brathwaite (1996, 29) correctly note, "curriculum concerns are some of the most damaging elements in our students' schooling, and this is an area that has attracted much attention in the Black community and among educators." Not surprisingly, it was also an area that generated the most discussion and sometimes anger and emotion among the students in my study. In fact, the question of racial bias in the curriculum content, as well as eurocentrism in school courses and texts, were also recurring themes in the student narratives. All complained that the curriculum had little relevance for their lives and, as one of them put it,

> I really didn't feel as though I got any education from school as far as Black education was concerned ... I didn't learn anything about Black history in high school. There was no subject [in Black studies] for you to take, and in regular social studies classes, they didn't discuss anything Black or African. They might have said something about slavery once or twice but they didn't really say anything in depth and they didn't say anything positive. (Codjoe 1997, 172)

This theme was echoed again and again by the students. Having grown up in West Africa before immigrating to Alberta with her parents, Akosua (I have used pseudonyms to ensure the anonymity of the students) thought courses in Canadian schools would be more inclusive and reflect its entire people. However, she found out in high school that

> Canadian history just seems to be concerned about White Canada. Except, maybe, the States, because they're so close to the States, they're not really concerned about other countries. I never knew anything about the history of Blacks in Canada until I joined Ebony [a Black youth club in Edmonton]. That's when I started to realize, "Oh, Blacks have been here for this long. I've talked to some Black families, too, here in Alberta and found that their roots have been here for a long time, and it's like I never knew." (Codjoe 1997, 172)

Another student, Kwabena, born outside of Canada, found that

> [a] lot of the history was about World War I, World War II – European history. There was very little African history. You find that a lot of the students hardly knew anything about Africa whatsoever. All they knew was what they saw on TV or what portrayed Blacks in the most negative way. (Codjoe 1997, 172)

Kweku, also born outside of Canada, found this Eurocentric emphasis "frustrating" at times,

> because we heard so much about the French and English and stuff. Amazingly, they don't even talk very much about the Natives. You'd think there'd be a lot more on that. It is frustrating because, I mean, the Blacks here did contribute a lot. We [Blacks] were one of the first immigrants here in Canada. I do feel that there should be a lot more mentioned about us, most definitely. (Codjoe 1997, 173)

This last point was often mentioned by the African students born in Canada. They are hurt by what one of them, echoing Willis (1995), called "a sin of omission." For example, Abena, born here in Alberta, narrated that

> in some of my classes [e.g.] in social studies, when they did mention anything that had to do with Black people, it was generally that the Blacks came over. They were slaves. In English, you'd read a book, Tom Sawyer or something, and it is "Nigger this, Nigger that," every second word, and I found that, in the end, I started to verbalize "Why do you always portray the negative aspects of Black life?" I found that a lot of my teachers just

would almost automatically say something, and they'd turn to me because they would expect me to give them a response because I wasn't going to be quiet about it. So, I thought it just made me more outspoken in the end, which was to my benefit. It made me learn more about Black history on my own than in school. (Codjoe 1997, 173)

Kwadjo, also born in Alberta and trying to make some sense of this, said he does not think that "the big problem is that the teachers are hidden Klansmen, [although] you still find teachers who have really bigoted attitudes and that sort of thing." He believes that "the real problem is that we're just invisible to the curriculum." He explains further:

> I took social studies in high school and the history course – that was supposed to be an enriched history course. The history course was actually subtitled "History of Western Europe." They didn't even make a secret out of it. So all the civilizations of the earth that were brown were left out. We didn't discuss China until the twentieth century. The first mention of Africans was not Egypt, or Nubia, or Mali, or Songhai, or great Zimbabwe. The first mention was the slave holocaust, which was called the slave trade. (Codjoe 1997, 173–74)

On this last point, it also came out unanimously during the focus group discussions that Black education in Alberta's schools, if mentioned at all, "tends to start and stop with Martin Luther King and Malcolm X. That's about it. There are a whole lot of other historical Black figures – music, science, you name it. Even in this country alone, there are a lot nobody knows about" (Codjoe 1997, 174). I was curious to know how all this made them feel in class and school, and so I asked them to tell me about it. Interestingly enough, although they were hurt and marginalized by the whole experience (one dropped out of school because of it, although returned later), most told me they were not surprised. They had expected it. They had been forewarned. As Alberta-born Abena said,

> I wasn't really surprised because I remember actually being told by someone before I went to [mentions school attended], I was told, "You're not going to learn anything about Black education." In fact, they said something about how the teachers there weren't very fond of Black students. (Codjoe 1997, 174)

In fact, during the focus group discussions with students, many said they were "furious" because "if you're willing to learn about other cultures, my culture might as well be known, too" (Codjoe 1997, 174). A few got into arguments with their teachers. Kwame, born in Alberta, relates one such experience:

One time, I got into a big argument with a teacher. We were doing the history of the world. When it came to the history of Africa, the teacher said Africa's history started from 1773 [*sic*] when the White man came. I said this is foolishness. Africa's history didn't start with the arrival of the White man. I pointed out to the teacher that when it came to do the history of Russia, he talked about way back in when they were still in [inaudible], that's their history. But when he talked about the history of Africa, the only thing he talked about was when the White man came. That's my experience with Black things in Alberta's schools. Always, it's not Black things. It's when the White people came and how the Black people kind of fitted in. That's about it. (Codjoe 1997, 174–75)

But perhaps the most important aspect mentioned by the students was the damage the impact of the absence of African studies in the school has on Black students. This comment by Kofi, an African immigrant, was typical:

There was nothing on anything that was Black-related or Black-successful in the academic area. I think if there was, even if it was just a small thing, a Black child would feel that they had something to associate themselves with in the academic sense. This would make them more motivated to achieve as well, because right now, they just feel that maybe some kids feel that education is a White thing. But it's [education] not something that they should be ashamed of. (Codjoe 1997, 175)

This was echoed by Ekua, born in Alberta of mixed African and Canadian parentage, who added that

I'm no academic genius, but when you have a sense of what your people have done, it helps you get through the school system, too. It helps you get through different things because you feel that your people have made a contribution to where you are. (Codjoe 1997, 175)

What I found remarkable about these students was that, though the schools made no effort to introduce or teach them about African studies, they made the effort on their own, and as one said, "I learned about Black history more on my own than in school" (Codjoe 1997, 175). Some regretted this and commented that it's not fair that they should have to learn their own history outside school, when European history is being taught in school.

As can be seen from the above student narratives, the curriculum in Canadian schools is at odds with the experiences, backgrounds, hopes, and wishes of students of African descent. The continued marginality of these students within the school system has created a situation in which African-Canadian students lack any sense of identification and connectedness to the school. Canada's schools have failed to respond to the direct needs of the African-Canadian student and to incorporate African peoples' history and experiences into the existing curriculum. This "sin of omission," as Willis calls it, has "[allowed] the cultural knowledge of culturally and linguistically diverse children to be ignored, devalued, and unnurtured as valid sources of literacy acquisition" (Willis 1995, 34). According to Giroux, "the issue here is that the school actively silences students by ignoring their histories; ... by refusing to provide them with knowledge relevant to their lives" (1986, 10). It becomes depressing when one discovers that this situation is not unique to the African-Canadian students interviewed for my study. Indeed, my research findings on this topic are shared by many others. For example, in her interviews with other Black students in Edmonton, Spencer concluded that "the pinnacle of discontent for all groups of Black students was the heavy emphasis on European history in the social studies curriculum" (1995, 110). Among the students Spencer interviewed, there was a general perception that the social studies curriculum portrayed Black people as "passive, rather than active, participants in society" (1995, 111). Where Blacks were represented in the curriculum, the students perceived it as often in negative terms.

At a conference of Black youth in Edmonton in March, 1995, to commemorate the International Day for the Elimination of Racial Discrimination, conference participants also said the Alberta school curriculum does not reflect the cultural diversity of Canada. Echoing the students in my study, the following were typical comments: "The school curriculum is designed to put *Whites first*; Blacks are non-existent; the school curriculum portrays Blacks as slaves, not as accomplished people" (Lendore-Mahabir 1995, 8). A teacher at the Black Heritage School in Calgary was surprised to discover that some Black students arrive at the school never having read a book written by, or about, a Black person (Adams 1993). On this, another teacher also observed that: "A Black kid can go through five years of high school and never read a Black author. This is an era when the 1992 Nobel prize for literature was won by Toni Morrison, and the 1993 prize for poetry by Derek Walcott" (cited in Ruby 1995, A21). It is no wonder that "an examination of Alberta texts revealed in 1984 that there still were anti-minority biases in books across Alberta" (Kilgour 1994, 7). In fact, according to Winks (1971), in over fifty history texts on the Canadian market by 1960, not one published after 1865 makes the slightest reference to Canada's Black population (see also Hill 1960).

Underscoring the points raised by these Black students and those I interviewed for my study is the observation made by Henry and Tator that "from the perspective of the educational institutions themselves, the issue which has been the focal point of multicultural and race relations policies and practices has been the curriculum" (1991, 16). The weight of the school curriculum in the education of Black students is thus recognized by educators and by recent studies. For example, an entire section of the *Draft Report on the Education of Black Students in Toronto Schools* is devoted to a discussion of curriculum matters. The report notes that "The inclusion of Black Studies in the regular curriculum, some parents say, would enhance the self-respect of Black students and generate the respect of teachers and other students for Blacks. At the same time, the inclusion of Black Studies as an optional credit course at the secondary level would be of interest not only to Black students but to other students in the same way that languages and cultures of other people are of interest to persons of different backgrounds" (cited in Brathwaite 1989, 209; see also O'Malley 1992 and Aoki et al. 1984). Another report noted that "[o]ften [in] schools in which the student population is predominantly Black ... the school curriculum is largely reflective of European presence, settlement, and development of Canada and, as such, provides little or no incentive for Black Canadians to develop their African heritage. Courses in Black history, a spotlight on Black achievements, an appreciation of Black culture – these are things for which the African-Canadian student hungers, often in vain" (Towards a New Beginning 1992, 78).

There is a feeling among Black educators, as well as African-Canadian students and parents, that because the school curriculum is one of the most important elements of education and is the carrier of the philosophy, culture, and national agenda of any country, the mismatch between African-Canadian students' cultures and that of Canadian schools goes a long way to "reinforce feelings of limited self-worth and cultural isolation by ignoring the historical contributions of African-Canadians or devaluing their culture" (Black Learners Advisory Committee 1994, 41 [hereafter BLAC 1994]; see also Bristow et al. 1994 and Walker 1980). The culture in Canadian schools, according to Hoo Kong, is that "in general, textbooks tend to present the perspectives of White, upper-class, Anglo- and French-Canadian males. Consequently, many textbooks do not acknowledge African-Canadians as active participants in the shaping of our nation's history" (Hoo Kong 1996, 58). Adds the *BLAC Report on Education*, "When you examine the Nova Scotia curriculum, the Black community hardly seems to exist at all" (BLAC 1994, 41). Richardson echoes the same point when he writes that "The shelves of the history and social issues sections of Canadian bookstores have long been devoid of books by and about Canadians of African descent. Indeed, one might infer from public school history and social studies texts that Black people have had nothing to contribute to Canadian society" (1995, 36). And on the "350th Anniversary of Blacks in Canada," Hill and Bruner aptly note that

> The history of Canada, according to the usual view of history, is told in
> White and Red: White for larger-than-life creators of momentous events;
> Red for the native Indians. But a deeper look reveals another distinct colour – Black. There is an almost total void in knowledge of Black heroes,

coloured commandos who defended Canada against the Americans in the 1780s on the Detroit frontier; of Black politics, Tories who rallied against William Lyon Mackenzie's 1837 rebels; of religious development, establishment of the Baptist faith by runaway slaves; of Black slaves, who were both bound and freed on Canadian soil. (1978, 10)

In reference to these important omissions from Canadian school curricula, Winks further observes that

Indeed, most White Canadians would not have learned that there were Negroes in Canada at all had they relied upon their formal schooling. Textbooks forgot that Black men existed after 1865, and only a few Canadian books gave even passing reference to the influx of fugitive slaves in the 1850s. Most did not mention Canada's own history of slavery, and none referred to Negroes – or separate schools – after discussing the American Civil War. C. D. Owen's 1842 text for use in Nova Scotian schools contained a single reference to the long Negro involvement with the province: Blacks "are perpetually begging and receiving charity." In the twentieth century, those few books which purported to discuss social problems for a school-age audience were imported from the United States, and readers not unnaturally assumed that the racial problems revealed in such books were unique to the Republic. (1971, 363)

The impact of this exclusion from the curriculum on Black learners has been analyzed by numerous educators and effectively summed up by Asante as follows: "Lacking reinforcement in their own historical experiences, they [Black students] become psychologically crippled, hobbling along in the margins of the European experiences of most of the curriculum" (cited in BLAC 1994, 40). As a matter of fact, the monocultural content of the school curriculum, including testing and grouping practices, as well as the expectations of educators for Black and minority children, have been established as the major barriers to educational achievement and equality (King 1993). On this point, a 1995 report by the Black Learners Advisory Committee in Nova Scotia, *A Legacy of Inequality*, noted that Black students suffer and fail in the school system because little is said about the contributions of Blacks to the development of the province (cited in *The Globe and Mail*, 1995). It lends support to what the National Alliance of Black School Educators has aptly observed: "Academic excellence cannot be reached without cultural excellence" (cited in BLAC 1994, 18).

The "persistent *invisibility* of Black studies and Black history within the [Canadian school] curriculum" (Yon 1994, 124), as shown above, has been described by Hoo Kong as "exclusionary history" – "the conscious and/or unconscious omission of historical perspectives that conflict with Anglo-Canadian males' interpretation and representation of past events and people, as well as the omission of ethnic or racial groups, such as Black Canadians, from history textbooks" (1996, 59). This exclusionary history also reveals how African-Canadian students are affected by the subtle forms of racism reflected in the school's curriculum. Indeed, in their book, *Teaching Prejudice*, McDiarmid and Pratt (1971) indicate that prejudicial attitudes and negative references to Blacks are widespread in the textbooks used in Ontario schools. So, when all is said and done, we currently have in Canadian schools what Asante calls "a White self-esteem curriculum – that is, a curriculum that, by design or effect, reinforces White students' self-esteem" (Asante 1992, 21). The dogma says that Western (European) knowledge is the sum total of what students should learn. That's why "in many schools, learning starts not with what students bring to class, but with what is considered *high-status knowledge*, that is, the *canon*, with its overemphasis on European and European [Canadian] history, arts, and values. This seldom includes the backgrounds, experiences, and talents of [Black and minority] students in schools" (Nieto 1994, 399). Regarding the subtle forms of racism reflected in this kind of curriculum, Maclear poses this question: "In classrooms, where the absence of African-Canadians in curricular content is still more the rule than the exception, what messages are being sent to Black students as to their participation in Canadian society?" (1994, 66).

CONCLUSION

To sum up and corroborate the thesis of this chapter, I would argue that the *exclusionary curriculum* discussed above constitutes a *hidden curriculum*, because it "often reinforces [Canadian] society's prejudicial view that [African] students ... are incapable and inferior" (Irvine 1990, 8). According to Irvine, "the hidden curriculum is the *unstated but influential knowledge*, attitudes, norms, rules, rituals, values, and beliefs that are transmitted to students through structure, policies, processes, formal content, and the social relations of school" (1990, 5; emphasis added). This hidden curriculum, separate from the "formal curriculum" or what is actually taught in schools, also refers to "the different beliefs, assumptions, attitudes, and expectations that teachers bring to the school with them," and particularly, "the different social relations that are formed and the underlying organizational structures and practices of schooling" (Yon 1994, 139). Further, I agree with Yon that "the hidden curriculum has received less attention than the formal curriculum, because it addresses what is essentially intangible, the very *ethos* of schooling that is difficult to pin down" (139). My point here, again agreeing with Yon (1994, 134), is that, in Canada, "the school's hidden curriculum can cause students to feel marginalized. This is the aspect of schooling through which the subtle and sometimes unintentional forms of racism manifest themselves."

For example, in a "personal reflection" on "Confronting a History of Exclusion," Hoo Kong made the following observation to illustrate the "sometimes unintentional forms of racism": "By ignoring or omitting the faces and experiences of African-Canadians in a society where race is often used to define people, the history curriculum not only alienated me from what I was supposed to believe was the history of my country, but also rendered me, a Black female, as a non-contributing *newcomer*" (Hoo Kong 1996, 62). Similarly, James Walker notes, in *A History of Blacks in Canada: A Study Guide for Teachers and Students*, that in "the Anglo-dominated schools, they [African students] have been taught that the heroes are White, the accomplishments have been attained by Whites, the nation was built by Whites, all of which leaves Blacks as intruders, or at best, hangers-on in a flow of history that ignores them" (cited in Hoo Kong 1996, 62–63). And according to Shadd, many Canadian children are being taught that "Blacks and other People of Colour are newcomers, or worse, *foreigners*, who have no claim to Canadian heritage except through the generosity of immigration officials," thus creating the "myth that Canada is a *White* country" (1989, 152). This lends credence to the thesis that "the groups who exercise the most power within society heavily influence what knowledge becomes legitimized and widely disseminated" (Banks 2002, 22). Indeed, the nature of what is defined as history underpins this process. I am reminded of Wright's observation that "we have listened only to the history of the winners," because the winners, who often are conquerors, write the history that "when it has been digested by a people, becomes myth. Myths are so fraught with meaning that we live and die by them" (1992, 4–5). In fact, in his book *History as Mystery*, Parenti (1999) attacks a number of popular historical myths in an attempt to challenge mainstream history and to show how history's victors distort, manipulate, and suppress the documentary record in order to perpetuate their power and privilege.

Well, it is time to hear the side of the *losers*. That is why, fortunately, African students and scholars and Black educators in North America are mounting oppositional challenges to the status quo and the dominant paradigm (McLaren and Gutierrez 1994). They follow the tradition of DuBois and others who earlier challenged European and racist assumptions of Africans. The students in my study and other minority youth and women have begun to offer a more systematic challenge to the structure of existing school knowledge and the assumptions and practices that undergird the curricula of schools and universities in northern industrialized societies. For example, they are demanding democratization and diversity in the curriculum and course offerings, in particular, incorporating learning about African roots and African cultural achievement, both on the Continent and in the diaspora; critiquing and challenging racist biases in existing school knowledge; and recruiting and hiring minority teachers and administrators. As Livingstone aptly observes,

[c]ollective reflection by subordinate groups leads to recognition not
only of the roles of dominant groups in constructing established beliefs
and practices, but also of their own roles in that process and of their own
potential power to reconstruct such beliefs and practices. Their own emer-
gent collective critiques of the status quo lead directly to some manner of
engagement of alternative possibilities in both conceptual and practical
terms. (1987, 8–9)

Wood points out that such a new critical approach would "celebrate the contributions of working people, women, and minorities to our general cultural pool
and would be the point of departure for providing students with their own
cultural capital" (1998, 177). It is a strategy that proposes to reconstruct the
dominant curriculum by bringing the "uninstitutionalized experiences of marginalized minorities ... to the *centre* of the organization and arrangement of
the school curriculum" (Wood 1998, 177). Giroux places the debate in proper
perspective with this summary:

We live at a time in which a strong challenge is being waged against mod-
ernist discourse in which knowledge is legitimized almost exclusively
from a European model of culture and civilization. In part, the struggle
for democracy can be seen in the context of a broader struggle against
certain features of modernism that represent the worst legacies of the
Enlightenment tradition. And it is against these features that a variety of
oppositional movements have emerged in an attempt to rewrite the relationship between modernism and democracy. (1990, 2)

On this note, I share Dei's conclusion that "on both analytical and practical levels, [the students' narratives] bring to the fore the dilemma of searching for an
appropriate centrality of the experiences, histories, and cultures of the diverse
student body in curriculum and classroom pedagogical practices to facilitate
youth learning" (Dei 1996, 57). It is a *transformative* approach to knowledge
construction that strives to reach towards a more accurate, more inclusive understanding of Canadian society and its diversity.

REFERENCES

Adams, Sharon. 1993. Coping with Racism is Part of Tutoring of Black Students.
Edmonton Journal, October 31.
Aoki, T., W. Warner, S. Dahlies, and B. Connors. 1984. Whose culture? Whose heritage?
Ethnicity within Canadian social studies curricula. In *Cultural Diversity and
Canadian Education*, ed. J. R. Mallea and J. C. Young, 265–89. Ottawa: Carleton
University Press.

Apple, Michael W. 1978. Ideology, reproduction, and educational reform. *Comparative Education Review* 22, no. 3: 367–87.

———. 1990. *Ideology and Curriculum*. 2nd ed. New York: Routledge.

———. 1992. The text and cultural politics. *Educational Researcher* 21, no. 7: 4–11, 19.

———. 1995. *Education and Power*. 2nd ed. New York: Routledge.

Apple, Michael W., and Landon E. Beyer, eds. 1998. *The Curriculum: Problems, Politics, and Possibilities*. Albany: State University of New York Press.

Aronowitz, Stanley, and Henry A. Giroux. 1985. *Education under Siege: The Conservative, Liberal and Radical Debate over Schooling*. South Hadley, MA: Bergin and Garvey.

Asante, Molefi K. 1992. Afrocentric curriculum. *Educational Leadership* 49, no. 4: 28–31.

Banks, James A. 1981. *Multi-Ethnic Education: Theory and Practice*. Boston: Allyn and Bacon.

———. 1993. The canon debate, knowledge construction, and multicultural education. *Education Researcher* 22, no. 5: 4–14.

———. 1995. The historical reconstruction of knowledge about race: Implications for transformative teaching. *Education Researcher* 24, no. 2: 15–25.

———. 1996. Transformative knowledge, curriculum reform, and action. In *Multicultural Education, Transformative Knowledge, and Action: Historical and Contemporary Perspectives*, ed. J. A. Banks, 335–48. New York: Columbia University, Teachers' College Press.

———. 2002. Race, knowledge construction, and education in the USA: Lessons from history. *Race, Ethnicity, and Education* 5, no. 1: 7–27.

Barrett, Stanley R. 1987. *Is God a Racist? The Right Wing in Canada*. Toronto: University of Toronto Press.

Beyer, Landon E., and Michael W. Apple. 1998a. *The Curriculum: Problems, Politics, and Possibilities*. 2nd ed. Albany: State University of New York Press.

———. 1998b. Introduction. In *The Curriculum: Problems, Politics, and Possibilities*, 2nd ed., ed. L. E. Beyer and M. W. Apple, 3–17. Albany: State University of New York Press.

Black Learners Advisory Committee [BLAC]. 1994. *BLAC Report on Education: Redressing Inequity: Empowering Black Learners*, vol. 1: *Summary*. Halifax: Black Learners Advisory Committee.

Bloom, Allan. 1987. *The Closing of the American Mind: How Higher Education Has Failed Democracy and Impoverished the Souls of Today's Students*. New York: Simon and Schuster.

Brathwaite, Keren. 1989. The Black student and the school: A Canadian dilemma. In *African Continuities,* ed. S. W. Chilungu and S. Niang, 195–216. Toronto: Terebi.

Brathwaite, Keren, and Carl E. James, eds. 1996. *Educating African-Canadians*. Toronto: James Lorimer.

Bristow, Peggy, et al. 1994. *We're Rooted Here and They Can't Pull Us Up: Essays in African-Canadian Women's History*. Toronto: University of Toronto Press.

Bullivant, Brian. 1983. Multiculturalism: Pluralist orthodoxy or ethnic hegemony? *Canadian Ethnic Studies/Études ethniques au Canada* 13, no. 2: 1–22.

Campbell, Murray. 1989. Fighting back: Canadian Blacks have become alarmed over a recent series of race-related incidents. *Globe and Mail*, 21 January, D1–D2.

Cannon, Margaret. 1995. *The Invisible Empire: Racism in Canada*. Toronto: Random House.

Chavanu, Bakari. 1996. Resisting the high school canon. *Rethinking Schools* 10, no. 4: 1, 6–7.

Cheng, Charles W., Emily Brizendine, and Jeannie Oakes. 1979. What is "an equal chance" for minority children? *Journal of Negro Education* 48, no. 3: 267–87.

Christensen, Carole P., and Morton Weinfeld. 1993. The Black family in Canada: A preliminary exploration of family patterns and inequality. *Canadian Ethnic Studies/Études ethniques au Canada* 25, no. 3: 26–44.

Code, Lorraine. 1991. *What Can She Know? Feminist Theory and the Construction of Knowledge*. Ithaca, NY: Cornell University Press.

Codjoe, Henry M. 1997. *Black Students and School Success: A Study of the Experiences of Academically Successful African-Canadian Student Graduates in Alberta's Secondary School*. Ph.D. diss., University of Alberta, Edmonton.

———. 1998. Pre-college/university education of Ghanaians and other Africans in North America: A Canadian perspective. *Ghana Review International* 52: 10–11.

———. 1999. The schooling experiences of African students in Canadian schools. *International Journal of Curriculum and Instruction* 1, no. 1: 67–94.

———. 2001a. Can Blacks be racist? Reflections on being "too Black and African." In *Talking about Identity: Encounters in Race, Ethnicity, and Language*, ed. C. James and A. Shadd, 277–90. Toronto: Between the Lines.

———. 2001b. Fighting a "public enemy" of Black academic achievement – The persistence of racism and the schooling experiences of Black students in Canada. *Race, Ethnicity, and Education* 4, no. 4: 343–75.

D'Oyley, Vincent, and Harry Silverman, eds. 1976. *Black Students in Urban Canada*. Toronto: Ministry of Culture and Recreation.

D'Souza, Dinesh. 1991. *Illiberal Education: The Politics of Race and Sex on Campus*. New York: Free Press.

Dei, George S. 1994. Afrocentricity: A cornerstone of pedagogy. *Anthropology and Education Quarterly* 25: 3–28.

———. 1996. Black/African-Canadian students' perspectives on school racism. In *Racism in Canadian Schools*, ed. M. I. Alladin, 42–61. Toronto: Harcourt Brace.

———. 1999. The denial of difference: Reframing anti-racist praxis. *Race, Ethnicity, and Education* 2, no. 1: 17–37.

Dei, George S., and Irma M. James. 1998. "Becoming Black": African-Canadian youth and the politics of negotiating racial and racialized identities. *Race, Ethnicity, and Education* 1, no. 1: 91–108.

Estrada, Kelly, and Peter McLaren. 1993. A dialogue on multicultural and democratic culture. *Educational Researcher* 22, no. 3: 27–33.

Eze, Emmanuel C., ed. 1997. *Race and the Enlightenment: Reader*. Cambridge, MA: Blackwell.

Farrell, Bill. 1991. DuBois and the boys' club of the "great books." *These Times*, September 11–17, 20.

Flecha, Ramon. 1999. Modern and postmodern racism in Europe: Dialogic approach and anti-racist pedagogies. *Harvard Educational Review* 69, no. 2: 150–71.

Foner, Eric. 2002 [online]. *Changing history*. *The Nation*, September 23 [cited 14 January 2004]. (www.thenation.com/doc.mhtml?i=20020923&s=foner).

Foucault, Michel. 1980. *Power/Knowledge: Selected Interviews and Other Writings, 1972–1977*, ed. C. Gordon. New York: Pantheon.

Ghosh, Ratna. 1995. New perspectives on multiculturalism in education. *McGill Journal of Education* 30, no. 3: 231–38.

Giroux, Henry A. 1986. The politics of schooling and culture. *Orbit* 17, no. 4: 10–11.

———. 1990. Introduction: Modernism, postmodernism, and feminism: Rethinking the boundaries of educational discourse. In *Postmodernism, Feminism, and Cultural Politics*, ed. Henry Giroux, 1–59. Buffalo, NY: State University of New York Press.

Globe and Mail. 1995. Nova Scotia Earmarks $1-Million to Fight Systemic Racism in Schools. *The Globe and Mail*, Toronto, June 30, A3.

Goldberg, David T. 1993. *Racist Culture: Philosophy and the Politics of Meaning*. Oxford: Blackwell.

Head, Wilson. 1975. *The Black Presence in the Canadian Mosaic: A Study of Perception and the Practice of Discrimination against Blacks in Metropolitan Toronto*. Toronto: Ontario Human Rights Commission.

Henry, Annette. 1993. Missing: Black self-representations in Canadian educational research. *Canadian Journal of Education* 18, no. 3: 206–22.

Henry, Frances, and Carol Tator. 1991. *Multicultural Education: Translating Policy into Practice*. Ottawa: Department of Multiculturalism and Citizenship.

Herrnstein, Richard, and Charles Murray. 1994. *The Bell Curve: Intelligence and Class Structure in American Life*. New York: Basic.

Hexham, Irving. 2002. *Recognizing academic bias* [cited 18 February 2002]. (www.ucalgary.ca/-Hexham/Study/T-1.html).

Hill, Daniel G. 1960. *Negroes in Toronto: A Sociological Study of a Minority Group*. Toronto: Department of Political Economy, University of Toronto Press.

Hill, Daniel G., and Arnold Bruner. 1978. Heritage of overcoming: The 350th anniversary of Blacks in Canada. *Globe and Mail*, 19 August.

Hirsch, Eric D., Jr. 1987. *Cultural Literacy: What Every American Needs to Know*. Boston: Houghton Mifflin.

Hoo Kong, Nancy A. 1996. Confronting a history of exclusion: A personal reflection. In *Educating African-Canadians*, ed. K. Brathwaite and C. E. James, 58–68. Toronto: James Lorimer.

Irvine, Jacqueline J. 1990. *Black Students and School Failure: Policies, Practices, and Prescriptions*. New York: Praeger.

James, Carl E. 1990. *Making It: Black Youth, Racism, and Career Aspirations in a Big City.* Oakville: Mosaic.

James, Carl E., and Keren Brathwaite. 1996. The education of African-Canadians: Issues, contexts, and expectations. In *Educating African-Canadians,* ed. K. Brathwaite and C. E. James, 13–31. Toronto: James Lorimer.

Kilgour, David. 1994. Whither racism? *Canadian Social Studies* 29, no. 1: 6–7.

King, Sabrina H. 1993. The limited presence of African-American teachers. *Review of Educational Research* 63, no. 2: 115–49.

Ladner, Joyce A., ed. 1973. *The Death of White Sociology.* New York: Vintage.

Lee, Enid. 1992. *Letters to Marcia: A Teacher's Guide to Anti-Racist Education.* Toronto: Ontario Cross-Cultural Communication Centre.

Lendore-Mahabir, Merle. 1995. *Issues Associated with Racial Intolerance and Inequality and Proposals for Their Resolution.* Edmonton: Council of Black Organizations.

Levine, Lawrence W. 1996. *The Opening of the American Mind: Cannons, Culture, and History.* Boston: Beacon.

Lewis, Stephen. 1992. *Consultative Report on Race Relations.* Toronto: Ontario Ministry of Citizenship.

Livingstone, David W. 1987. Introduction. In *Critical Pedagogy and Cultural Power.* ed. Livingstone, D. W. et al., 1–14. New York: Bergin and Garvey.

Maclear, Kyo. 1994. The myth of the "model minority": Re-thinking the education of Asian Canadians. *Our Schools/Our Selves* 5, no. 3: 54–76.

Maher, Frances A., and Mary Kay Tetrault. 1994. *The Feminist Classroom.* New York: Basic Books.

McDiarmid, Garnet, and David Pratt. 1971. *Teaching Prejudice: The Content Analysis of Social Textbooks Authorized for Use in Ontario Schools.* Toronto: Ontario Institute for Studies in Education.

McKague, Ormond, ed. 1991. *Racism in Canada.* Saskatoon: Fifth House.

McLaren, Peter, and Kris Gutierrez. 1994. Pedagogies of dissent and transformation: A dialogue about postmodernity, social context, and the politics of literacy. *International Journal of Educational Reform* 3, no. 3: 327–37.

Mensah, Joseph. 2002. *Black Canadians: History, Experiences, Social Conditions.* Halifax: Fernwood.

Minnich, Elizabeth K. 1990. *Transforming Knowledge.* Philadelphia: Temple University Press.

Morrow, Raymond A., and Carlos A. Torres. 1995. *Social Theory and Education: A Critique of Theories of Social and Cultural Reproduction.* Albany: State University of New York Press.

Nieto, Sonia. 1992. *Affirming Diversity: The Sociopolitical Context of Multicultural Education.* New York: Longman.

———. 1994. Lessons from students on creating a chance to dream. *Harvard Educational Review* 64: 392–426.

Noffke, Susan E. 1998. Multicultural curricula: "Whose knowledge?" and beyond. In *The Curriculum: Problems, Politics, and Possibilities,* 2nd ed., ed. L. E. Beyer and M. W. Apple, 101–16. Albany: State University of New York Press.

Ogbu, John U. 1991. Immigrant and involuntary minorities in comparative perspective. In *Minority Status and Schooling: A Comparative Study of Immigrant and Involuntary Minorities*, ed. M. Gibson and J. U. Ogbu, 3–33. New York: Garland.

O'Malley, Sean. 1992. Demand quality education, Black parents told. *Globe and Mail*, 20 August.

Ovando, Carlos J., and Karen Gourd. 1996. Knowledge construction, language maintenance, revitalization, and empowerment. In *Multicultural Education, Transformative Knowledge, and Action: Historical and Contemporary Perspectives*, ed. J. A. Banks, 297–322. New York: Columbia University, Teachers' College Press.

Parenti, Michael. 1999. *History as Myth*. San Francisco: City Lights.

Pinar, William F. 1993. Notes on understanding curriculum as a racial text. In *Race, Identity, and Representation in Education*, ed. C. McCarthy and W. Crichlow, 60–70. New York: Routledge.

Ravitch, Diane, and Chester E. Finn, Jr. 1987. *What Do Our 17-Year-Olds Know: A Report on the First National Assessment of History and Literature*. New York: HarperCollins.

Richardson, Robert. 1995. Let no one off the hook. *Canadian Forum* 74, no. 841: 36–38.

Roman, Leslie, and Linda Christian-Smith, with Elizabeth Ellsworth, eds. 1988. *Becoming Feminine: The Politics of Popular Culture*. Philadelphia: Falmer.

Rosenblum, Karen E., and Toni-Michelle Travis. 2000. Framework essay: Constructing categories of difference. In *The Meaning of Difference: Americans' Constructions of Race, Sex, and Gender, Social Class, and Sexual Orientation*, ed. K. E. Rosenblum and T.-M. Travis, 1–33. Boston: McGraw-Hill.

Rothenberg, Paula, ed. 2001. *Race, Class, and Gender in the United States*, 5th ed. New York: Worth.

———. 2004. Many voices, many lives: Some consequences of racial, gender, and class inequality. In *Race, Class, and Gender in the United States*, 6th ed., ed. P. Rothenberg, 333–35. New York: Worth.

Ruby, Clayton. 1995. We have a lot to learn from this royal commission. *Toronto Star*, 15 March, A21.

Sardar, Ziauddin, and Merryl Wyn Davies. 2002. *Why Do People Hate America?* New York: Disinformation Company.

Sarup, Madan. 1991. *Education and the Ideologies of Racism*. Stoke-On-Trent, UK: Trentham.

Schlesinger, Arthur M., Jr. 1991. *The Disuniting of America: Reflections on a Multicultural Society*. New York: W. W. Norton.

Shadd, Adrienne. 1989. Institutionalized racism and Canadian history: Notes of a Black Canadian. In *Seeing Ourselves: Exploring Race, Ethnicity and Culture*, ed. C. E. James, 151–55. Oakville: Sheridan College.

Solomon, Patrick. 1992. *Black Resistance in High School: Forging a Separatist Culture*. Albany: State University of New York Press.

Spencer, Jennifer R. 1995. *Under the Gaze: The Experiences of African-Canadian Students in Two Edmonton High Schools*. Unpublished M.A. Thesis, Department of Educational Policy Studies, University of Alberta, Edmonton, Alberta, Canada.

Sultana, Ronald G. 1995. Ethnography and the politics of absence. In *Critical Theory and Educational Research*, ed. P. L. McLaren and J. M. Giarelli, 113–25. Albany: State University of New York Press.

Takaki, Ronald. 1993. *A Different Mirror: A History of Multicultural America*. Boston: Little, Brown and Co.

Thorsell, William. 1996. Despite the republicans' "American dream," the U.S. is clearly fragmented. *Globe and Mail*, 17 August, D6.

Towards a New Beginning. 1992. *The Report and Action Plan of the Four-Level Government/African-Canadian Community Working Group*. Toronto.

Walker, James. 1980. *A History of Blacks in Canada*. Ottawa: Ministry of Supply and Services, Canada.

Williams, Walter. 2002. Celebrating multiculturalism. *Daily Citizen*. Dalton, GA, 2 January, 4a.

Willis, Arlette I. 1995. Reading the world of school literacy: Contextualizing the experience of a young African-American male. *Harvard Educational Review* 65, no. 1: 30–49.

Winks, Robin. 1971. *The History of Blacks in Canada*. New Haven, CT: Yale University Press.

Wood, George H. 1998. Democracy and curriculum. In *The Curriculum: Problems, Politics, and Possibilities*, 2nd ed., ed. L. E. Beyer and M. W. Apple, 177–98. Albany: State University of New York Press.

Wright, Ronald. 1992. *Stolen Continents: The Americas through Indian Eyes since 1492*. Boston: Houghton Mifflin.

Yin, Robert K. 1984. *Case Study Research: Design and Methods*. Newbury Park, CA: Sage.

Yon, Daniel. 1994. The educational experiences of Caribbean youth. In *The Caribbean Diaspora in Toronto: Learning to Live with Racism*, ed. F. Henry, 120–47. Toronto: University of Toronto Press.

5

RACISM IN CANADIAN CONTEXTS:
Exploring Public & Private Issues
in the Educational System

George S. Dei

INTRODUCTION

I BEGIN THIS DISCUSSION with some words of caution. In speaking of race/racism, I am not creating it; rather, I am pointing to what already exists. Silence cannot wish away the problem of racism. In addition, I am writing from my social position as a male, Canadian educator of African descent teaching in a post-secondary institution. I therefore speak from the position of someone who is privileged but one who simultaneously faces social discrimination having to deal with day-to-day racist and racialized practices. While I acknowledge my privileged position and the contradictions that come with it, I also share responsibility in the search for viable solutions to racism in Canadian contexts. In doing so, I borrow from Stuart Hall's (1996, 447) words of caution that we must continually recognize that "we all speak from a particular place, out of a particular history, out of a particular experience, [and] a particular culture." The limits of our knowing do not invalidate our experiential and academic knowledge of racism.

In this chapter, therefore, I present a cursory overview of how I see racism and race relations working in Canadian society. Admittedly, any attempt to interrogate racism within society is a large and complex undertaking, given the different and diverse manifestations of society. Nevertheless, I partake in this discursive practice to show both the historical and contemporary connections of racism as it manifests itself in society. The learning objective is to critically examine the historical and contemporary manifestations of racism, specifically, the nature and context of racism in Canadian society pointing to the extent to which racism is viewed as a social or political problem. The discussion proceeds to reflect on the nation-state/governmental responses to the problem of racism, as well as the role of local community organizations in resisting/addressing racism through anti-racist initiatives. I utilize personal experience/reflections as an important knowledge base to highlight the nature and extent of racism within a specific societal institutional sector – schooling and education.

The chapter draws on my personal, subjective experiences, and I do not, in any way, attempt to project such experiences onto others. It would be presumptuous on my part to do so, and I respect the views of those who do not share the experiences I speak about. I also hold a powerful conviction that the issues discussed here will resonate with many others. There will always be allies in the struggles of the racially minoritized to have their experiences, cultures, and histories represented in the conventional school setting, workplace, and other institutional settings. Throughout this discussion, I use the word *minoritized* in the sense of power relations within the social setting. I speak of a process of minoritization, in which groups are denied access to power and their agency is structurally constrained by local and national politics of the dominant. The term *minoritized* does not mean minority groups lack agency and the power to resist. On the contrary, it (the term) gestures to the constant practice of placing these groups in subordinate power relations with the dominant group(s), primarily through the distribution of valued goods and services of society.

As a person of African descent, I have no qualms about being described as a racial minority faculty. In fact, I see myself as such. I am also working with a broader definition of *exclusion*. My broad concerns in this chapter are with the institutionalized processes of *othering*, which feeds racism and racist practices; the social construction of *otherness*, and the historic failure and outright refusal to include and to centre the experiences, histories, cultures, and knowledge systems of non-European peoples in Euro-American contexts. I also concede that there are macro- and micro-differences (or distinctions) in terms of gender, sexual orientation, ability, socioeconomic status, race, ethnicity, and histories that need to guide the discussion of racism and oppression in society. The facts of race, ethnicity, gender sexuality, ability, and history differentially impact upon the experiences of every member of society. However, such differences should not prevent a critical analysis of the situation that minoritized bodies face in mainstream, hetero-patriarchal institutions (e.g., in schools, workplaces, union halls, and so on). It is important that an understanding of the subjective, lived experiences of the minoritized be situated within a wider structural context, particularly in external social conditions and processes.

At the theoretical level, this chapter is positioned within an anti-racist, discursive framework. This framework seeks to challenge both the exclusionary politics of social institutions and institutional settings, and the universal claims to truth that have historically been propagated by conventional, dominant systems. The anti-racist agenda interrogates power relations in society and the rationality for dominance. The anti-racist agenda also validates difference and diversity by addressing questions of race, representation, and identity in institutional settings (e.g., homes, families, workplaces, schools, and union halls). In terms of communicative practice, the anti-racist, pedagogical strategy (like other forms of liberatory pedagogy) posits and nurtures avenues for marginalized, excluded, and silenced groups to challenge dominant hegemonic discourses, ideas, and interests, definitions of knowledge, and conventional (Euro-centred) approaches to learning.

The anti-racist framework can assist in understanding how our racial, class, and gender identities are implicated in our ways of knowing and in knowledge itself. That framework also helps us to understand how our race, gender, or class position implicates us in both particular and diverse interests in the institutions in which we work. Many times our voices can be heard differently when we seem to be saying the same things. The readings of discourses on bodies have historically worked to position us differently in the academy in terms of the politics of our work. It is not surprising that Black scholars are often heard speaking only about race, even when they are articulating the intersections of difference. Anti-racism pedagogy problematizes the manner in which patriarchal relations of schooling engage some students and faculty while disengaging others. The anti-racist stance calls on educators to acknowledge their relative power and privileged positions in society, and to interrogate what such power and privilege has done, and continues to do, for some people.

In examining and interrogating the exclusionary politics of social systems and institutions, certain questions have to be asked: For example, what are the prevailing definitions of racism within Canada? What are the lessons of history in understanding racism in Canadian contexts? Whose interests are being served by social and institutional practices of racial exclusions? How do the relations of power within our social system hegemonize the norms and values of mainstream Canadians? Do all subjects have equal access to available resources, materials, and valued goods of the society? Who and what are excluded from the seating of major players in society? How do those who are racially minoritized resist their subordination? Finally, what avenues exist in society for subordinated groups to voice their concerns and aspirations?

Race and racism have become an unsettling issue for most Canadians. A common [dominant] view or position is that the less said about these terms, the better it is for society. The hegemonic view of racism is that it is simply negative and must be swept under a carpet (see also Tatum 1999). The degree to which academic knowledge produces, sustains, or subverts such problematic general understandings is still a debatable matter. The hostility towards the assertion of racism in society by dominant groups reaches its highest level when the anti-racist worker also heralds the saliency of race in Canadian society. As Tatum (1999, 60) has observed, "some dimensions of our identities are reflected more saliently than others, a distinction made apparent by the energy we invest in their examination." Dei (1996, 1999) addresses the situational and contextual variations in intensities of oppression that make it possible for the anti-racist worker to notice that, while oppressions may be similar, they are not equal in their consequences, given the history and context of oppressive practice. I share Winant's (1997) insights in asserting that the contemporary Euro-American/Canadian scene can be characterized as an open denial of the significance of race in academic discourses. Race repeatedly takes a back seat in *progressive* politics. This fact is coupled with the call for a trans-racial politics devoid of a politics of identity. Many so-called progressive workers have also resorted to strictly class-based criteria in formulating social policy for equity and justice. In such an atmosphere, many minorities, including African-Canadians, are losing their sense of entitlement and belonging to Canadian citizenship.

In Canadian public, official, and academic discourses, one could argue that there are commonsense definitions of race relations, as opposed to critical anti-racist perspectives about what terms, such as *race, racism, anti-racism,* and *race relations,* mean. There are varied definitions of racism ranging from the denial of the importance of race to a liberal acknowledgement that speaks of race relations in the multicultural sense of *getting to know each other* and *let us get along.* In this view, culture, as opposed to race, is the central concept. The question of conflict among groups is muted, and group differences are read largely as misunderstandings, perceived ignorance, and a lack of knowledge. Racism is hardly seen as a power issue, as in, "Who has the power to construct difference?" Racism is also hardly seen in the refusal to acknowledge and problematize what is designated as different. Race relations are individual, interpersonal relations understood as simply prejudice and the simple acts of the racist self. Racism is perceived as a *personal* and an interactional problem, and to this end, anti-racist work can be about raising consciousness. Racism is not about structural relations between groups competing for access to the valued goods and services of society. Neither is racism institutionalized in daily social practices. A liberal discourse of colour-blind society erases race. How such discourse of *not seeing colour* is itself not innocent is never highlighted for public discussion. After all, if one does not see colour, then there is no recognition of *White* power and privilege. We are all the same.

As many others have noted, the denial of racism is an integral and central part of the Canadian identity (Razack 1998, 11). There are also critical perspectives on racism that see racism as a system of structural, material, and ideological advantage that some groups have over others in society. This discourse unmasks *Whiteness* as a racial category anchored in a powerful identity (see also Frankenberg 1993; Levine-Rasky 2002). It seeks to reconfigure *Whiteness* as problematically *dominant*. Whiteness has become the *norm*, but it is not, and should not be, the norm. Racism is seen as a conscious/calculated strategy to establish group material and symbolic advantage. Race relations are relations of dominant and subordinate groups. Racism is a relation of power used to privilege and punish groups on the basis of their perceived physical and cultural differences. The social reality of many racial minorities in Canadian society can be problematized in a critical sense as subjects located in the lower end of a hierarchical and highly contested power structure. Many of the challenges faced by bodies of colour can be understood as historic problems of social inequality and of differential levels of influence within the wider social setting. The so-called visible minorities are generally in a subordinate position in relation to groups and individuals that have power to subject them to unequal and differential treatment. The structures of institutionalized racism, sexism, and classism can create obstacles to the attainment of educational and professional goals.

Racism is power. It is institutional, systemic, and cultural. In fact, racism as a system, in which one group exercises power over another on the basis of real, perceived, or imagined physical and cultural differences, has had numerous and persistent effects in Canadian history. I highlight *history* because, as Rodriguez (1998, 2000) argues, when it comes to speaking about racism, we cannot step outside of our histories. There are those who would want to amputate history from the discussion of Canadian society, in part, because this history is of a troubling past. We must resist this call to amputate the past, because the present is itself constitutive of what it is not, the past (see also Lattas 1993). The importance of the history of racism is also for us to learn from the past and to see how the past continues to shape and influence the present.

HISTORY OF CANADIAN RACISM

The primary manifestation of racism was European imperial expansion in the *New World*, characterized by land and resource acquisitions from Indigenous populations. In Canada, from the arrival of the French in 1535 to the Royal Proclamation in 1763, there were many instances of overt racism visited on the Indigenous population: European claims and occupations of Aboriginal land; the enslavement of Aboriginal peoples by European traders; the founding of the

Hudson's Bay Company in 1670; and the opening of the first residential school by Jesuits in Upper Canada in 1680. The introduction of slavery in Canada in 1608, culminating in the presence of over 4,000 Black slaves in Canada as far back as 1750, can be claimed as part of the history of racism in Canada (see Walker 1981). With the settlement of White Europeans in Canada came the *civilizing mission* directed towards Aboriginal peoples through legislation and education. As the colonization of Aboriginal peoples intensified amidst local resistance, immigration and employment policies and practices were explicitly aimed at making Canada a White nation and/or keeping power and privilege in the hands of Whites, despite the fact of a gradually more diversified citizenry.

As racism shaped White Canadians' dealings with the Aboriginal inhabitants of this land, racist practice also defined the historic immigration policies followed by Canadian governments over the years. Thomas (2001) notes that, for much of Canada's history, official immigration policy has been racist and exclusionary. The regulation of early entry into Canada was through a mechanistic process that ensured that Canada would be peopled by members of a particular stock. In 1896–1905, Clifford Sifton (Minister of the Interior) wanted English and Scottish settlers in the West. In the relatively prosperous times of 1946–1957, the Canadian government reappraised its prewar policy, allowing more immigrants. Social absorption was pursued to the extent that the would-be immigrants were similar to Canadians, that is, White Canadians of Western European stock. Initially, only close family members from Asia, for example, were allowed. Black Caribbean females were admitted, but only as domestic servants in the 1950s (see Calliste 1991, 1993). In fact, the government was opposed to large-scale immigration from the Orient to preserve the *White Canada* policy for the next fifteen years. Under the point system in 1967, the proportion of immigrants coming from the West Indies, the Middle East, Asia, and Africa increased sharply from less than 20 percent to over 40 percent in the late 1960s and early 1970s (Ramcharan 1995).

Looking at Canada's history, it can be argued that racism shaped national and provincial educational policies, work practices, and the pursuit of justice. Nowhere is this clearer than in looking at Canada's immigration policy/system. Immigration law is closely related to the composition of Canadian society from the perspectives of race and ethnicity, class, and gender. Immigration policy has been, and is, an instrument for social, political, and economic engineering projects of Canadian governments. This agenda is cloaked in language that upholds global human rights and domestic multiculturalism.

Racism was the reason for denying Japanese Canadians access to some of the valued goods and services of society in British Columbia during World War II. Racism is to blame for the imposition of the head tax on Chinese immigrants; "the denial of landing for the *Komagata Maru*," a ship carrying South Asians off the coast of Vancouver at the turn of the century; the race riots in Nova Scotia in the late 1800s; the segregation of African-Canadians in the educational system in Ontario until the 1960s; the treatment of nurses from racialized groups in the 1970s and 1980s; the denial of employment opportunities for racialized peoples; the documented over-representation of racialized group members in the prison systems in Manitoba, Nova Scotia, and Ontario; persistent differential access to services, such as housing, health care, social assistance, and recreational facilities; the imposition of limits on access to property; and differential treatment in the criminal justice system (see Centre for Social Justice 2001).

Walker (1981) and Calliste (1991, 1993, 1993/4) amply demonstrate the exclusionary practices that Blacks, particularly Caribbean immigrants, had to endure as they sought entry to Canadian society. Today, the primary manifestation of racism is the pervasiveness of institutional racism in the educational system, employment, media, and immigration. There are continuing instances of overt individual and institutional acts of racism and physical violence directed particularly at non-White populations. How has the Canadian government attempted to deal with acts of discrimination?

STATE RESPONSE TO RACIAL DISCRIMINATION AND THE DIVERSITY QUESTION

To understand the state's response to race issues in Canada, we need to look critically at official action in terms of enacting acts to affirm the rights of Canadian citizens. Butler (2001) provides a historical sequence of policy initiatives by the Canadian national and provincial governments to affirm individual rights. The year 1948 marked the *Universal Declaration of Human Rights*. Since this date, Canada has tried to ensure that its domestic human rights policies are in line with those of the international community. At the federal level, a *Canadian Bill of Rights* was passed in 1960. The *Act for the Recognition and Protection of Human Rights and Fundamental Freedoms* states, in part, that "it is hereby recognized and declared that in Canada there have existed and continue to exist without discrimination by reason of race, national origin, colour, religion or sex, the following human rights and fundamental freedoms, namely:

a) the right of the individual to life, liberty, security of the person and enjoyment of property, and the right not to be deprived thereof except by due process of law,
b) the right of the individual to equality before the law and the protection of the law,
c) freedom of religion,
d) freedom of speech,
e) freedom of assembly and association, and
f) freedom of the press.

On 17 April 1982 a *Canadian Charter of Rights and Freedoms* was enacted. This was part of a package contained in law called the *Constitution Act, 1982*. One section of the charter, section 15.1, states that "Every individual is equal before and under the law and has the right to the equal protection and equal benefit of the law without discrimination and, in particular, without discrimination based on race, national or ethnic origin, colour, religion, sex, age or mental or physical disability." On 12 July 1988, *Bill C-93, An Act for the Preservation and Enhancement of Multiculturalism in Canada*, was also passed. Within official discourse, multiculturalism has since referred to the government policy of promoting cultural diversity in Canadian society.

The province of Ontario provides a clear example of the diversity of Canadian society. Ontario has a population of over 10 million people that contains 37 percent of Canada's total population and slightly over 49 percent of Canada's *visible minority* groups. When consideration of ethnicity/nationality is included, nearly half of all people in Canada who reported origins other than British or French resided in Ontario (Statistics Canada 1993; see also Statistics Canada 2001). Statistics Canada (1993, 1) notes that "over half of all persons in Canada, reporting West Asian, South Asian, African, Caribbean, and Black single ethnic origins, lived in Ontario." According to the same source, in 1991, 66 percent of the total 345,445 peoples of African descent (African, Black, and Caribbean) in Canada were living in Ontario. The city of Toronto is seen as one of the world's most ethnoculturally diverse cities, and it continues to be a primary destination for immigrants to Canada. In any given year, the city receives almost one-quarter of all new arrivals to Canada. In 1996, 47 percent of the population was foreign born, and nearly 40 percent were members of a visible minority. More recent Statistics Canada (2001) figures reveal that this trend is increasing (see also Smith, Mirza-Beg, and Anderson, 2003; Statistics Canada 2003).

Official recognition of this growing diversity is not questioned. As Abramovitz (2001) notes, embedded in Canadian institutions is the recognition that cultural diversity is a hallmark of contemporary societies, that we are a *mosaic*, not a *melting-pot*. To this end, the Government of Canada has sponsored multiculturalism as a state policy. Unfortunately, many critics are quick to point out that multiculturalism in fact does nothing to address racism or redress issues of inequity. Such liberal ideological dynamics are "grounded on an allegedly neutral and universal process of consciousness construction that is unaffected by racial, class, and gender differences" (Abramovitz 2001, 1). The ideological appeal of consensus and similarity erases both the dynamics and the relational aspects of difference. The unexamined sameness of liberal multiculturalism allows educators and cultural producers to speak the language of diversity while normalizing Eurocentric culture as the tacit norm everyone references (Kincheloe and Steinberg 1998, 11).

One would argue that while good intentions abound, the problem has always been how to translate these noble intentions into concrete actions that make a difference in the lives of peoples, particularly those who are racially minoritized. The state's response to racism and anti-racism initiatives needs to be more proactive; otherwise they can simply be termed a politics of containment and accommodation. Canada has benefited greatly from the absorption of immigrants. There can be little doubt that there would have been tremendous cost to the country if adult immigrants arriving in Canada in the last two decades had been raised and educated in Canada. Immigration has been seen as a way to address human power shortages, particularly for skilled personnel. The Conference Board of Canada has projected that there will be one million skilled workers in Canada by 2020 (see Ghafour 2001). While official policy recognizes and welcomes immigrants, not much is done to ensure that the talents and skills brought into the country are fully harnessed. Although a sizeable number of immigrants have high educational levels, they have had problems accessing employment opportunities. In 1999, a total of 196,871 immigrants arrived in Canada, of which 133,201 were classified as skilled and business classes (see Ghafour 2001). Forty percent of the immigrants arriving in Canada had first degrees. Yet a good number of highly qualified and educated immigrants recount stories of disappointment in terms of the inability to secure jobs commensurate with their educational qualifications (Ghafour 2001).

The foregoing discussions have implications for social action. It is imperative that these figures translate into the provision of social and economic rights and services to adults and children that the above numbers represent. Two of the most important of these rights are elementary and secondary education. The diversity of society is the diversity of the classroom (see Board of Education 1993). The challenge to family, community, teachers, administration, and other educational stakeholders is to address questions of educational equity, social difference, and identity and knowledge production in the school system and beyond. While research demonstrates the effects of racism on students' engagement and disengagement from school, policy responses have been relatively silent on race and equity issues.

A number of research studies have documented the extent of racism in schools (see Canadian Alliance of Black Educators [CABE] 1992; Black Educators' Working Group [BEWG] 1993; Board of Education 1988; Brathwaite 1989; Solomon 1992; James 1990; Brathwaite and James 1996; Dei et al. 1995; Dei et al. 1997; Alladin 1996). Again, schooling in the province of Ontario is a good example that points to the challenge of educational inclusivity within the context of diversity and difference. As with other parts of Canada, the racialized contexts of Ontario call for measures to address the question of the exclusion and marginality of some populations. In Dei et al. (1995) and Dei et al. (1997), the authors show how some students leave school or become disengaged from the Canadian school system because of the complex dynamics of the *cultures, environments,* and *organizational lives* of mainstream schools. Disengaged students and *dropouts* are very critical of the structures of public schooling, articulating their concerns around differential treatment because of their race and having to deal with an exclusive curriculum.

Furthermore, they are dissatisfied with communicative and pedagogic practices that fail to adequately explore the complexities of experiences that have shaped, and that continue to influence, human growth and development. The students also complain of the paucity of Black and other racial minority teachers in the school system (see Dei et al. 1995). These concerns are pervasive in students' voices to the extent that they emerge in response to seemingly unrelated questions or descriptions. When students speak to the low expectations of some teachers, the tendency for Caribbean students to be stigmatized as *violent, unruly, and criminal,* and for African students to be characterized as having language difficulties, they are referring to how racialized bodies are read or regarded in school systems.

CONFRONTING OPPRESSIVE AND EXCLUSIVE ENVIRONMENTS: THE ISSUE OF PHYSICAL REPRESENTATION OF DIVERSE BODIES

In ending this discussion, I cannot overemphasize the strategies of action and responses to racism. It is important to speak of anti-racist resistance in order to convey the message that there are many Canadians fighting and resisting racism. Within many Canadian communities, there are committed individuals working in collectivities to deal with the scourge of racism and other forms of oppression. Anti-racist organizations have emerged over the years and engaged in coalition politics to deal with the interlocking systems of oppression that we all continually face in our daily lives (see Robertson 1999). These are grassroots initiatives cementing the origins of anti-racist politics in Canada within local communities (see Dei and Calliste 2000; Calliste and Dei 2000). The activities of such bodies need to be supported and sustained. I see the question of power as central to a discussion of anti-racist change to deal with racism and other forms of oppression. I maintain a view that addressing the power inequities that exist in society is crucial to a fundamental restructuring of our institutions to serve a diverse body politic. To this end, I conclude this essay by reflecting on one area of anti-racist change that is required to deal with racism within institutions. I want to focus my gaze on the educational system and address the importance of having diverse physical bodies in positions of power and influence. While I understand that these bodies may, by themselves, be insignificant and that what is required is structural change of the system, I would argue for a place for having bodies in places as *structural hegemonic rupturing* of the status quo. The essay began by identifying my location (the academy), and it ends with the same location.

Indisputably, within Canadian institutions of higher learning, there are very few *instructors of colour* in any capacity (tenured, tenure-stream, or contractual positions). The lack of adequate representation of racial minority faculty can make the presence and work of a few minority scholars in the academy very demanding indeed. This is particularly so when it comes to matters dealing directly with one's community of identification. Admittedly, the feeling of isolation may be tempered by the realization that there are other colleagues who may share similar political concerns. In fact, in pursuing anti-racism and anti-oppression work, I find it helpful to join forces with other colleagues (faculty and students) who share a similar political project, to question Euro-Canadian/American dominance of what constitutes valid knowledge and how such knowledge should be produced and disseminated internally and internationally.

Engaging in an educational project to change the Eurocentric nature of Canadian schooling is, however, a risky undertaking. In educational institutions staffed by senior colleagues who are predominantly White and male, one cannot live without the *fear* of reprisal, however unfounded, particularly if the minority faculty's academic and political work identifies the structures of White male privilege as the main target of academic and political critique (see Dei 1993). Since there are so few racial minority faculty in our educational institutions, the pressure is on those few to be appropriate *role models* for members of their race and also to provide academic guidance for racial minority students within the system. The problem with this positioning arises when one is seen as the spokesperson for others. I believe that the history of exclusion of certain bodies in our institutions provide us all with an important lesson: those few minoritized bodies *who get through the door* have an obligation to be responsive to the needs and concerns of those traditionally excluded and keep those doors open. Doing so will require playing a politics of inclusion of the bodies historically excluded.

Our schools also need a diverse physical representation of bodies to deal with the *marginal curriculum.* Taylor (1994) discusses the sometimes not so subtle nuances through which Black/African-Canadian educators "despite counted-for qualifications, have been marginalized in Canadian colleges and universities" (Taylor 1994, 8). For the critical educator, it does not take long to recognize that existing structures within which learning, teaching, and administration of education take place in Canada contribute, both directly and indirectly, to the marginalization of non-White peoples. Dei (1993) has argued that Canadian schools have historically not presented a complete account of the ideas and events that have shaped human growth and development. For example, it is has been argued by many critical educators and students that Canadian textbooks and school pedagogical practices have not always presented an insightful and comprehensive account of the historic roles and achievements of Black/African peoples, First Nations peoples, and other Canadian ethnic minorities. Many Anglo-European authors have written off non-European peoples' cultures, histories, and lived experiences, as well as their contributions to society (see also Calliste 1994).

Many schools are now slowly admitting that information presented about Africans, Asians, and First Nations peoples is usually scanty or distorted, and that they sometimes only reinforce prejudicial ideas. While this is gradually changing, much remains to be done. The works of peoples of colour, women, and gays and lesbians are not visible on the majority of the reading lists of academic courses. School administrators have usually supported only a handful of courses on non-European peoples in the schools' curricula. Such tokenist approaches to dealing with questions of difference and diversity in schooling have been helpful to no one. Even the small numbers of such courses that have been put in place are usually the first to be threatened by budget cuts.

The point of this critique is that these concerns are readily acknowledged when raised by Euro-Canadian scholars rather than by the minority educator. This has implications for the professional development of minority faculty in terms of the creation of counter and oppositional knowledge. This is particularly so for those whose academic and political work recognizes the pedagogic need to confront the challenge of diversity in Canadian schools and the development of a pedagogy that is inclusive. Many African educators have joined the requisite alternative and non-exclusionary educational perspectives to inform a multi-ethnic, pluralistic society. Through various ways and on diverse pedagogical platforms, community groups and educators are questioning the Eurocentricity of Canadian schooling and education. They are questioning the theoretical and pedagogic inadequacies of, and political intolerance for, a hegemonic discourse that does not correspond to the lived experiences of non-White peoples, and that does not lead to a deeper understanding and integration of race, gender, sexuality, class, or social processes. Counter and oppositional forms of knowledge and oppositional discourses, such as African-centered education, have been put forward (see Asante 1987 and 1991), but these ideas, instead of being taken up seriously by mainstream education, are being marginalized. The irony of it all is that many of the harshest critics of such counter knowledges have oftentimes not even read a complete text on the discourse. They have heard worn-out criticism by another scholar (who happens to know a bit of the discourse) and just decided to go along with it, to run with it.

It is part of the paradox of the academy that, while there is some insistence on academic freedom, there is no corresponding emphasis on the issue of academic responsibility. The seduction of *academic freedom* is so powerful that it glosses over the perpetuation of harm and oppression, particularly on racially minoritized groups. I have always been struck by the exclusionary politics that can be fostered through language as a powerful medium of communication. Within academia, language can be used to mask and cultivate resentment and intolerance with possible consequences of further marginalizing minority faculty and students. A good example is contemporary debates on academic freedom. I feel compelled to ask these questions: What is the goal of education in society? Should our schools be in the business of sanctioning any form of education that really mis-educates people about the self-worth and collective worth of minorities and people who look different in society? What do we actually mean when we tacitly fail to challenge the view that the advancement of knowledge can somehow be served through the denigration of other peoples in society? What do students learn by the denigration of ethnic and cultural minorities, women, those who are physically challenged, or who are non-heterosexuals? Why is the defense of the *noble ideals* of free speech and individual freedom always carried out at the *expense*, or *on the backs*, of minorities and our concerns? What are the responsibilities of the academic community regarding research and classroom pedagogy that validate discrimination and promote racial prejudice under the cover of such concepts as academic freedom? Are not the noble ideals of academic freedom and educational excellence enhanced in a climate of educational equity?

As a minority faculty member, I do not broach the subject of academic freedom from a disinterested perspective. I see every form of education and scholarly writing as political. I do recognize the importance and significance of academic freedom. However, I am strongly opposed to freedom of speech and research without due regard to the social responsibility of the academic scholar. I do not believe in the search for knowledge for the sake of knowledge. I do not see it as mere coincidence that in the current discussions about academic freedom, those faculty who historically have wielded the most power in the colleges and universities are having their views heard.

Despite pretensions to the contrary, our schools are not autonomous entities. Schools, colleges, and universities do not stand apart from the wider society. The connection of our educational institutions to the wider community has with it certain restrictions and constraints. As educators and students, we are all restricted in many ways as a result of external and internal vagaries and conditionalities. State and provincial funding, for example, has implications for what we do, can do, and cannot do. Internally, schools, colleges, and universities operate within specified guidelines that in many senses restrict when, how, and what people can do. There is no absolute freedom anywhere in the confines of a modern educational setting. For example, younger, untenured faculty cannot simply publish anywhere and expect to get tenure and promotion. A tenured professor whose work is deemed not to carry maximum pedagogic and communicative effect as far as the university's clientele is concerned will soon find out that there is a cost. In effect, individuals are punished and rewarded to varying degrees according to what is conventionally accepted as constituting valid academic work. To a great extent, then, no one has that absolute freedom to do what they so please in the academic setting.

If education is to contribute to building and sustaining society, how is this goal served by education that does not teach about individual and group responsibilities? The historical absence of racial minority faculty, women, and other disadvantaged groups has implications for a critical debate about the place of academic freedom in contemporary society. Those who are most directly affected by the defense of absolute academic freedom as yet do not constitute a critical mass in our educational institutions. The academy is still a long way from providing members with the requisite tools to challenge those who traditionally have had the power to define others in society. It is thus grossly unfair to defend a right when only a few people have the luxury of using such a right.

Despite the presence of other colleagues and students who share concerns about unfettered academic freedom, the few minority faculty and students in our educational institutions still find their voices and concerns marginalized. In the debate over academic freedom, the marginalizing of certain voices carries a burden of psychological and emotional distress when it is realized that defenders of academic freedom – with all their good intentions – may unwittingly be trivializing the social ills of racism, sexism, classism, homophobia, and xenophobia. In my academic work as an anti-racist educator, I talk about the Eurocenteredness of Canadian education and White male privilege in society. This, to me, is not tantamount to denigrating Whiteness; therefore, it cannot be argued that anti-racist teaching causes emotional and physical threat to Whites privileged by their Whiteness. To argue thus is to silence the just struggle for social justice and fairness and to trivialize the physical and emotional pain that ethnic and cultural minorities, women, and others disadvantaged in society feel when their experiences, histories, and contributions are marginalized.

CONCLUSION

I conclude this discussion with suggestions of, and strategies about, ways to deal with the exclusion of racially minoritized bodies in our institutions. The complexities of the processes of exclusion that many minority faculty have to contend with in academia demands that concerted action be taken by various levels of educators, students, and administrators to find and institute appropriate solutions. There are already some measures in place in some schools, colleges, and universities. As was already pointed out, there are also many individuals within our educational institutions committed to addressing some of these concerns. However, we need to redouble our efforts and also search for alternative strategies to supplement existing measures of dealing with the general Whiteness of Canadian schooling and education.

Racially minoritized bodies themselves must actively explore and discover countermeasures to deal with many of the issues discussed in this chapter. We may enter into alliances with our progressive colleagues, students, and administrative staff. We may want to liaise with other groups in the schools and in the wider society who share our concerns. We could build and cement coalitions with other colleagues in other educational institutions and devise creative ways to share information and experiences and offer support to each other.

As educators, we should see that our work involves more than teaching our youth. We need to actively engage in a larger project, a project that seeks to bring into political existence our lived experiences. We must seek to defend the dignity of all people. We must seek to rupture the status quo for genuine educational and social transformation. We cannot conveniently ignore the challenges of our times. It is important for us to answer the question, 'What do we (as educators and, specifically, racially minoritized faculty) see as our roles and responsibilities in education?' Personally, I believe that we have a responsibility to be a *voice of difference*. By that, I mean to challenge the status quo, to rupture the racialized, hetero-patriarchal nature of our educational and institutional settings and its prevailing culture of dominance. It means that we should speak out boldly on pertinent issues of our time and question the structures within which learning, teaching, and administration of education take place in Canada. Unlike others, minority faculty simply cannot afford the luxury of silence. Of course, there are always going to be risks and consequences with doing *subversive* academic work, and the central question today is going to be whether we are all prepared to take the risk and the consequences that come with doing anti-racist work. It is no longer a simple question of, *Who can do anti-racist work?*

ACKNOWLEDGMENTS

I owe a great deal of intellectual debt to the students in my *SES 1924Y: Principles of Anti-Racism Education* class at the Ontario Institute for Studies in Education of the University of Toronto (OISE/UT) in the 2000–2001 academic year for the contributions they offered in discussing some of the major points covered in the first half of the chapter. I am thankful to Alana Butler for reading through and commenting on drafts of the chapter. Bathseba Opini of the Department of Sociology and Equity Studies (OISE/UT) also assisted with editing. The section of the chapter dealing with my personal reflections is culled from a presentation to students and faculty of the Ontario Institute for Studies in Education (OISE) during the speaker series organized by the Students from Africa and the diaspora (OSAD) in the fall of 1991. I would like to thank the audience for their comments and criticisms, as well as other colleagues within the institute who provided suggestions on improving the chapter.

REFERENCES

Abramovitz, Mary. 2001. State response to racism. Class presentation, SES 1921Y:
    Principles of Anti-Racism. Department of Sociology and Equity Studies,
    Ontario Institute for Studies in Education, University of Toronto.
Alladin, Ibrahim, ed. 1996. *Racism in Canadian Schools*. Toronto: Harcourt Brace.
Asante, Molefi. 1987. *The Afrocentric Idea*. Philadelphia: Temple University Press.
———. 1991. The Afrocentric idea in education. *Journal of Negro Education* 60, no. 2:
    170–80.
Black Educators' Working Group [BEWG]. 1993. *Submission to the Ontario Royal
    Commission on Learning*. Toronto: Black Educators' Working Group.
Board of Education, Toronto. 1988. *Education of Black Students in Toronto: Final Report
    of the Consultative Committee*. Toronto: Toronto Board of Education.
———. 1993. *The Every Secondary Student Survey, Part II: Detailed Profiles of Toronto's
    Secondary School Students*. Research Services, No. 204. Toronto, Toronto Board
    of Education.
Brathwaite, Keren. 1989. The Black student and the school: A Canadian dilemma.
    African Continuities/L'Héritage Africain, ed. S. Chilungu and S. Niang, 195–
    216. Toronto: Terebi.
Brathwaite, Keren, and Carl James, eds. 1996. *Educating African-Canadians*. Toronto:
    James Lorimer.
Butler, Alana. 2001. State response to racism. Class presentation, SES 1921Y: Principles
    of Anti-Racism. Department of Sociology and Equity Studies, Ontario
    Institute for Studies in Education, University of Toronto.
Calliste, Agnes. 1991. Canada's immigration policy and domestics from the Caribbean:
    The second domestic scheme. In *Race, Class, Gender: Bonds and Barriers*, ed.
    Jesse Vorst et al., 136–68. Toronto: Garamond Press.
———. 1993. Women of "exceptional merit": Immigration of Canadian nurses to Canada.
    Canadian Journal of Women and Labour 6: 85–102.
———. 1993/1994. Race, gender, and Canadian immigration policy: Blacks from the
    Caribbean, 1900–1932. *Journal of Canadian Studies* 28, no. 4: 131–48.
———. 1994. African-Canadian Experiences: The Need for Inclusion in the University
    Curriculum. Paper presented at the Diversity in the Curriculum Conference,
    University of Toronto, 7 February.
Calliste, Agnes, and George S. Dei, eds. 2000. *Anti-Racist Feminism: Critical Race and
    Gender Studies*. Halifax: Fernwood.
Canadian Alliance of Black Educators [CABE]. 1992. Sharing the Challenge, I,II,III: A
    Focus on Black High School Students. Toronto: Canadian Alliance of Black
    Educators.
Centre for Social Justice. 2001. *Canada's Creeping Apartheid*. Toronto: Centre for Social
    Justice.
Dei, George S. 1993. The challenges of anti-racist education in Canada. *Canadian Ethnic
    Studies/Études ethniques au Canada* 25, no. 2: 36–51.

———. 1996. *Anti-Racism Education: Theory and Practice*. Halifax: Fernwood.

———. 1999. The denial of difference: Reframing anti-racist praxis. *Race, Ethnicity, and Education* 2, no. 1: 17–37.

Dei, George S., L. Holmes, Josephine Mazzuca, Elizabeth McIsaac, and R. Campbell. 1995. *Push Out or Drop Out: The Dynamics of Black/African-Canadian Students' Disengagement from School*. Report submitted to the Ontario Ministry of Education and Training, Toronto.

Dei, George S., Josephine Mazzuca, Elizabeth McIsaac, and Jasmine Zine. 1997. *Reconstructing "Dropout." A Critical Ethnography of Black Students' Disengagement from School*. Toronto: University of Toronto Press.

Dei, George S., and Agnes Calliste, eds. 2000. *Power, Knowledge and Anti-Racism Education*. Halifax: Fernwood.

Frankenberg, Ruth. 1993. *White Women, Race Matters: The Social Construction of Whiteness*. Minneapolis: University of Minnesota Press.

Ghafour, Hamida. 2001. Immigrants dream has a rude awakening. *Toronto Star*, 17 June, A10.

Hall, Stuart. 1996. New ethnicities. In *Stuart Hall: Critical Dialogues in Cultural Studies*, ed. S. Hall, D. Morley, and K.-H. Chen, 441–49. London: Blackwell.

James, Carl. 1990. *Making It: Black Youth, Racism, and Career Aspirations in a Big City*. Oakville, ON: Mosaic.

Kincheloe, Joe L. and Steinberg, Shirley R. 1998. "Addressing the Crisis of Whiteness: Reconfiguring White Identity in a Pedagogy of Whiteness." In J. L. Kincheloe, S. R. Steinberg, N.M. Rodriguez, and R. E. Chennault, eds. *White Reign: Deploying Whiteness in America*. New York: St Martin's Press.

Lattas, Andrew. 1993. Essentialism, memory, and resistance: Aboriginality and the politics of authenticity. *Oceania* 63: 242–67.

Levine-Rasky, Cynthia, ed. 2002. *Working through Whiteness: International Perspectives*. Albany: State University of New York Press.

Ramcharan, Subhas. 1995. Anti-racism and diversity. In *Canadian Diversity: 2000 and Beyond*, ed. S. Nancoo and S. Ramcharan, 235–49. Toronto: Canadian Educators' Press.

Razack, Sherene. 1998. *Looking White People in the Eye*. Toronto: University of Toronto Press.

Robertson, Angela. 1999. Continuing on the ground: Feminists of colour discuss organizing. In *Scratching the Surface: Canadian Anti-Racist Feminist Thought*, ed. E. Dua and A. Robertson, 309–29. Toronto: Women's Press.

Rodriguez, Nelson. 1998. Empty the content of Whiteness: Toward an understanding of the relation between Whiteness and pedagogy. In *White Reign: Deploying Whiteness in America*, ed. J. Kincheloe, S. Steinberg, N. Rodriquez, and R. Chennault, 39–62. New York: St. Martin's.

———. 2000. Projects of whiteness in critical pedagogy. In *Dismantling White Privilege: Pedagogy, Politics, and Whiteness*, ed. N. Rodriguez and L. Villaverde, 31–62. New York: Peter Lang.

Smith, E., N. Mirza-Beg, and J. Andersen. 2003. *Ensuring Cultural Diversity and Social Cohesion for Visible Minorities in Canada: Tools for Measurement*. Ottawa: Canadian Council on Social Development.

Solomon, Patrick. 1992. *Black Resistance in High School: Forging a Separatist Culture*. New York: State University of New York Press.

Statistics Canada. 1993. *Census 1991*. Ottawa: Statistics Canada.

———. 2001. *Census 2001*. Ottawa: Statistics Canada.

———. 2003. *Census of population: Immigration, birthplace, birthplace of parents, citizenship, ethnic origin, visible minorities, and Aboriginal peoples*. Ottawa: Statistics Canada, *The Daily*, 21 January.

Tatum, Beverly. 1999. Lighting candles in the dark: One Black woman's response to White anti-racist narratives. In *Becoming and Unbecoming White: Owning and Disowning a Racial Identity*, ed. C. Clark and J. O'Donnell, 56–77. Westport: Bergin and Garvey.

Taylor, S. 1994. Black academics face racism. *Share*. Toronto: Toronto Black Community, 16, 8.

Thomas, Roslyn. 2001. State response to racism. Class presentation, SES 1921Y: Principles of Anti-Racism. Department of Sociology and Equity Studies, Ontario Institute for Studies in Education, University of Toronto.

Walker, James. 1981. *A History of Blacks in Canada*. Ottawa: Ministry of State-Multiculturalism.

Winant, Howard. 1997. Behind blue eyes: Whiteness and contemporary U.S. radical politics. In *Off White: Readings on Race, Power and Society*, ed. M. Fine, L. Weis, L. Powell, and L. Mun Wong, 40–53. New York: Routledge.

SECTION III

The Socio-Economic Context & Contests
of the African-Canadian Experience

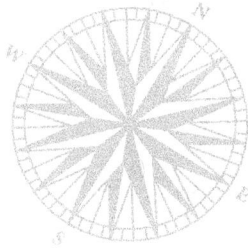

6

AFRICAN IMMIGRANTS & THE LABOUR MARKET:
Exploring Career Opportunities, Earning
Differentials, & Job Satisfaction[1]

Samuel A. Laryea and John E. Hayfron

INTRODUCTION

P RIOR TO 1961, the number of Africans immigrating to Canada was a mere trickle, under
5,000 per year. After 1970, however, the number of African immigrants arriving in Canada each
year increased dramatically. For example, during
the period 1971–2001, the number of African immigrant arrivals increased from 54,600 to 139,770,
bringing the number of immigrants of African
origin in Canada to 282,600 as of 2001.[2] The increasing flow of immigrants into Canada from
countries in Africa, as well as from the other developing countries, was a result of changes in Canada's
immigration policies.[3] Canada's pre-1967 immigration policies, shaped by the 1953 *Immigration Act*,
were essentially discriminatory. This is because
the 1953 act gave preferences to citizens of the so-
called *desirable* source countries, namely the United
Kingdom, other West European countries, and the
United States. Thus, individuals from these geopolitical regions could easily immigrate to Canada

without necessarily being screened on the basis of educational qualifications, work experience, language fluency, etc.

In 1967, Canada introduced the *points system*, making it possible for individuals with the needed skills, regardless of the country of origin, to immigrate to Canada. This change in immigration policy was necessitated by the need to recruit skilled workers for employers in the Canadian labour market. In addition, the new *Immigration Act of 1978* also established three entry gates under which immigrants could be admitted into Canada. These were the family class, the refugee class, and a composite class involving independent applicants, entrepreneurs, and assisted relatives.

Canada increasingly relies on immigration as a source of skills and knowledge. Using data from the 2001 census, Statistics Canada reports that immigrants who landed during the 1990s and were in the labour force in 2001 account for 70 percent of the net labour force growth in Canada during 1991–2001. By the year 2011, 100 percent of the net labour force growth in Canada will emanate solely from immigration (Statistics Canada-Cat. No. 11-001-XIE, The Daily, 11 February 2003). We expect a much bigger contribution from Africa if the current trend in immigration from the African continent continues. Of course, the push factor is partly tied to the deteriorating economic conditions in several African countries, while the pull factor is also partly tied to the perceived economic opportunities in Canada. Thus, a key question is whether African-born immigrants are performing better or more poorly in the Canadian labour market. This question is somewhat difficult to answer, given the scanty information about the economic performance of African immigrants in this market.

Apart from Grant (1999), who mentioned in a footnote that African-born immigrants in Canada experience a high rate of earnings growth (assimilation), previous studies have either made inferences about the economic performances of African immigrants using information on the performances of the entire group of Black immigrants in Canada, or have mentioned them only in passing while discussing the labour market performances of visible minorities in Canada. However, as shown in studies done elsewhere (see, for example, Dodoo 1997; Butcher 1984), African/Black immigrants are a heterogeneous group with differences in culture, skills, and labour market activities. Therefore, using a dummy variable, *visible minority*, in a regression analysis to capture earnings differentials between African-born immigrants and native-born Canadians would lead to a mis-specification of the earnings equation. It should also be noted that while all groups are heterogeneous, including the African-born immigrant population in Canada, the finer the category, the better.

In the United States, where there is a large population of immigrants of African origin, a number of recent studies (e.g., Dodoo 1991, 1997; Butcher 1984), have attempted to predict the economic performances of African immigrants in the American labour markets. For example, Dodoo's findings indicate that despite their higher educational attainment, the average African immigrant in the United States receives little, if any, premium for his/her education compared to Caribbeans or their native-born African-American counterparts. The findings of the American studies add to our curiosity, hence our efforts to ascertain how African-born immigrants are faring in the Canadian labour market.

Our aim in this interdisciplinary research effort is to examine the labour market performance of African immigrants from an economic perspective, measured in terms of earnings and occupational attainments. To have a meaningful measure of the labour market performances of African-born immigrants, we must identify a reference group for comparative purposes. For this reason, we use native-born Canadians as our reference group. In other words, we examine the data to ascertain whether earnings and occupational distributions differ for African-born immigrants and native-born Canadians with similar measurable skills in the labour market, circa 1991–96. We also distinguish African immigrants from the others (including Caribbean immigrants).

The chapter is organized as follows. We proceed with a descriptive analysis of the key variables of interest in the next section. This is followed by a discussion of the results from the regression analysis. Issues pertaining to occupational attainment and job satisfaction are then explored, leading to an outline of some policy prescriptions in the conclusion.

DESCRIPTIVE STATISTICS

We employ data from the 1991 and 1996 Canadian censuses, public use microdata files, to ascertain the performance of African immigrants in the labour market vis-à-vis Canadian-born workers and other immigrant groups. Census data have some limitations in correctly identifying various ethnic/immigrant groups. For example, peoples' recollection and construction of their ethnic and cultural background could be subjective. Despite methodological problems, census questions (on ethnic origin, visible minority, language, and so on) that are used to identify various immigrant groups remain a powerful tool in describing the changing landscape of ethnocultural and linguistic diversity in Canada (Bourhis 2003). Table 6.1 presents the distribution of average earnings, by gender, of African-born immigrants, the other immigrant groups, and native-born Canadians.

In 1996, African immigrant men working full-time earned $30,828 on average, compared to $26,317 for Asians, $36,354 for U.S./Europeans, $27,666 for Caribbean/Latin Americans, and $33,119 for native-born Canadians. Contrary to our expectation, African immigrant women working full-time earned slightly more on average than their Canadian-born counterparts; $25,274 compared to $24,471. Earnings for Asian women, Caribbean/Latin American women, and U.S./European women were $20,274, $22,446, and $25,304, respectively.

Table 6.1 Earnings of African Immigrants, Other Immigrants, and
Canadian-Born Workers, 1996

Annual Earnings	Africans	Asians	Caribbean & Latin America	U.S. & Europe	Canadian Born
Men	$30,828.7	$26,317.2	$27,666.3	$36,354.6	$33,119.5
Women	$25,274.8	$20,150.3	$22,446.9	$25,304.5	$24,471.4
Total (both sexes)	$28,750.5	$23,563.2	$25,207.5	$32,103.1	$29,461.3

Source: Authors' calculations based on the 1996 Canadian census data, Public Use
Microdata Files.

However, when one considers the total population as a whole, that is, both men
and women together, African immigrants working full-time earned less on average than Canadian-born workers; $28,750 compared to $29,461. The relevant
questions are: Why do the native-born Canadians earn more on average than
African-born immigrants in the Canadian labour market? Do the native-born
Canadians have more human capital (level of education and work experience)
than African-born immigrants? Do the occupational distributions differ for the
native-born Canadians and African-born immigrants? These are some of the
key questions we set out to address in the remainder of this chapter. To be able
to answer them, we begin with a descriptive analysis of the 1996 census data
(descriptive statistics of the 1991 data are not reported here, but can be obtained
from the authors upon request).

Table 6.2 presents the distributions of educational levels of African immigrants, Asian immigrants, U.S./European immigrants, Caribbean/Latin
American immigrants, and the Canadian-born men and women. In 1996 a
higher proportion (56%) of African-born male immigrants possessed a bachelor's degree or higher, compared to 45 percent of Asian men, 26.7 percent of
Caribbean/Latin American men, 29.8 percent of U.S./European men, and 26.6
percent of native-born Canadian men. Considering the men with less than
a high school diploma, we find that 8.5 percent of African immigrant men
have less than a high school diploma compared to 23.1 percent of Asians, 24.7
percent of Caribbean/Latin Americans, 23 percent of U.S./Europeans, and 23.7
percent of Canadian-born men.

Focusing on the women, the sample statistics show that a higher proportion (46%) of African women possessed a bachelor's degree or higher in
1996, compared to 41.3 percent of Asians, 24.8 percent of Caribbean/Latin
Americans, 31.3 percent of U.S./Europeans, and 31.2 percent of the Canadian-
born women. Just like their male counterparts, fewer female African immigrants (9.7%) have less than a high school education, compared to 23.7
percent of Asians, 20.1 percent of Caribbean/Latin Americans, 22.2 percent of

Table 6.2 Highest Level of Schooling for African Immigrants, Other Immigrants, and All Canadians, 1996

	Africans	Asians	Caribbean & Latin American	U.S. & European	Canadian Born
MEN					
Less than high school (%)	8.51	23.11	24.70	22.94	23.65
High school certificate (%)	9.42	11.08	13.15	10.15	15.26
Trades certificate (%)	3.05	1.96	4.64	6.81	5.51
Other non-university (%)	23.45	18.90	30.80	30.32	28.94
University (%)	55.57	44.96	26.70	29.78	26.63
N	1,868	9,685	4,052	18,464	26,846
WOMEN					
Less than high school (%)	9.67	23.69	20.11	22.16	16.54
High school certificate (%)	12.83	13.10	13.73	14.87	17.89
Trades certificate (%)	2.88	1.64	4.07	3.50	2.95
Other non-university (%)	28.90	20.23	37.34	28.18	31.44
University (%)	45.72	41.34	24.75	31.28	31.18
N	1,076	7,814	3,540	11,588	18,332

Source: Authors' calculations based on the 1996 Canadian census data, Public Use Microdata Files.

Notes:

1. This and all following tables restrict the sample to ages 16–64.
2. In addition, the sample pertains to full time workers, excluding residents of the Atlantic provinces.
3. A 20 percent sample was used for the Canadian-born population.

U.S./Europeans, and 16.5 percent of Canadian-born women. By all accounts, African-born immigrants have a higher level of education than either the native-born Canadians or the other immigrant groups.

Having examined the educational distribution of the African immigrants, we now turn to their occupational distribution. As shown in Table 6.3, African immigrants are well represented in all the occupational categories or skill levels. Our interest is in knowing what proportion of the highly qualified, African-born immigrants are employed in professional or managerial positions (Skill level IV) relative to native-born Canadians with the same level of education.

As can be observed in Table 6.3, 43.4 percent of African-born immigrant men are employed in high-skilled occupations (skill level IV), compared to 29.1 percent of Asian men, 30.8 percent of U.S./European men, 19 percent of Caribbean/Latin American men, and 25.3 percent of Canadian-born men. The distribution in the low-skilled occupation (skill level I) shows that 8.4 percent

Table 6.3   Occupational Distribution of Men and Women Aged 20–64

Occupations	Africans	Asians	Caribbean & Latin America	U.S.A. & Europe	Canadian Born
MEN					
Skill Level IV (%)	43.42	29.09	19.03	30.77	25.29
Skill Level III (%)	22.48	26.7	29.1	36.36	34.28
Skill Level II (%)	25.7	31.79	37.61	23.15	29.91
Skill Level I (%)	8.4	12.42	14.26	9.72	10.52
WOMEN					
Skill Level IV (%)	32.06	19.81	19.12	26.35	26.52
Skill Level III (%)	22.03	18.44	19.38	25.79	26.92
Skill Level II (%)	36.34	45.89	46.78	37.02	37.98
Skill Level I (%)	9.57	15.86	14.72	10.83	8.58

Source: Authors' calculations Based on the 1996 Canadian Census, Public Use Microdata Files.
Notes:
1. Level IV Occupations: Senior Managers; Middle and other Managers; Professionals.
2. Level III Occupations: Semi-professional and Technicians; Supervisors; Foremen/women; Administrative and Senior Clerical; Sales and Service.
3. Level II Occupations: Clerical Workers; Sales and Service; Semi-skilled Manual Workers.
4. Level I Occupations: Sales and Service; Other Manual Workers.

of African immigrant men are employed in low-skilled occupations, compared to 12.4 percent of Asian men, 9.7 percent of U.S./European men, 14.3 percent of Caribbean/Central American men, and 10.5 percent of Canadian-born men.

Considering the distribution for women, Table 6.3 shows that 32.1 percent of African-born immigrants are employed in high-skilled occupations, compared to 19.8 percent of Asians, 19.1 percent of Caribbean/Latin Americans, 26.4 percent of U.S./Europeans, and 26.5 percent of native-born Canadians.

Similarly, 9.6 percent of African-born immigrants are employed in low-skilled occupations (skill level I), compared to 15.9 percent of Asians, 10.8 percent of U.S./Europeans, 14.7 percent of Caribbean/Latin Americans, and 10.5 percent of the Canadian born. The descriptive analysis of the raw data provides useful information about the distribution of earnings and human capital endowments among the immigrant groups and the native-born Canadians. For example, the analysis shows that despite the fact that African-born immigrants, particularly men, have a higher average level of education and work in high-skilled occupations, they still earn less than the native-born Canadians.

Nevertheless, it should be noted that the descriptive statistics only provide a partial explanation for why observed earnings differ for African-born immigrants and native-born Canadians in the Canadian labour market. For this reason, we employ a multivariate framework to analyze the earnings disparities more formally.

REGRESSION RESULTS

The pooled regression for immigrants and the Canadian born and the data used to estimate the earnings function are discussed in the appendix. In what follows, we interpret the results from the multiple regression analysis. The estimated coefficients from both the reduced model and the full model and t statistics are reported in Table 6.4a (columns 1–3).

Overall, most of the estimated coefficients are of the expected signs and have t statistics that are statistically significant at conventional levels (1% and 5%).

Beginning with the estimated earnings function for men aged 20–64, the results in column (1) show that the coefficient estimates of all the region of origin dummy variables except for U.S./European have negative signs and are statistically different from zero. For example, the coefficient of the African dummy variable (–0.126) implies that African-born male immigrants earn, on average, 12.6 percent less than Canadian-born men. As expected, male immigrants from Europe and the United States earn 11.4 percent more than Canadian-born men on average. The coefficients of the remaining region of origin dummy variables can be interpreted in a similar fashion. It is not clear what the region of origin dummy variables are capturing. However, if region of origin plays an important role in earnings determination in Canada, then the significantly negative coefficient of the African dummy variable will imply a kind of discrimination. Of course, the argument for discrimination is not strong, since we have not controlled for other socioeconomic variables.

In column 3, we introduce the interaction terms in addition to the socio-economic variables. Before we discuss the estimated coefficients of the interaction terms, we discuss briefly the estimated rate of return to some key variables of interest. The results in column 3 show that the rate of return to potential experience for an average immigrant is 3.2 percent in the first year and 2.9 percent after five years. This is consistent with the human capital theory, which holds that earnings rise with experience at a diminishing rate. The cohort dummy variables measure the earnings penalty experienced by newly arrived immigrants, while the years since migration (*YSM*) variable measures the return to length of stay in Canada. For example, immigrant men who arrived in Canada between 1991 and 1996 earned 29.7 percent less than those counterparts who arrived before 1955 (*the reference category*). However, the earnings of these immigrants are predicted to increase by 1.3 percent with

Table 6.4a Regression Results for Annual Earnings, Immigrants and Canadian-Born Men, Pooled 1991 and 1996 Data

Variable	(1) Estimate	(1) T-Value	(2) Estimate	(2) T-Value	(3) Estimate	(3) T-Value
Intercept	10.298	2,531.53	6.268	223.57	6.274	219.79
Region of origin – *Canadian born (reference)*						
U.S./Europeans	0.114	18.27	−0.129	−3.93	−0.123	−3.67
Africans	−0.126	−30.24	−0.173	−4.80	−0.225	−5.07
Asians	−0.249	−30.24	−0.206	−5.87	−0.228	−6.31
Caribbean/Latin Americans	−0.226	−20.03	−0.182	−5.19	−0.195	−5.30
Others	−0.283	−16.15	−0.196	−5.40	−0.221	−5.27
Education – *High school or less (reference)*						
Trades			0.102	10.57	0.087	6.30
Post–secondary education			0.128	24.13	0.127	16.66
University BA			0.268	32.90	0.255	21.60
University MA			0.336	32.18	0.337	20.09
University Ph.D.			0.481	24.91	0.321	7.23
Experience			0.032	43.14	0.032	43.14
Experience squared			−0.00053	−35.42	−0.00054	−35.48
Married			0.146	28.91	0.145	28.81
Years since migration (YSM)			0.014	6.90	0.013	6.76
YSM squared			−0.00022	−5.38	−0.00022	−5.26
Visible minority			−0.109	−9.11	−0.107	−8.86
Year of immigration – *Before 1955 (reference)*						
Cohort 1956–60			−0.049	−3.05	−0.049	−3.03
Cohort 1961–65			−0.048	−2.29	−0.049	−2.33
Cohort 1966–70			−0.052	−2.28	−0.053	−2.29
Cohort 1971–75			−0.057	−2.26	−0.057	−2.25
Cohort 1976–80			−0.067	−2.47	−0.066	−2.40
Cohort 1981–85			−0.077	−2.68	−0.075	−2.59
Cohort 1986–90			−0.164	−5.36	−0.163	−5.34
Cohort 1991–96			−0.297	−8.83	−0.297	−8.83
Language ability – *Neither English nor French (reference)*						
English only			0.081	4.66	0.076	4.28
French only			−0.006	−0.32	−0.012	−0.60
Both English and French			0.080	4.32	0.076	4.02
Log of weeks worked			0.853	163.57	0.853	163.52
Hours worked – *40–44 hours (reference)*						
30–39 hours			0.007	1.07	0.007	1.07
45 hours or more			0.068	13.59	0.069	13.64

Table 6.4a (continued)

Other CMAs and non–CMA (reference)				
Montreal		–0.051	–6.44	–0.051	–6.49
Toronto		0.105	18.84	0.105	18.83
Vancouver		0.076	9.64	0.077	9.72
Census time period – Census 1991 (reference)				
Census 1996		–0.055	–11.29	–0.055	–11.26
Interactions terms – Canadian born* all education levels (reference)				
U.S./European* trade				0.023	1.08
U.S./European* PSE				–0.011	–0.95
U.S./European* university BA				0.004	0.23
U.S./European* university MA				–0.042	–1.86
U.S./European* university Ph.D.				0.166	3.28
African* trade				0.018	0.24
African* PSE				0.039	1.11
African* university BA				0.081	1.99
African* university MA				0.124	2.54
African* university Ph.D.				0.207	2.27
Asian* trade				0.135	3.18
Asian* PSE				0.018	1.11
Asian* university BA				0.032	1.66
Asian* university MA				0.042	1.56
Asian* university Ph.D.				0.224	3.66
Caribbean/Latin American* trade				–0.048	–1.09
Caribbean/Latin American* PSE				0.009	0.44
Caribbean/Latin American* university BA				0.070	2.15
Caribbean/Latin American* university MA				0.032	0.73
Caribbean/Latin American* university Ph.D.				0.345	3.30
Sample size (N)	109362	109362		109362	
R – squared	0.022	0.389		0.389	

Sources: Canadian census data, Public Use Microdata Files, 1991 and 1996.

Notes:
1. Dependent Variable = Natural Log of Annual Earnings.
2. The sample is based on individuals aged 20–59 years in 1991 and 25–64 in 1996, working full–time. The full immigrant sample was used, as opposed to 20 percent for the Canadian–born population.
3. The regression also controls for occupation and the industry of employment. Full regression estimates are available upon request from the authors.

Table 6.4b Regression Results for Annual Earnings, Immigrants and Canadian-Born Women, Pooled 1991 and 1996 Data

	(1)		(2)		(3)	
Variable	Estimate	T-Value	Estimate	T-Value	Estimate	T-Value
Intercept	9.937	2044.57	5.882	192.24	5.850	186.04
Region of origin – *Canadian born (reference)*						
U.S./Europeans	0.023	2.97	−0.135	−3.30	−0.119	−2.87
Africans	−0.025	−1.21	−0.108	−2.41	−0.115	−2.17
Asians	−0.201	−21.68	−0.126	−2.92	−0.106	−2.40
Caribbean/Latin Americans	−0.121	−9.98	−0.144	−3.34	−0.133	−2.98
Others	−0.185	−7.92	−0.150	−3.32	−0.156	−3.04
Education – *High school or less (reference)*						
Trades			0.038	2.65	0.058	2.78
Post–secondary education			0.119	19.44	0.129	14.76
University BA			0.284	31.05	0.321	24.57
University MA			0.358	28.46	0.418	21.22
University Ph.D.			0.519	13.38	0.533	6.50
Experience			0.024	29.61	0.024	29.74
Experience squared			−0.00044	−25.05	−0.00045	−25.19
Married			0.005	0.95	0.005	0.94
Years since migration (YSM)			0.014	6.16	0.015	6.25
YSM squared			−0.00024	−4.87	−0.00025	−4.90
Visible minority			−0.052	−3.75	−0.052	−3.72
Year of immigration – *Before 1955 (reference)*						
Cohort 1956–60			−0.059	−2.89	−0.059	−2.91
Cohort 1961–65			−0.072	−2.79	−0.071	−2.75
Cohort 1966–70			−0.064	−2.23	−0.060	−2.10
Cohort 1971–75			−0.084	−2.63	−0.080	−2.51
Cohort 1976–80			−0.079	−2.30	−0.075	−2.20
Cohort 1981–85			−0.115	−3.18	−0.111	−3.08
Cohort 1986–90			−0.139	−3.66	−0.133	−3.49
Cohort 1991–96			−0.267	−6.42	−0.258	−6.21
Language ability – *Neither English nor French (reference)*						
English only			0.104	6.10	0.114	6.54
French only			0.0005	0.02	0.013	0.66
Both English and French			0.124	6.68	0.133	7.02
Log of weeks worked			0.855	161.5	0.855	161.46
Hours worked – *40–44 hours (reference)*						
30–39 hours			0.046	8.10	0.047	8.25
45 hours or more			0.081	10.6	0.080	10.50

Table 6.4b   (continued)

Other CMAs and non–CMA (reference)

Montreal	0.00083	0.09	–0.0003	–0.03
Toronto	0.174	27.74	0.173	27.39
Vancouver	0.130	14.45	0.128	14.24

Census time period – Census 1991 (reference)

Census 1996	–0.004	–0.76	–0.005	–0.87

Interactions terms – Canadian born* all education levels (reference)

U.S./European* trade	–0.029	–0.90
U.S./European* PSE	–0.028	–2.12
U.S./European* university BA	–0.056	–2.79
U.S./European* university MA	–0.065	–2.44
U.S./European* university Ph.D.	–0.004	–0.04
African* trade	–0.152	–1.62
African* PSE	0.009	0.24
African* university BA	–0.004	–0.07
African* university MA	–0.026	–0.40
African* university Ph.D.	–0.086	–0.37
Asian* trade	–0.072	–1.41
Asian* PSE	–0.0003	–0.02
Asian* university BA	–0.081	–3.84
Asian* university MA	–0.175	–5.18
Asian* university Ph.D.	–0.043	–0.34
Caribbean/Latin American* trade	0.030	0.59
Caribbean/Latin American* PSE	–0.015	–0.75
Caribbean/Latin American* university BA	–0.071	–1.99
Caribbean/Latin American* university MA	–0.098	–1.89
Caribbean/Latin American* university Ph.D.	–0.002	–0.01

Sample size (N)	78243	78243	78243
R – squared	0.008	0.424	0.424

Sources: Regression estimates are based on the 1991 and 1996 Canadian census data, Public Use Microdata Files.

Notes: 1. Dependent Variable = Natural Log of Annual Earnings.
2. The sample is based on individuals aged 20–59 years in 1991 and 25–64 in 1996, working full-time. The full immigrant sample was used as opposed to 20 percent for the Canadian-born population.
3. The regression also controls for occupation and the industry of employment. Full regression estimates are available upon request from the authors.

an extra year of residence in Canada, implying that the initial adjustment costs in adapting to conditions in the Canadian labour market dissipate over time.

The pooled regression presupposes that the socioeconomic characteristics, such as education, potential experience, et cetera, are the same for native-born Canadians and immigrants. In this case, the statistically significant coefficients of the interaction terms *(country of origin * educational level)* are of interest to us, since they measure the earnings differentials between native-born Canadians and immigrants across educational levels. For example, the results show that the estimated return to a bachelor's degree is 25.5 percent for Canadian-born men, 13.6 percent for U.S./European immigrant men, 11.1 percent for African immigrant men, 5.9 percent for Asian immigrant men, and 13 percent for Caribbean/Latin American immigrant men. The estimated return for a master's degree is 33.7 percent for Canadian-born men, 17.2 percent for U.S./European immigrant men, 23.6 percent for African immigrant men, 15.1 percent for Asian immigrant men, and 17.4 percent for the Caribbean/Latin American immigrant men. Similarly, the estimated return for a doctorate is 32.1 percent for Canadian-born men, 36.4 percent for U.S./European immigrant men, 30.3 percent for African immigrant men, 31.7 percent for Asian immigrant men, and 47 percent for Caribbean/Latin American immigrant men.

Comparing African-born immigrant men to native-born Canadian men, we find that the estimated returns to university degrees for African-born immigrant men are smaller relative to that of their Canadian-born counterparts. However, the differential rate of return narrows with increases in educational qualifications. For example, African immigrants with a bachelor's degree earn 14.4 percent less than the Canadian born with the same level of education. They earn 10.1 percent less and 1.8 percent less than their Canadian-born counterparts at the master's and doctorate degree levels, respectively. This finding is consistent with the finding in Dodoo (1991), which suggests a lower return to education for African immigrant men in the United States.

Table 6.4b shows the results for women. Women also receive positive returns (2.4%) to potential experience and length of stay in Canada (1.5%). Considering the interaction terms, the results show that the estimated return for a bachelor's degree is 32.1 percent for Canadian-born women, 14.6 percent for U.S./Europe, 20.2 percent for African-born immigrants, 13.4 percent for Asian immigrants, and 21.8 percent for the Caribbean/Central American immigrants. The estimated return for a master's degree is 41.8 percent for the Canadian born, 23.4 percent for U.S./European immigrants, 27.7 percent for African immigrants, 13.7 percent for Asian immigrants, and 18.7 percent for the Caribbean/Latin American immigrants. The estimated return for a doctorate is 53.3 percent for the Canadian born, 41.4 percent for U.S./European immigrants, 33.2 percent for African immigrants, 38.4 percent for Asian immigrants, and 39.8 percent for Caribbean/Latin American male immigrants, respectively. Unlike their male counterparts, the differential returns to the highest level of education between African-born female immigrants and their Canadian-born counterparts increases with the level of education.

OCCUPATIONAL ATTAINMENT AND JOB SATISFACTION

In this section, we examine the individual occupational attainments for two major reasons. First, it is consistent with the human capital model that suggests a positive relationship between occupation and earnings. Second, we assume that an individual derives some degree of job satisfaction if his or her skills are properly matched to the job or occupation he or she is in. For example, an individual with an engineering degree will have a higher level of job satisfaction if they are employed as an engineer than if they work as a taxi driver.

The first assumption is captured by the inclusion of occupation dummy variables in the earnings function. The second assumption, individual job satisfaction, is psychological in nature and does not lend itself readily to direct measurement. However, we can use the odds ratio derived from the estimated coefficients in the logistic regression to make inferences about individual occupational attainments. If the odds ratio for any of the explanatory variables is greater than one, this would imply that a unit change in that variable increases the odds of an individual being employed in a specific occupational category. On the other hand, if the odds ratio is less than one, a unit change in the explanatory variable decreases the odds of an individual being employed in this particular occupational category.[4] For the purposes of our investigation, we define the odds ratio as the probability of an individual being in a high-skilled occupation divided by the probability of an individual not being in this particular occupational category.

Moreover, by comparing the odds ratios calculated for the various ethnic groups, we will, at least, be able to answer the question of whether or not African-born immigrants and Canadian-born individuals with similar observable skills have equal probabilities of finding employment in high-skilled occupations. We focus mainly on the occupational attainments of university graduates. This is not to suggest that non-degree holders are not important. However, it should be easier to document the existence of underutilization of immigrant skills if we concentrate on high-skilled individuals than on low-skilled individuals.

The calculated odds ratios are depicted in Table 6.5 for both men and women. Table 6.5 shows that the probability of employment in the high-skilled occupations differs for the male African-born immigrants, as well as the other ethnic groups. For example, an African-born immigrant with a university degree obtained at any level is less likely to work in a high-skilled occupation. In particular, the odds ratios for master's and doctorate degree holders are particularly low; 0.29 for master's degrees and 0.39 for doctorate holders.

Table 6.5 Odds Ratios of Being in Skill Level IV Occupations, Men and Women Aged 20–64

	USA/Europe	Africans	Asians	Caribbean/ Central America
MEN				
BA	0.95	0.44	0.58	1.28
MA	0.68	0.29	0.43	0.79
PhD	1.08	0.39	1.18	1.115
WOMEN				
BA	0.91	0.55	0.45	0.91
MA	0.76	0.63	0.41	0.96
PhD	0.63	0.15	0.62	1.1

Similarly for women, Table 6.5 indicates that African-born immigrant women with doctorates are less likely to work in a high-skilled occupation.

The calculated odds ratios are also smaller for Asian women (0.14) and U.S./European women (0.6). On the whole, Caribbean/Latin American immigrant women tend to perform better in terms of employment in high-skilled occupations. Based on the calculated odds ratios, we argue that since the likelihood of working in a high-skilled occupation is relatively low for African immigrants, they are more likely to be in less-skilled and lower paying occupations. This may offer a partial explanation for why the observed average earnings are lower for African immigrants than for their Canadian-born counterparts.

DISCUSSION

The main conclusions from the previous two sections are that there are significant earnings gaps between African-born immigrants and their Canadian-born counterparts. This occurs even though African-born immigrants tend to have a higher level of education than their Canadian-born counterparts.

Second, African-born immigrants are less likely to be employed in a high-skilled occupation, implying an underutilization of their skills. This may partly explain the low returns on their education. Previous studies in Canada seem to suggest the existence of race-based barriers in the Canadian labour market. The type of barrier varies by gender and racial origin of immigrants (Li 2000). The oft-cited barrier has to do with the non-recognition of foreign credentials, as well as with employment discrimination against visible minorities with identifiable linguistic and racial features (Henry and Ginzberg 1985; Scassa 1994; Pendakur and Pendakur 1998).

Furthermore, our analysis also produced some interesting findings worth investigating in future research. For example, Asian immigrant men seem to do better or have better odds in working in high-skilled occupations than African immigrant men with similar characteristics, while the reverse holds for women. In addition, Caribbean/Latin American-born female and male immigrants have greater odds of working in high-skilled occupations compared to their African-born counterparts (See Table 6.5). It is not very clear what drives these results, and we are hesitant to speculate, because it is beyond the scope of this chapter. Moreover, our focus here is to compare African immigrants to their Canadian-born counterparts.

CONCLUSIONS AND POLICY IMPLICATIONS

According to the human capital theory, because people's abilities and productivities differ, they have different earnings potentials. Individual productivities depend on the amount of human capital accumulated over time through formal schooling and on-the-job training. This implies that the more human capital accumulated, the higher the returns or earnings.

Based on the human capital theory, we examined the labour market outcomes (earnings and occupational attainments) of immigrants of African origin, Asian origin, U.S./European origin, and Caribbean/Latin American origin, using native-born Canadians as our reference group. We did this analysis for men and women working full-time and aged 20–64.

The analysis shows that the returns to education are consistent with the human capital theory, since for each immigrant group, as well as for the Canadian born, the predicted earnings tended to rise with level of education. However, human capital theory failed to explain why African-born immigrants earned less, on average, than Canadian-born individuals with the same level of education. The popular explanation given in most studies (see Basavarajappa and Verma 1985; Basran and Zong 1998; Rajagopal 1990) for the observed differential returns to education is the immigrants' inability to transfer their skills from the countries of origin to the Canadian labour market. While we are unable to distinguish between pre- and post-migration education in our data, it is plausible to argue that where one obtained his or her education is important in such an analysis. We also found that the differences in the returns to education in the Canadian labour market are both ethnic- and gender-specific. Evidence exists that female immigrants in the Canadian labour market experience a double earnings penalty (see Beach and Worswick 1993; Shamsuddin 1998).

What implications do our findings have for public policy? Our findings suggest that there will be an economic gain for Canada if the federal and provincial governments take adequate steps to address the issue regarding foreign credential recognition.[5] In other words, this will reduce the amount of skill under-utilization or *brain waste*, especially among Africans, in the economy. A similar argument has been made in several studies, including Mensah (2002) and Reitz (2001). Reitz (2001), for example, argues that the costs of skill under-utilization, which includes non-recognition of foreign credentials, amounted to 10.9 billion dollars as of 1996.

The challenge, however, will be to bring the professional bodies, trade associations, employer associations, and provincial governments together around the same table to map out a solution as different interests and jurisdictional issues are involved. Secondly, the federal government, working with the professional bodies and the provinces, can also institute skills-bridging programs for African immigrants. Such programs can assist African immigrants to acquire the necessary Canadian work experience whilst simultaneously upgrading their skills.

Finally, foreign credential recognition, though important, is just one of many barriers to the economic integration of African immigrants. Emphasis should also be placed on social capital acquisition, especially the bridging type. As Kunz (2003, 34) contends, "bridging capital is essential for immigrants to expand their networks beyond their own ethnic community and to acculturate into the receiving society." This exposes them to more social and economic opportunities.

APPENDIX

I. The Data

The data used in this analysis came from the 1991 and 1996 Canadian censuses, respectively. The sample selection was restricted to individuals aged 20–59 from the 1991 sample, and 25–64 from the 1996 sample, respectively. These individuals worked full-time and were neither students nor residents of the Atlantic Provinces, which were excluded from the sample because the year of immigration variable was coded differently compared to the other provinces. Moreover, very few African immigrants live in the Atlantic Provinces.

For the African-born sample, we used the place of birth variable, POBP (values = 29 to 30 in the 1996 census and value = 26 in the 1991 census), to identify the African immigrant population. The other immigrant groups were also selected using the place of birth variable. We also randomly selected 20 percent of the native-born Canadians (non-immigrant sample) to be used as a reference group in the analysis. All the observations with missing information were excluded from the analysis. These restrictions resulted in a working sample of 1,868 for African immigrant men, 26,846 Canadian-born men, 1,076 African immigrant women, and 18,332 Canadian-born women.

The variables included place of birth (Origin), age, highest level of schooling (Educ), marital status (1 = married), years since migration (YSM), years since migration squared, visible minority status, year of immigration, language ability (= 1 if individual speaks both English and French), occupational categories, annual earnings, logarithm of weeks worked, hours worked, census time period (D_{1996}) (= 1 if individual belonged to 1996 sample), and census metropolitan area (CMA). The CMA was set equal to one if the individual was a resident of Montreal, Toronto, or Vancouver. In the absence of actual work experience, we computed potential experience (Exp) as *age – years of schooling – 6.*

II. Earnings Equation

In order to predict the earnings differentials between African immigrants and the Canadian born, we estimated the following pooled regression for immigrants and Canadian-born men and women,

(1)

$$LnEarn = \alpha_0 + \beta_1 Educ + \beta_2 Exp + \beta_3 Expsq + \beta_4 YSM + \beta_5 YSMSQ + \delta Origin + D_{1996} + \beta_i Z + u.$$

Where the natural logarithm of earnings (LnEarn) is regressed on the traditional human capital variables, such as education (Educ) dummy variables, potential experience (Exp), potential experience squared (ExpSq), years since migration (*YSM*), and years since migration squared (YSMSQ). We also included cohort-specific dummy variables (Cohort), meant to capture the quality of arrival cohort (see Borjas 1985), region of origin (origin), marital status, visible minority status, language ability, and a host of other socio-economic variables (*Z*). The error term is *u.*

REFERENCES

Basavarajappa, K. G., and R. Verma. 1985. Asian immigrants in Canada: Some findings from the 1981 census. *International Migration* 23, no. 1: 97–121.

Basran, Gurcham S., and Li Zong. 1998. Devaluation of foreign credentials as perceived by non-White professional immigrants. *Canadian Ethnic Studies/Études ethniques au Canada* 30, no. 3: 6–23.

Beach, Charles M., and Christopher Worswick. 1993. Is there a double-negative on the earnings of immigrant women? *Canadian Public Policy* 19, no. 1: 36–53.

Borjas, George. 1985. Assimilation, changes in cohort quality, and earnings of immigrants. *Journal of Labour Economics* 3: 463–89.

Bourhis, Richard Y. 2003. Measuring ethnocultural diversity using the Canadian census. *Canadian Ethnic Studies/Études ethniques au Canada* 35, no. 1: 9–33.

Butcher, Kristin F. 1994. Black immigrants in the United States: A comparison with native Blacks and other immigrants. *Industrial and Labour Relations Review* 47: 265–84.

Dodoo, Francis. 1991. Earnings differences among Blacks in America. *Social Science Research* 20: 93–108.

——. 1997. Assimilation differences among Africans in America. *Social Forces* 76, no. 2: 527–46.

Grant, Mary L. 1999. Evidence of new immigrant assimilation in Canada. *Canadian Journal of Economics* 32: 930–55.

Henry, Frances, and Effie Ginzberg. 1985. *Who Gets the Work? A Test of Racial Discrimination in Employment.* Toronto: Urban Alliance on Race Relations and the Social Planning Council of Metropolitan Toronto.

Kunz, Jean. 2003. Social capital: A key dimension of immigrant integration. *Canadian Issues* April: 33–34.

Li, Peter S. 2000. Earning disparities between immigrants and native-born Canadians. *Canadian Review of Sociology and Anthropology* 37, no. 4: 289–311.

Mensah, Joseph. 2002. *Black Canadians: History, Experiences, Social Conditions.* Halifax: Fernwood.

Pendakur, Krishna, and Ravi Pendakur. 1998. The colour of money: Earnings differentials among ethnic groups in Canada. *Canadian Journal of Economics* 31, no. 3: 518–48.

Rajagopal, Indhu. 1990. The glass ceiling in the vertical mosaic: Indian immigrants to Canada. *Canadian Ethnic Studies/Études ethniques au Canada* 22, no. 1: 96–105.

Reitz, Jeffrey G. 2001. Immigrant skill utilization in the Canadian labour market: Implications of human capital research. *Journal of International Migration and Integration* 2, no. 3: 347–78.

Scassa, Teresa. 1994. Language standards, ethnicity, and discrimination. *Canadian Ethnic Studies/Études ethniques au Canada* 26, no. 3: 105–21.

Shamsuddin, Abul F. 1998. The double-negative effect on the earnings of foreign-born females in Canada. *Applied Economics* 30: 1187–1201.

Statistics Canada. 2003. *The Daily, February 11,* Catalogue No. 11-001-X1E, Ottawa: Industry Canada.

NOTES

1   The views expressed in this chapter are those of the authors, and should not be attributed to Human Resources and Skills Development Canada or the Government of Canada.

2   See Statistics Canada, Catalogue No. 97F0009XCB011002, 2003.

3   The influx of African immigrants to Canada was influenced, not only by favourable immigration policies in Canada (pull factors), but also by push factors. These include the deteriorating economic and political conditions on the African continent. In addition, wars between rival factions in countries such as Somalia have also fueled the African refugee population in Canada.

4   The odds ratios are calculated from the estimated coefficients from the logistic regression. This classification is based on the 1991 Standard Occupational Classification (SOC).

5   We must say that the government is aware of these problems facing new immigrants and has made specific commitments in the 2003 budget to promote foreign credential recognition issues and language programs. Consequently, in the 2003 budget, the Federal Government will invest $41 million in these programs over the next two years to help new Canadians integrate better into the labour market.

7

THE GENDER DIMENSIONS OF THE IMMIGRANT EXPERIENCE:
The Case of African–Canadian Women in Edmonton

Adenike O. Yesufu

INTRODUCTION

IT IS COMMON KNOWLEDGE that the experiences of immigrants vary from group to group. However, very little distinction is made among the various ethnic groups; all are lumped together as *visible minorities*. As a group, Canadians of African descent, specifically continental Africans, have received limited attention in both academic and popular writings, and their experiences tend to be homogenized under the category of Black (see Cassidy, Lord, and Mandell 2001). In the same vein, many analysts have homogenized the experiences of African-Canadian women under the broad rubric of *women of colour*. African women are thus lost in a maze of data describing the experiences of women of colour. There are few studies on the labour market experiences of continental African women in Canada (see Elabor-Idemudia 2000, 1999; Moussa 1993).

In 1999, six Black female researchers, including the author of this paper, set out to investigate the experiences of Black women in Edmonton as a basis for understanding the broader experiences of Black women in Canada. The research specifically sought to examine the relationship between their educational training and their economic status in Canada. A major objective was to identify and systematically document the barriers to education and employment faced by Black women in Canada. The study involved all categories of Black women: Black women from Sub-Saharan Africa and from the Caribbean, and Canadian/American Black women. Recognizing the differences among the groups of women after the initial administration of the questionnaire, focus group discussions were conducted with the various groups of women to elicit deeper meaning and understanding from them. During the course of that research, I conducted two focus group discussions specifically with the Black women from Africa on their experiences in Canada. This paper presents discussions from the focus groups.

The findings from the focus group discussions show considerable difficulties for the women in finding jobs appropriate to their skills and qualifications. Many of the women attribute their failure in the job market to their minority status and the fact that some of them obtained their credentials from African institutions of higher education. The narratives also illustrate difficulties in securing jobs even after they undergo further training and receive accreditation from recognized Canadian institutions. As bread-winners for their families, these women accepted any job that would "simply pay the bills" so that, in some cases, their student-husbands could pursue their education.

These women's experiences have significant implications for the ongoing debate about the lack of recognition of foreign degrees in Canada, the racialized identities that could determine employability, and the stability of the family. The study is divided into three major sections. The first section provides a brief historical overview of the experiences of African-Canadian women in the labour market. The second addresses the nature of the research process, while the third reports and discusses the findings of the study. Based on these findings, the third section also offers some policy options before proceeding to a summary and conclusion.

THE CANADIAN LABOUR MARKET
AND CONTINENTAL AFRICAN WOMEN: AN OVERVIEW

Despite Canada's policy of multiculturalism, meant to promote the equality of all people irrespective of race, ethnicity, gender, or social class, the reality shows otherwise. For example, studies on women of colour (read as Black in this chapter) as a whole have indicated their over-representation in low-end manufacturing and service sectors in comparison to Canadian-born women (see Leah 1991; Boyd 1986; Ng 1988). Comparatively few women of colour have attained the expected economic autonomy their educational attainments should command. Thus, middle-class *colourless women* (read as

White) continue to reap most of the benefits of the feminist revolution compared to their counterparts of colour (Elabor-Idemudia 2000; Bannerji 1993; Schecter 1998).

African-Canadian women, like other Black women and women in general, play very crucial roles in keeping together families and communities. In writing about Black women's history, African women are usually left out of the picture (Cooper 2000). African women thus constitute a minority within a minority, and they have long endured discrimination and exclusion in Canada. They continue to be exploited as cheap domestic labour, and they also experience racism (see Cassidy, Lord, and Mandell 2001). African women, like other Black women, are in many cases, found at the very bottom of the labour force. They seem to face double discrimination, both as women and as Blacks. Often, their immigrant status does not improve the situation. On the whole, African women encounter discrimination with regard to accessing social services and resources, asserting their legal rights, and securing economic autonomy. Certainly, there is an urgent need to explore the specific experiences and the challenges that continental African women face in Canada.

There is no question that education and training are required in order to be gainfully employed or to permeate the professional enclaves. However, the preliminary investigation that preceded this research suggests that a significant number of African-Canadian women were highly educated with extensive experience in their fields of specialization. Yet their economic status in paid work and in the overall society did not reflect their educational credentials. Overall, Black women are at the bottom of the income ladder, earning 27 percent less than other female and immigrant populations (Calliste 1991).

In other words, despite a history that covers many years of settlement in Canada, African-Canadians, even those with Canadian citizenship, have not shed the stereotypical images of immigrants; perpetual outsiders and visitors to a foreign land (Ghosh 1996). The images are often frozen in time and space, and apply to subsequent generations of Canadians of African descent. These images and the related practices continue to exist despite the supposed integration and tolerance encouraged by Canada's *Multiculturalism Act* of 1988. Despite the prevailing stereotypes, the high educational level among African-Canadians shatters the pervasive stereotype of the "backward, savage, primitive" Africans (House-Midamba 1991).

THE RESEARCH AND GENERAL PROFILE
OF AFRICAN-CANADIAN WOMEN

The specific objectives of this study were to identify and systematically document the barriers to education and employment faced by African women in Canada and to assess the impact of these barriers on their pursuit of economic autonomy. The study was also conducted with a view to making recommendations for viable strategies that could enhance the economic autonomy of African women in Canada. As mentioned earlier, the current study centered mainly on the two focus group discussions with fifty Black women of African origin living in Edmonton. The two focus groups were made up of randomly selected groups of twenty-five women each. The focus groups allowed for a rich sharing of experiences among the women. Participants found themselves in a conducive atmosphere where they felt free to revisit old memories, evaluate their present status, and pose questions about their future. They shared experiences that offered considerable insights into their initial aspirations and present frustrations in the struggle to attain economic autonomy in Canada.

The African women who participated in these group discussions came from various parts of Africa: some from East African countries, such as Kenya, Tanzania, and Uganda; some from Central African countries like the Congo and the Cameroun; some from the Horn of Africa, specifically Ethiopia and Somalia; and still others from West African countries, namely Nigeria, Ghana, Liberia, and Sierra Leone. The majority of the African women who participated in the focus group discussions immigrated to Canada as adults. A large percentage of them were married with children and came to Canada with their husbands. Many of the women have children born in Canada. Hence, with little or no roots in Canada, most of these women have made Canada their home.

FINDINGS OF THE GROUP DISCUSSIONS

General Expectations and Educational Background

Virtually all the participants came to Canada with very high expectations in terms of the prospects their new home initially held for them. They saw Canada as a land of opportunity where they would be able to pursue higher education in fields of their choice. Their education and training, they assumed, would propel them to the highest echelons of their professions. But upon arrival in Canada, they were confronted with a *catch twenty-two* dilemma. They were deemed not to have the needed Canadian training for jobs, and since nobody would give them jobs to obtain the needed Canadian experience, they were left in a quandary. Experience prerequisites continue to push a good number of the African women into training and retraining for Canadian jobs. Perhaps their initial expectations flowed from their educational backgrounds and from the perception of Canada abroad as a meritocracy and a land of opportunity.

Overall, the African women who participated in this study could be described as well educated. Over 80 percent of the respondents have post-secondary education. Thirty percent of those have earned bachelor and higher degrees at the tertiary level. Less than 3 percent were without a high school diploma. It is also important to stress that over half of the women acquired their highest level of education in Canada. Only about 37 percent of the women in the group obtained their credentials from African institutions.

The general theoretical argument is that education and training are required in order to be gainfully employed or to enter the professional occupations. Data from the participants in the focus groups indicate that the women were educated and skilled, and had extensive experience in their fields of specialization. Their incomes, however, did not reflect their training and experience. Many of them had an annual income of under $15,000, and the rest earned incomes under $30,000. A number of the women who participated in the focus discussions were highly qualified in their fields of specialization but were generally under-employed. For example, there were lawyers, accountants, computer programmers, high school teachers, secretaries, and engineers who were working as housekeepers and nannies and in other menial, low-paying jobs with no job security and no opportunity for advancement.

Barriers to Labour Market Participation

African women are confronted with several barriers to labour market participation. The major problem is the question of foreign educational credentials in Canada. This is a serious challenge to these African women, even though only 37 percent had educational credentials outside Canada. For the over 50 percent who had educational credentials from Canadian institutions, the earlier foreign degrees did not put them in a better position. There are a number of academic assessment centers in Alberta that evaluate credentials obtained outside Canada, for example, the International Qualifications Assessment Services. However, many Canadian employers are not impressed by the evaluations provided by such institutions, because they often accept the prevailing stereotypical aspersions cast on educational credentials from certain regions of the world, including some countries in Africa. For Julia, stereotyping was a factor in the unwillingness of some employers and instructors to recognize educational credentials from the African continent:

> Hopefully, people will begin to know more about Nigeria or about Africa and begin to see that when you come in with a bachelor of science degree, it's the same thing as a bachelor of science degree in Canada, and it's not inferior. But a lot of it is ignorance. The employers don't know what you can do, and they're not prepared to give you a chance. Occasionally you might be lucky to get somebody who is willing to give you a chance.

It is arguable that such discriminatory treatment stems from ignorance. However, in a racially segregated labour market, such assessments attached to an applicant's credentials do not improve one's chances of being seriously considered for a job.

Most of the African women came to Canada under the family class, in many cases to join their husbands who came to study in Canada. They came with young children or started a family in Canada. Usually, their husband's aspirations as the head of the household and their children's welfare took first priority in their lives. Even for the few who came with tertiary educational credentials, their plans for retraining took a back seat to these priorities, which also dictated the nature of employment opportunities they could seek in the interim. In addition to their domestic responsibilities, many provided significant financial support to the family, especially the more recent immigrants for whom there was no established male breadwinner. Those who were able to weather the vagaries of employment in Canada had to slot themselves into racially segmented and gendered occupations in nursing, home care services, childcare, and house cleaning.

Higher education did not necessarily help the majority of the women get jobs in their occupation. Those who came to Canada with higher qualifications and years of experience in their profession pointed out that such assets hardly commanded them highly paid employment. Those with a strong support base in the family and community opted for retraining, while the rest found themselves less prepared for the struggle and settled for lower paying jobs. Those without the necessary social support either gave up totally on paid work or sought alternative economic opportunities far below their initial expectations. Many decided to be self-employed.

Those who were not self-employed found that their capacity to access available jobs was often determined by social trends. Occupations such as nursing and childcare recorded significant shortages, thereby opening the door for minority applicants. The women explained that Black women in general, and African women in particular, who came into these occupations fared better in terms of accessing and advancing in jobs. One reason was that most of these jobs were available on a part-time basis and so came without benefits. In an atmosphere where job opportunities were scarce, the women accepted the few that came along.

In general, the focus group discussions revealed considerable frustration in their search for gainful employment in their occupations in order to attain economic independence. With an average age of thirty-five, most of the women would normally be approaching the peak of their careers. However, a significant number were still looking for work in their fields of specialization years after their arrival or retraining in Canada. For some, Canadian education and training opened doors to better job opportunities, but for Mary, additional educational qualifications did not automatically open doors to a professional occupation:

> Before I went to NAIT [Northern Alberta Institute of Technology], the
> only thing that I could do is work in a daycare ... I also worked as an

aide in the hospital. That was the only thing I could do. But after I went to NAIT, the door opened a little for me, because I now had something Canadian to show them, so that sort of opened the door a bit.

Those who retrained earned the needed Canadian training but still faced the challenges of acquiring Canadian job experience. Gladys and her husband found the catch twenty-two difficult to live with:

> So both of us retrained and came back, but suddenly the jobs that were all over the place were not there any more. We went for a number of interviews, even as a bank teller in a bank. You go for an interview, and you do very well in the aptitude test.... They call to say, "Sorry you didn't get the job." May I ask why? "Oh we took somebody who was better suited for the position." And that doesn't tell you anything.

Obviously, Canadian training does not necessarily open the door to Canadian experience. As most of the women strongly argued, African immigrant women must deal with both the hostilities that are visited on newcomers, as well as the systemic discrimination that Canadian Blacks have always lived with. It is therefore not surprising that many Black women gave up their dreams at some point and settled for less. Often, the only jobs available were at the lower ranks. Some of the women in the study had been looking for jobs in their fields for more than ten years. Over this period, they worked exclusively in jobs unrelated to their previous occupations.

Only a few of the women managed to secure jobs in their areas of specialization. These women reported difficulties in advancing their professional and economic status. This was especially true for women working in the public sector, who described the process of promotion and mentorship as a *big boys club* where they stood twice disadvantaged as females and as Blacks. In such an environment, the ability to access training for promotion was also problematic:

> Because of the in-crowd, big boys club mentality, you cannot cross that barrier. They see Black women only in a service-oriented position, and they cannot see you in upper management.

Despite the barriers these women faced in the pursuit of economic autonomy in Canada, on one hand, they continued to believe in education and training as keys to getting into professional jobs. On the other, they also argued that educational qualifications do not necessarily guarantee a job for Black women in the competition for paid employment. In many cases, discriminatory practices against visible minorities are structurally ingrained, and any attempts to restructure would require very serious and concrete steps.

About 80 percent of the women were wage earners. Some were self-employed and sold various products. Some of them had small-scale hair salons or janitorial/cleaning services. The majority had worked as cooks, waitresses, janitors, housekeepers, childcare givers, clerks, sales agents, and community healthcare providers. For most, these business ventures were geared primarily towards family subsistence. Although managing a business was very time consuming, demanding, and stressful, they were relieved at the end of the day when the family had food on the table, and the bills were paid.

Self-employment was the reluctant choice for some of the women. Most of them saw self-employment as *doing something*, and recognized that it was not the best substitute for professional activities in one's area of specialization. A remarkable finding was that the self-employed women did not seek any public or private financial assistance outside the family. Nine of the twelve women who were self-employed indicated that their businesses were financed through either personal capital or private loans from family members and close friends. Upon further probing, it became clear that a good number of the women were unaware of funding sources outside the family unit. Saddled with the burden of family survival, the women did not have time to pursue funding from other sources. Thus, with little public or community support, most of the self-employed businesses relied on financial support from immediate family or close friends.

The focus group discussions revealed that the women were less likely to be dependent on public assistance through transfer payments. The women's discussions displayed a strong sense of self-worth and pride (this might account for their willingness to forge independent economic arrangements outside the public sphere). Their source of self-worth and pride can perhaps be located in their pre-Canadian life experiences. Given their educational background, some of the women left behind an already established life and history, a life in which they were both independent and self-reliant. Hence, they were less likely to apply for social welfare handouts even when entitled to it. These African women claimed they would prefer to risk their health doing two or three jobs to keep their families afloat, rather than queue for handouts from government. Even for women with husbands in school, dependence on public support was an option they would consider only as a last resort.

The choice the women made to rely on private, rather than public, sources of financing for their business or support undermines the generally held belief that immigrants are heavily reliant on the social safety net for their economic and social survival. If the experiences of the women in this study group can be confirmed in other studies, it would demonstrate that the notion of immigrants being the greatest beneficiaries of the social safety net is just another myth about immigrants in Canada.

DISCRIMINATION BY EMPLOYERS, RESOURCES, AND SOCIAL SUPPORT

The majority of the women claimed that they were discriminated against based on their race. Their experiences clearly show that even as they were striving to meet Canadian requirements in paid work, the attitudes of employers significantly affect their prospects. Discriminatory practices are subtle and attitudinal in nature in most cases. For example, the women explained that they always had to carry the label of outsiders invading an environment where they were not equipped with the necessary identities. Even in institutions where employment equity policies were supposed to be in place, they noted that Black women were still not able to access jobs in the higher levels of the organizations where they worked.

In the midst of what were obviously frustrating working conditions, some of the women reported satisfaction in their jobs. This is surprising, given the fact that more than half were employed in the service sector in occupations unrelated to their training and previous experience. When questioned further about what seemed a facade of general satisfaction, several themes emerged. It appears that despite the challenges of the work environment, the fact they were working and contributing to the family's wellbeing was a source of satisfaction.

However, almost all the focus group members made allusions to their high level of dissatisfaction in Canada. They construed those levels as a major determinant of their emotional health. Although this study did not set out to investigate the women's emotional health, it is important to mention the feelings of disappointment clearly etched on the faces of the subjects during the focus group discussions. Two major issues underpin those feelings: inadequate access to information and the lack of social support. Repeatedly, the women described their unsuccessful attempts to seek information to enable them to settle into their new environment, even though, as stated earlier, they were ignorant of funding sources outside the family network. Most of the participants came to Canada under the family and independent classes. In the former class, for example, there is an assumption of financial guarantees. They are not expected to work outside the domestic sphere and are thus confined to the realm of childcare and housework. That policy "in effect, reproduces traditional gender ideology with regard to the sexual division of labour. The sponsorship agreement of ten years [implicit in the family class] puts these women into a dependency relationship with their male principal applicants. Their dependent status is maintained and perpetuated by various institutional processes which have negative implications" (Elabor-Idemudia 2000, 91). Their domestic status and obligations often forced them to place their professional aspirations on the back burner, making their husband's and children's futures their first priority. Together with those who came under the independent class, the barriers in the labour market shattered their initial aspirations over time. Most of them shared their frustrations as they tried to reconcile their aspirations with the realities of being an African immigrant in Edmonton. Apparently, an immigrant woman's best bet is to seek out available resource centres upon arrival. Such centres provide a head start in what is certainly a long journey. Women who were able to access the relevant information and help found it made a big difference in their confidence levels and their ability to find work.

The women also indicated a need for social support, especially for new immigrants. For women with younger children in need of pre- and after-school care, juggling paid work and childcare has been a very trying experience, one that also limited the range of economic opportunities they could explore. Since some of these women did not come to Canada with landed immigrant status, there was little or no social assistance. International students often do not qualify for any significant childcare subsidy. However, those with landed immigration status at the point of entry to Canada saw a rosy economic future in terms of employment opportunities, but they soon realized that progress in working towards that future was elusive. The lack of childcare subsidies and a social support network basically crippled any attempts to make headway in expanding or advancing their employment opportunities. It is also important to contextualize some of the above experiences. The fact remains that it is not easy to navigate one's way in a new environment. However, the initial and subsequent settlement pains for the women were worsened by their racialized ethnic identities.

CONCLUSION

This study examined the experiences of African women in Canada using a purposive sample drawn from the City of Edmonton. The focus group discussions provided the opportunity to explore the African women's aspirations and to highlight the barriers they face in Canada. Their attempts to gain access to meaningful and appropriate employment to attain economic autonomy have not quite been successful. Their levels of education, training, and employment experiences in their countries of origin, as well as in Canada, did not enhance their chances, as they had previously expected.

The focus groups discussions turned into a powerful medium where many of the women got to know about each other's existence, shared common problems, and compared coping strategies. They subsequently began to explore various ways they could provide support, both individually and as a group. In the discussions, the women spoke as a group and as individuals. They shared common experiences that illustrate their resilience in a struggle many women in the mainstream cannot even relate to. The focus group discussions revealed their frustrations with life in Canada, as well as their resolve to continue the struggle, at least to help their children earn a better place in the future. The majority of the women had not fared as well as they had expected in their new home. This study's findings reinforce the need to further explore and document the experiences of various other immigrant groups if the broader society is to better understand the unfolding dilemmas, tensions, and problems of settling in Canada.

Canada has introduced various measures over the years to improve the prospects of those affected by racial discrimination. Legislative instruments and policies, for example, the *Multiculturalism Act*, the *Canadian Charter of Rights and Freedoms*, the *Employment Equity Act*, and other anti-discrimination laws have not addressed the myriad difficulties the women expressed in the focus group discussions. A major problem is the existence of attitudinal, structural, and systemic issues, giving the impression that there are still numerous individuals and organizations who would prefer to maintain the status quo with its inherently unequal structures and practices.

While the majority of the women eke out a living, they usually work in occupations far below their levels of training and/or previous experience. The reasons for this downgrading of occupational status or lack of opportunities for finding employment in their occupations are: the lack of recognition of foreign education, training, and experience; discrimination and stereotyping by employers; and inadequate access to information about life in Canada. The difficulties in the accreditation of foreign credentials continue to limit the ability of African professional women to contribute effectively to the economy of the place they have adopted as home.

This research was conducted with an eye to effecting change within both the public and private sectors and in non-profit agencies. To ensure this, direct interventions are needed at the institutional and community levels. At the institutional level, considerable effort must be geared towards training Canadian employers in cultural sensitivity so as to change their attitudes regarding minorities. There is a need to focus on measures that will promote employment equity in all employer communities. The larger policy question is about the process of evaluating foreign degrees. As indicated earlier, there are institutions that evaluate foreign credentials. The problem is that some employers do not accept the legitimacy of the evaluations because of stereotypical values and attitudes. Perhaps public sector institutions can take a leadership role in this regard by highlighting the legitimacy of the accreditation process and hiring some of the people with foreign credentials. This would have a demonstrable effect on private sector institutions.

There are some conceptual difficulties that require clarification at the level of policy. This starts with the struggle to name and define the African woman. Power relations are embedded in the terminology, a reflection of social and political realities (Agnew 1996). For the African women, the term *visible minority* is ill defined and refers to an inferior and inadequate state. The term *Black woman* recognizes the history of slavery, a condition that does not apply to her. For the African women, these terms do not represent the reality of their situations.

The African woman's lot and history is different from the Caribbean woman, from other Black women in the diaspora, and even from Canadian-born Black women. These terms only serve to perpetuate the perceived inferiority of all non-White women. The African woman is not poor and deprived when she arrives in Canada, considering the substantial costs of migration. Many African women arrive in Canada educated and endowed with the ability to provide for themselves and their families. They usually have a history of some level of financial comfort. As soon as they arrive in Canada, their previous history and experience are eradicated, and they become inconsequential within the system. Thus begins their marginalization and the patronizing attitude of the mainstream. Their emigration from a Third World country should not confer on them a homogeneity with women who are separated from each other by different histories of colonialism and class membership (Agnew 1996). There is no common identity to justify the inclusion of African women in the various categories described, except to be recognized as African women. Given the unique experiences of the women in the focus group, it would be necessary to recognize their differences vis-à-vis categories like *non-white, racial minority, women of colour*, and even *Black women*.

The study has confirmed that the experiences of African women in Canada are quite different from those of other Black women. All Black women have tended to be lumped into one basket, yet their needs are different. The cultural differences within the broader Black communities would have to be recognized. Since there is nothing like a Black community in Canada, lumping all Black people into one category and expecting common experiences will only continue to negatively impact policy measures to address the concerns of the women in this study. To be defined as Black, it seems, is to accept discrimination and an inferior position in society. From positions of relative independence, the transition of the African women in this study to being a member of a visible minority, with its implicit powerlessness, is difficult to deal with, especially within the context of racialized identities. Racism, in its brutality and lack of honesty, continues to be a reality in Canada for racialized bodies (Akwani 2002).

At the broader level, it seems that some sections of the Canadian society would wish the African to be a more subdued person, to be eternally grateful for the privilege of being allowed into Canada, and to appreciate the illusion of opportunities of a better life. It is always very difficult for some Canadians to accept Africans as Canadian citizens, hence the *twisted eyebrow* when an African announces him/herself as a Canadian. This has made it more difficult for the Africans, particularly the African woman, to bond with any community. The African lives in virtual isolation, estranged from the others who see her/him as *inferior* and as coming from a continent in shambles. The larger mainstream society relates to him/her as a colonizer would relate to the colonized.

In the absence of strong inter- and intra-community bonds and the lack of institutional support, the African woman continues to struggle, suffering in silence, even smiling in suffering. She continues to absorb the misery of racism and the gradual erosion of her core identity. Therefore, a more inclusive atmosphere, one where African women can interact and compete with others without fighting to be recognized as equal citizens at every juncture, should be established. The development of strategic alliances, not only among various African women groups, but also with other women's groups, especially racialized groups, would provide the context for capacity building and an atmosphere in which women can support each other, talk about their concerns, and share resources for improving their situations.

There is also a need to support a fair representation of African women in training and employment preparation. There should be representative interventions for African women in general with various government and other policy-making bodies that maintain strategic partnerships with agencies and institutions best able to deal with African women's specific concerns. There is a need for strategies directed at a more equitable distribution of rewards and opportunities. African women are under-represented in higher paying occupations; especially upper- and middle-level management in Canadian organizations. Breaking the barriers to these upper- and middle-level occupations can expand opportunities for African women who, according to this study, are usually well educated.

As shown by this study, a small percentage of African women who participated in the group discussions are self-employed. Obviously, this small minority found self-employment, despite its limitations, an option that aligns better with their perceived domestic responsibilities. It is also very likely that better access to credit may encourage other African women to become self-employed. For many African women, a woman's place is in her business, and many have been successful at doing just that. For example, the market women of Africa have been a known phenomenon since the colonial days (see Clark 1994). With a conducive system, they could contribute to the economy of Canada in more ways than the system can imagine.

Finally, success for African women cannot be achieved without the considerable commitment of both public and private groups, commitment that should be reflected in policies, programs, and practices. Political authorities should begin to demonstrate some significant awareness regarding the special and peculiar plight of all immigrant women by paying attention to the differences that exist among them. Canada needs to wake up to the needs of the people it has so *graciously* brought into the country through a very long, tedious, and expensive immigration process. The significant efforts and financial resources expended on encouraging people to migrate to Canada should not be allowed to go to waste.

REFERENCES

Agnew, Vijay. 1996. *Women from Asia, Africa, and the Caribbean and the Women's Movement in Canada*. Toronto: University of Toronto Press.

Akwani, Obi. 2002 [online]. *Oh Canada! Lament of the Black Canute Experience* [cited 15 December 2002]. (www.imdiversity.com/villages/global/Article_Detail. asp?Article_ID=18463).

Bannerji, Himani, ed. 1993. *Returning the Gaze: Essays on Racism, Feminism, and Politics*. Toronto: Sister Vision.

Boyd, Monica. 1986. Immigrant women in Canada. In *International Migration: The Female Experience*, ed. R. J. Simon and C.B. Brettell. Totowa, NJ: Rowman and Allanheld.

Calliste, Agnes. 1991. Canada's immigration policy and domestics from the Caribbean. In *Race, Class, Gender, Bonds and Barriers*, ed. J. Vorst et al. Toronto: Garamond.

Cassidy, Barbara, Robina Lord, and Nancy Mandell. 2001. Silenced and forgotten women: Race, poverty, and disability. In *Feminist Issues: Race, Class and Sexuality*, 3rd ed., ed. N. Mandell, 75–107. Toronto: Prentice Hall.

Clark, Gracia. 1994. *Onions Are My Husband: Survival and Accumulation by West African Market Women*. Chicago: University of Chicago Press.

Cooper, Afua. 2000. Constructing Black women's historical knowledge. *Atlantis* 25: 39–50.

Elabor-Idemudia, Patience. 1999. Gender and the new African diaspora: African immigrant women in the Canadian labour force. In *The African Diaspora: African Origins and New World Self-Fashioning*, ed. I. Okpewho, C. B. Davies, and A. A. Mazrui, 234–53. Bloomington: Indiana University Press.

———. 2000. Challenges confronting African immigrant women in the Canadian workforce. In *Anti-Racist Feminism: Critical Race and Gender Studies*, ed. A. Calliste and G. S. Dei, 91–110. Halifax: Fernwood.

Ghosh, Ratna. 1996. *Redefining Multicultural Education*. Toronto: Harcourt Brace.

House-Midamba, Bessie. 1991. Economic Self-Sufficiency and the Role of the African Market Women. Paper presented at the fourth annual meeting of the African Studies Association. St. Louis, MO.

Leah, Ronnie. 1991. Linking the struggles: Racism, sexism and the union movement. In *Race, Class, and Gender: Bonds and Barriers*, ed. Jesse Vorst et al., 169–200. Toronto: Between the Lines.

Moussa, Helene. 1993. *Storm and Sanctuary: The Journey of Ethiopian and Women Refugees*. Dundas, ON: Artemis.

Ng, Roxanna. 1988. *Politics of Community Services: Immigrant Women, Class, and the State*. Toronto: Garamond.

Schecter, Tanya. 1998. *Race, Class, Women, and the State: The Case of Domestic Labour*. Montreal: Black Rose.

SECTION IV

Place, 'In-Between' Spaces, & the
Negotiation of Identities

8

BORDER CROSSINGS & HOME–DIASPORA LINKAGES AMONG AFRICAN–CANADIANS:
An Analysis of Translocational Positionality, Cultural Remittance, & Social Capital

Wisdom J. Tettey and Korbla P. Puplampu

INTRODUCTION

SIGNIFICANT SOCIO-ECONOMIC DEVELOPMENTS in this era of globalization and internal political strife have pushed many people out of their countries of origin to explore possibilities for survival in other places. Concomitant with these transnational movements are innovations in the field of technology that attenuate the barriers posed by time and space – what Giddens (1985) calls *time-space distanciation*. As a result of these processes, some observers contend that there is no longer the need to draw a distinction between temporary and permanent migration. In advancing this view, Richmond (2002, 713) opines that "globalization has facilitated worldwide network linkages with friends and families in the former country, and with the international labour market." Consequently, *transilience*, which he defines as the ability to move back and forth between two or more countries and cultures, has become a fact of life. A corollary to these processes of shifting locations and attachments is the reconfiguration of people's identities in ways that are anti-essentialist and that transcend fixed notions of self, location, culture, ethnicity, and citizenship.

These understandings of the ethos of people in motion have been at the basis of the concept of hybridity. A key contribution of this concept has been to pursue analyses that help to "overcome the victimology of transnational migrants, empowering them, linking the past with the present" (Anthias 2001, 620). To capture the multiple complexities that characterize immigrants' *in-between* status (Bhaba 1998) and to give the concept of hybridity a more encompassing essence vis-à-vis issues of belonging, otherness, and identity, it is important that we explore other dimensions of immigrants' experiences. To advance this purpose, Anthias (2001) proposes the idea of *translocational positionality* that allows us to interrogate other constructions of difference (beyond culture) based on various identifiers and signifiers. Such a tool makes it possible to look beyond immigrant communities as homogenous groups bound together by a collective identity in relation to others. It opens up analytical insights into different narratives of belonging and otherness, not only in the context of the host society, but of the societies of origin, as well. As Anthias (2001, 633) argues,

> [c]ollective identities involve forms of social organization postulating boundaries with identity markers that denote essential elements of membership (which act to *code* people), as well as claims that are articulated for specific purposes. The identity markers (culture, origin, language, colour, and physiognomy, etc.) may themselves function as resources that are deployed contextually and situationally. They function both as sets of self-attributions and attributions by others. By focusing on location/dislocation and on positionality, it is possible to pay attention to spatial and contextual dimensions, treating the issues involved in terms of processes rather than possessive properties of individuals. (see also Dirlik 1999)

In the following discussion, we use the framework of translocational positionality to analyze the multiple ways in which first generation African-Canadians connect with their communities/countries of origin in spite of the spatial distanciation that their location in Canada imposes. The rationale behind using this framework stems from the fact that it allows us to escape the constraints of a binary division between subjectivity, on the one hand, and cultural determinism, on the other. Rather, what we have is a dialectical approach that facilitates the appreciation of the multiple, simultaneous, fluid, and sometimes conflictual, positions occupied by individuals and groups as they negotiate their sense of self and consequent attachments to cultures, ethnicities, places, and nations.

We must acknowledge at the outset that connections to home and our perceptions of it also reflect different experiences, interests, and rationales. As

Shami (1998, 633) observes, "even with the formation of collective approaches to the homeland, people who journey back and forth, their motivations, aims, representations, and the kinds of landscapes they construct as they travel these circuits vary significantly." It is in this respect that Shain and Barth's (2003) distinction among core, passive, and silent members of the diaspora is useful to keep in mind as we discuss the relationships between African-Canadians and their home countries, especially within the public sphere. While core members are at the forefront of articulating their connections to the homeland and mobilizing their compatriots, passive members tend to be on the margins but are ready to make themselves available for purposes initiated by the core. Silent members are generally not involved in diaspora affairs, but they may respond to the needs of their communities of origin in times of crisis, whether in Canada or at home.

Related to these distinctions is how individuals and groups define *home*. The extent of one's involvement in both a geographical and deterritorialized home is partly determined by his/her definition of the term. Home, in the context of this chapter,

> is *where one best knows oneself* – where *best* means *most* even not always
> *happiest*. Here, in sum, is an ambiguous and fluid but yet ubiquitous no-
> tion, apposite for charting the ambiguities and fluidities, the migrancies
> and paradoxes, of identity in the world today ... [B]eing at *home* and being
> *homeless* are not matters of movement, of physical space, or of the fluid-
> ity of socio-cultural times and places, as such. One is at home when one
> inhabits a cognitive environment in which one can undertake the routines
> of daily life and through which one finds one's identity best mediated – and
> homeless when such a cognitive environment is eschewed. (Rapport and
> Dawson 1998, 9–10)

As they construct and interpellate a sense of belonging, home, location, and dislocation, the experiences of African-Canadians are based on a concept of place that traverses the physical boundaries of a particular state, though it in-corporates it. For them,

> [p]lace is at once a physical construct and a mental imaginary. Thus, while
> people may be separated from the physical construct of *home* as a result
> of immigration and other forms of geographical mobility, they tend to
> retain their attachment to that space through mental connections and
> outward practices that invoke that geographical location. This is the case
> even though signifiers of their cultures of origin are adapted to their new
> settings, new cultures, and by new generations. (Tettey 2004, 129, see also
> Svas˘ek 2002, 497–98)

BORDER CROSSINGS: IDENTITY, HYBRIDITY,
AND THE REPLICATION OF HOME CULTURES

The literature has been divided between those who emphasize the assimilating capacities of host cultures and those who contend that the impacts produced by contact between immigrants and host cultures result from complex processes of negotiation, adaptation, and reinvention (see Faist 2000, 215). As a result of these processes, immigrants retain elements of their cultures of origin even as they adjust to the norms and practices of their new environment. Williams (2002) examines how the intersection of physical and social space affects the sense of identity among immigrants and their daily practices. He argues that diaspora life is characterized by a definitive and situated culture. Consequently, immigrants practice familiar rites in new settings and give new meanings to familiar practices and rituals, which are then exhibited during interactions among compatriots.

In this section we explore various means by which African-Canadians engage with their cultures of origin as forms of national, ethnic, or racial expression, as well as manifestations of resistance to mainstream Canadian society. We draw on the theory of *cultural remittance* to examine the practices, imaginings, nostalgias, and yearnings that link African-Canadians to the countries and communities from which they have journeyed. Burman (2001, 277) defines cultural remittance as:

> Gestures sent to an elsewhere (often conceived as home but not the only home), exceeding goods and money sent. Such gestures join points within a diasporic sphere that are not necessarily spatially contiguous, and bring to the fore imagination as social practice ... with transformative potential. Cultural remittances play out in, and transform, diasporic locales ... and they are often addressed to both the elsewhere evoked and the mainstream context [of the host countries in which immigrants are located].

Before analyzing the phenomena transferred through cultural remittance, it is important to clarify how culture is being used here. We base our analysis on Anthias' (2001) three dimensions of culture – (1) culture as content or product; (2) culture as process or mechanism; and (3) culture as form or structure. The first refers to cultural attributes and artifacts that are linked to particular locales or communities and provide an illustration of their symbols and practices. The second dimension pertains to the understanding of culture as an expression of a world view. It serves as the basis on which culture as content/product is built, but it is distinct from it. Finally, culture as form or structure refers to the patterns of knowledge and actions that characterize a society, and to their institutionalization within defined structures and processes. Aberrations from these patterns lead to the application of relevant sanctions. Far from being assimilated into mainstream Canadian society, African-Canadians are engaged in an "extraordinary process of periphery-induced creolization in the metropolis" (Patterson 1994, 104) as they manifest elements of the three dimensions of culture enunciated above.

Many African-Canadians, irrespective of how long ago they immigrated, appear to have a stronger connection to the cultures of their homelands than to mainstream Canadian culture. An online poll of South Africans living abroad, including those in Canada, bears this out (see RainBowNation n.d.). Part of the reason for the nostalgia that Africans feel for home is the fact that it offers the best cognitive environment for their routines and for their assertions of self. These feelings also stem from their marginalized location within Canadian society and the perception that they are second-class citizens. Many well qualified professionals end up in low end jobs that underutilize their skills and potentials (Tettey 2001). Abusharaf (2002) documents the case of the Sudanese exile community in North America that shows how engineers have become taxi-drivers, and teachers and lawyers have had to survive as gas station attendants. Consequently, many struggle to maintain a sense of self-worth based on the status and respect they enjoyed in their countries of origin, and they long for the benefits derived therefrom. This process can be at once emotionally soothing and painful, as they try to resolve the dissonance produced by the differences in their diaspora and home positionalities.

A fundamental value of African cultures is the link to ancestors. Africans maintain this connection by being buried in their ancestral homes. The desire to be in the midst of one's forebears has been at the base of efforts on the part of a significant number of African-Canadians to spend the twilight years of their lives in their country of birth (see White 2002). To accomplish this goal, many people invest a lot of resources in putting up buildings in their home countries where they hope to retire. In response to this desire, Africa-based real estate companies are making forays into Canada to woo potential clients. In July 2003, for example, a huge housing exhibition was organized by Ghanaian real estate developers for their compatriots in the Toronto area (Ghanaweb 2003a).

While the evidence seems to suggest that many of these people will not end up retiring to their home countries, the desire to build at home nevertheless continues to motivate many. There is constant concern with what most Africans consider to be the deplorable social and psychological state many elderly people in Canada find themselves in as they spend their last days in old peoples' homes. They contrast these homes, in particular, and the perceived anomie and loneliness of old age in Canada, in general, with the imagined emotional succor that elderly people in Africa enjoy through the constant flow of interactions with friends and extended family. It is worth acknowledging that the reality in Africa is slowly shifting away from this ideal, nostalgic image ingrained in people's minds as *modernity* creates changes in African social structures, and as families begin to experience trends similar to what these African-Canadians are worried about (see Charlton 1998; Apt 1996).

Theorists of intercultural communication argue that there are differences in time orientation among different cultures, and they categorize African societies as being among those which adhere to a non-linear, or polychronic, concept of time (Hall 1994). This attitude towards time, which does not dwell on strict schedules, continues to be a defining characteristic of diaspora Africans when they operate outside of the institutions and cultural parameters of mainstream Canadian society. It is not unusual for events to start behind schedule, ostensibly because both organizers and participants are operating within the framework of *African time*. The notion of African time is characterized by a tendency not to put much stock in scheduled start times. There is a belief that nobody really shows up on time, and that one should allow some time between the advertised starting time for a program and when it actually gets underway, in order not to have to wait unnecessarily. The following story illustrates the extent of this attitude and its carry-over into transnational settings:

> Last week [18 October 2003], for instance, international journalists in the UK were kept waiting by the king of Ghana's largest ethnic group who was visiting Alexandra Palace in north London at the climax of a Ghanaian trade exhibition, Ghana Expo 2003. The journalists had been informed that Otumfuo Osei Tutu II from the Ashanti would arrive at the exhibition at 1100. The time was changed to 1400, but the king did not show up until two hours later when the journalists had already packed and left. (British Broadcasting Corporation [BBC] News 2003)

The transposition of the concept of *African time* to the specific milieu of African diaspora activities is fascinating, because members of the diaspora adhere to the mainstream concept of time in their workplaces and in dealings with institutions outside their socio-cultural environment. The fact that they are able to apply appropriate time schemes to particular contexts is an indication of the dialectics of continuity and discontinuity that characterize the *in-between* spaces these communities occupy.

Africans organize several activities that enact rituals and events back home. These activities are, in Dabydeen's words (1988, 40), a "living link to ... ancestral history, our means of keeping in touch with the ghosts of *back home*." They include celebrations of national holidays, funerals, and child-naming ceremonies. Independence Day celebrations provide an opportunity for African-Canadians to reiterate their connections to the political histories of their countries of origin. For some, these occasions are an opportunity for anti-colonial resistance in the context of their new homes. It reminds them of the oppression, racism, and discrimination that their nations suffered under colonial rule and how that has shaped their circumstances in their contemporary locales. These perspectives on

Independence or Republic Day celebrations highlight the relationship between antecedents of contact and the current positionality of these immigrants. The way they are viewed by the larger society, irrespective of their standing in the context of their host societies, is largely a product of the colonial relations and the representations that they spawned. These representations become ingrained in the consciousness of members of the dominant society in Canada, who then relate to the Africans through the lenses of the images carved by the colonial and postcolonial experience.

Festivals, such as *Afrikadey* in Calgary, provide opportunities for Africans to share their cultures with the rest of the community. The essence of these festivals is not only to showcase the cultural traditions of the continent to other Canadians; it also serves the purpose of building bridges of cultural understanding among citizens. The following observations describing West Indian carnivals in the diaspora are applicable to the celebrations and observances within the African community in Canada:

> [They offer] a kind of social therapy that overcomes the separation and
> isolation imposed by the diaspora and restores to West Indian immigrants
> both a sense of community with each other and a sense of connection
> to the culture that they claim as a birthright. Politically, however, there
> is more to these carnivals than cultural nostalgia. They are also a means
> through which West Indians seek and symbolize integration into the met-
> ropolitan society, by coming to terms with the opportunities, as well as the
> constraints, that surround them. (Manning 1990, 35)

The observation of various rites of passage constitutes an important dimension of the home-diaspora connection for a lot of African-Canadians. In Africa, funerals are community events, and every member of the community is expected to help bereaved families organize a fitting burial for their departed relatives. This social obligation stems from a moral economy that requires reciprocal support from community members. The obligation is even more pronounced with members of the deceased's extended family, irrespective of where they may be resident. The same sense of community obligation that surrounds these activities in Africa is replicated by some Africans in the Canadian context, as well. Thus, it is not uncommon to see Africans organizing funerals for their relatives who have died in their home countries. These funerals are supported by compatriots who live in the cities where the event takes place, even though they may not know the deceased. Cash donations are made to help the bereaved person meet his or her obligations to kin in the country of origin. The sense of communal mobilization to support the bereaved in the Canadian context is heightened by the fact that relatives who are resident abroad are usually expected to bear a significant part of the funeral expenses, particularly if they are the children or siblings of the deceased. Their compatriots, understanding the onus that this responsibility places on the bereaved, do the best they can to offer their support.

Events and celebrations, such as those discussed above, provide opportunities for these African-Canadians to display their material culture, which constitutes the most visible marker of their connection to the African continent. As they dress themselves in the most elaborate apparels of their cultural groups and feast on traditional cuisines, they assert their pride in their cultures of origin and their continuing attachment to them. One very strong manifestation of Africans' desire to transfer their indigenous rituals and institutions, as well as attendant regalia, is the replication of chieftaincy among Ghanaians, especially Asantes (see Asanteman Council of North America (ACONA) n.d.). In an interview for the Asanteman Council of North America (ACONA) website, the chief of Asantes in Houston explains how the institution, in its diasporic incarnation, is legitimized:

> Traditionally Asante Chieftancy is by matrilineal inheritance, but here in the U.S., elections decide who becomes the next Asantefouhene [that is, chief of Asantes]. Permission is duly sought from the Royal Palace, (Manhyia), Kumasi, Ghana. A representative of the Asantehene [King of the Asante] is delegated to represent the Golden Stool to perform all the royal rites on behalf of the Asantehene. This legitimizes the elected Asantefuohene. (Asanteman Council of North America n.d.)

Like their compatriots in the United States, Asantes in Montreal and Toronto have *chiefs* whose role, while mainly symbolic, involves providing leadership in mobilizing members of their ethnic community for development projects at home. They also help organize cultural events, in addition to providing guidance and support to community members in a variety of areas.

Canada has become an important destination for the export of traditional African cultural products. Several businesses are springing up in large Canadian cities that provide these cultural items and cater, not only to the African population, but to other Canadians, mainly Blacks, who are interested in those items. These businesses sell African crafts, clothing, hair products, and food. The bulk of the inventory held by these establishments is food items. These developments reflect the pattern of ethno-specific cultural establishments among some ethnic groups in Canada (see Qadeer 1998). Access to familiar culinary ingredients and other cultural products has been described as a "powerful force influencing the processes of immigrant settlement, acculturation, and identity development" (Tsang et al. 2003, 372). Such access makes it possible for these immigrants to express their identities and cultural orientation in ways that recreate their cultures of origin in a foreign land.

Pendakur and Subramanyam (1996) found that family-based video watching seems to be of critical importance in helping Indians in the diaspora to reproduce their home cultures abroad. The impact of videos as a link to home countries does not, however, appear to be significant among African-Canadians at this point, even though some of the shops mentioned above do sell videos, for example, those coming from the nascent West African film industry. There are several reasons for this. The major one is that most of the videos on the continent are produced in PAL-format, whereas most North American homes operate on the NTSC system. This lack of compatibility discourages African-Canadians from patronizing the industry to an extent similar to their Indian counterparts. Efforts by vendors to address the problem by converting the original tapes into the NTSC format for commercial purposes affect the quality of the images, thereby reducing their market value.

Television programs that feature African stories or events are, however, a big draw for diaspora Africans. It is not unusual for Africans to phone one another to tune in to Canadian or American television programs or stories that touch on their continent. Positive stories or documentaries evoke nostalgia and a feeling of pride, whereas negative portrayals of the continent and its people either elicit complaints about negative stereotyping in the media or revulsion against those whose actions generate the negative representations carried by the media. There was general pride among Africans about the coverage given the 1994 multi-racial elections in South Africa and the success of Cameroon and Senegal in recent FIFA World Cup tournaments. On the other hand, the depictions of ubiquitous abject poverty (e.g., in World Vision ads), the devastation of HIV/AIDS, civil conflict, and political corruption create feelings of shame or critiques about the slant and accuracy of coverage. As pointed out earlier, the representation of the African continent in colonial and post-colonial times affects African-Canadians' ascribed identity. They cannot, therefore, escape connections to their home continent even if they choose to, because who they are in mainstream society is largely related to where they come from.

The fact that many Africans are glued to their television sets during international sporting events featuring their countries or an African representative (e.g., FIFA World Cup; Rugby World Cup; Cricket World Cup; African Cup of Nations) is evidence of their emotional attachment to their homelands. The Internet provides a unique opportunity for African-Canadians to keep abreast of developments in their home countries, as well as engage with one another and with others in the diaspora via online chat rooms, news sources, and so on (see Tettey 2002, 2004). Both online and offline social networks provide forums where mores and values that Africans consider to be fundamental to who they are, are validated and reinforced, particularly when they do not dovetail neatly with mainstream values. This attachment to a geographically distant, yet psychologically and emotionally proximate, space is a fundamental part of what defines most African-Canadians' sense of their Africanness. The above discussion bears out the assertion that "a new technology can be used to cognitively connect with what is a symbol of primordial essence" (Adams and Ghose 2003, 415). Music cassette tapes and compact discs (CDs) also provide a major and popular cultural link to the continent. Many African-Canadian homes have some form of indigenous African music or hybrid varieties from the continent reflecting transmutations that resulted from the blending of traditional African music with influences from elsewhere, particularly genres from Western popular culture. These tunes are the highlight of social gatherings and cultural events.

Beyond popular culture, the emergence of *African churches* in the diaspora has been identified as a growing phenomenon in the process of transnationalization (see Hepner 2003; Gerloff 2000). African-founded and led Christian churches are becoming a common sight in Canada's big cities (see Afro Drive n.d; Ghanaweb 2003b). Some estimates put the number of *Ghanaian churches* in Toronto alone at over sixty (*ExpoTimes* 2002). Even though they welcome people from all backgrounds, their core congregation is African. Part of the reason for their growth is the fact that they offer a spiritual environment their mostly African members can identify with. Members find the services in mainstream Canadian churches too sedate. They are therefore attracted to the African churches where the atmosphere replicates the exuberance, patterns, and forms of worship (e.g., dancing and drumming) common to Christian groups at home. As Hepner (2003, 270) notes with regard to Eritrean churches in the United States, the growth in these organizations is due largely to the fact that they "help maintain cultural patterns (religious belief systems and values, language, gender roles, dress, and socialization of youth)." Religious bodies also bring to the fore important questions about diaspora mobilization via religion and its implication for socio-economic and political developments at home. Furthermore, they respond to the spiritual vulnerabilities that are specific to the African community. For example, witchcraft and the fears that it generates are still a very big concern among Africans in Canada, even though they function in a society where these superstitions and the metaphysical trappings of this phenomenon do not hold much, if any, sway. African churches are able to address these concerns in ways that mainstream churches cannot.

Some of the Canadian churches are affiliated with churches in Africa and operate under the authority of the home churches. A recent development among some Ghanaian churches in Toronto illustrates these home-diaspora linkages:

> In a bold move to reverse the disturbing trend of Church divisions and
> multiplications in the Ghanaian-Canadian communities, the leader-
> ship of the Methodist Church have [*sic*] taken some positive action to
> re-unite the various factions of the Church starting with the factions in
> Toronto, Canada's largest city. Throughout the weekend of December
> 7 to 8 the leadership of the Ghana Methodist Church of Toronto and
> the Ghana Calvary Methodist United Church of Toronto met behind

closed doors in marathon negotiating sessions. These were under the spiritual guidance and supervision of the Presiding Bishop of the Ghana Methodist Conference, The Most Reverend Dr. Aboagye-Mensah and the Lay President of the Ghana Methodist Conference in Ghana, Mr Ato Essuman. (Ghanaweb 2003c)

SOCIAL CAPITAL AND THE TRANSNATIONAL MORAL ECONOMY

Remittances from sojourners abroad have, for over a century, been a critical link between immigrant communities and their places of origin. Their purposes and impacts have been varied. Fenianism in Northern Ireland derived much of its financial backbone from the Irish diaspora in the United States; the formative years of modern Greece are said to have been facilitated by its *absentee bourgeoisie*; the contribution of New York's *Little Italy* to the Italian tax roll exceeded that of several poorer provinces at the turn of the twentieth century; and Polish-Americans' contributions to the independence movement in their homeland earned them the accolade "fourth province of Poland" (Shain and Sherman 2001). Globalization processes and technological advancements have increased the role of remittances even more at the beginning of the twenty-first century, not only in relation to national-level endeavours, but at the meso- and micro-levels of communities and families, respectively. Richmond (2002) notes the importance of remittances in the relationship between immigrants from developing countries and their families in home countries. For example,

> such transfers were the only means of income for between 70 and 80 percent of the Somali population. It is estimated that in an average year, a staggering US$200 million to $500 million is transferred to Somalia through the hawalad system. By contrast, just $60 million was injected into the Somali economy last year through international humanitarian aid. (Africa Action 2001)

Official estimates of Somalis living abroad in 2001 stood at just under 400,000. Of these, Canada had 70,000, the second largest number after the Gulf states, which had about 120,000 (Africa Action 2001). It is reasonable to assume that the contributions of these Canadian residents to the remittances mentioned above will be significant.

National and ethnic associations have provided avenues for disbursing social capital, as well. What is significant about these, as well as continental, associations is that their formation has a lot to do with adaptation to a different environment in which these migrants share a collective position as subalterns within the dominant Euro-American culture. In such an environment, solidarity with others of similar racial, ethnic, or geographical provenance becomes a key ingredient for cultural adaptation and integration. The relational character of identity is borne out by Cusack's (1999) analyses of ethnic creation in Africa. In twentieth century Nigeria, processes of modernization led to rapid migration into large urban centers characterized by isolation and difference, which in turn, spawned the mobilization of an Igbo ethnicity. He also argues that being away from home played a major role in mobilizing migrant labourers along ethnic lines in Southern Africa. Similarly, Africans in a North American context, defined largely by the racialization of identities, are willing to subordinate the fragmentations that characterize their relations at home to a unity of purpose at different levels – ethnic, national, regional, religious, and continental (see Leblanc 2002). Abdusharaf (2002) describes Sudanese associations that transcend ethnic, religious, and regional differences as they juxtapose themselves vis-à-vis other groups in North America.

The objectives of ethnic associations are tailored towards meeting the needs of specific sub-national groups in the diaspora and at home. Contrary to the view that cultural differences will be eliminated in the era of modernity, there is a significant body of scholarship that contests the argument that "mobilization along ethnic lines dissipates with modernity" (Paul 2000, 25). Based on the extent of ethnically-based diaspora organizations, the evidence seems to suggest that ethnicity retains its ability to act as a catalyst for collective identity and mobilization. Individuals who share common backgrounds see their identities and their obligations, not only in relation to their host societies, but to their communities of origin and ethnic groups, as well. Hall (1999) points out that the process of globalization has intensified commitments to the local.

> The local, as far as the African diaspora is concerned, is not only the physical here and now, but also an imaginary or *distant* local. This imaginary local is defined by cultural affinity and shared origin, and though groups or individuals may be physically removed from their communities or ethnic groups, they nevertheless maintain ethical, cultural, and pecuniary obligations and linkages. They exhibit these through mobilization of their social capital towards specific projects to benefit their compatriots. (Tettey 2004, 131)

Examples of such mobilization abound in the African-Canadian community. In November 2003, members of the Agona Association of Canada, representing a particular area in Ghana, presented 3.3 million cedis (about CAD$500) to a local hospital in their hometown to defray the medical expenses, and hence secure the release, of a nineteen-year old man who had undergone surgery for a typhoid perforation. The association took the initiative after learning on the Internet that hospital authorities had detained the man because he and his family could not settle his medical bill (Ghanaweb 2003d). The connection between this action and the Internet is instructive. It shows how sojourners in the new physical ecology that has resulted from transmigration are taking advantage of the space-time compression capabilities of the new media ecology represented by the Internet to meet their obligations within the framework of a moral economy. The above example supports Faist's (2000, 196) assertion that "communities without propinquity link through reciprocity and solidarity to achieve a high degree of social cohesion and a common repertoire of symbolic and collective representations."

An intriguing phenomenon among some African-Canadians that sustains their links to families at home is the reverse of the *satellite children* phenomenon.

> The *satellite children* or *satellite kids* phenomenon is a result of a relatively new pattern of migration. The term *satellite kids* was first used in the late 1980s to describe children whose parents are Chinese immigrants to North America, mainly from Hong Kong and Taiwan, who have returned to their country of origin after immigration. The typical pattern is for the father to return to the country of origin to pursue economic advantages while the mother and the children try to settle in the new country. There are also cases of the mother returning or both parents returning. The family is divided by immense geographical distance, although regular visits are not uncommon. (Tsang et al. 2003, 360)

In the context of African-Canadians, economic necessity, the multi-step process of migration in some cases, and a desire to raise children in an environment and with values that are less permissive than is perceived to be the case with mainstream Canadian values, lead to people coming to Canada without their nuclear families. Thus, unlike the Chinese pattern described above, children and/or spouses (usually wives) stay back in Africa while the parent/partner makes a sojourn in search of better opportunities. In situations involving political refugees, an individual is compelled to leave his/her country without the family, and it may be a while before they re-unite.

Another dimension of the *astronaut family* (Tsang et al. 2003) arrangement involves cases where spouses choose to stay behind in the home country because they have good jobs which they are not willing to sacrifice in hopes of gaining commensurate or better positions in Canada. The discussion above regarding the deskilling and frustrations that many professionals have to deal with (Tettey 2001) discourages such people. They would rather get together regularly in Canada or their home countries than be subjected to the vicissitudes of life abroad. Many people in mainstream society have difficulty understanding how families can be separated by a vast ocean, sometimes for extended periods of time, when couples are still *together*. In some cases, there are perceptions that Africans involved in these arrangements are not committed to their families. These observers do not comprehend the complex economic, cultural, or political rationales behind these arrangements.

Interpersonal communication via e-mail and telephone also makes it easier for African-Canadians to be in touch with their friends and families and to be involved with issues and activities at home. This interaction is not only initiated from the diaspora, but originates from home countries, as well. The expansion in telephone services across the African continent and the springing up of Internet cafes in many urban areas in the last decade has made this possible. The downside of these technological advancements for Africans in the diaspora is the increased pressure that the ease of access imposes in terms of financial and other solicitations from friends and family, and the inability to escape the customary social obligations that continuous familiarity with events at home demand. Many African-Canadians acknowledge that there was less pressure in the period before the mid-1990s, when collect calls could not be made to Canada from many African countries. This meant that their physical distance shielded them from all but the most important occurrences in their home communities and within their families. As Dahan and Sheffer (2001, 85) observe, "the growing sophistication, availability, low costs, and ease of utilization of distance shrinking technology" have significant value for home-diaspora engagement.

TRANSNATIONAL POLITICS AND THE DIASPORIZATION OF CIVIL SOCIETY

While much has been written about civil society, the analyses have tended to dwell on domestic groups (see Hepner 2003). Where cross-national civil society has been addressed, the focus invariably tends to be restricted to transnational groups mobilized to address issues with global resonance, such as the anti-globalization movements. Not much attention has been paid to the emerging phenomenon whereby civil society activities pertaining to particular states are being *diasporized*, that is, how political engagement by citizens are being deterritorialized as a result of migration. To deal with the undertheorization of this phenomenon, Hepner (2003, 286) proposes "the concept of transnational civil society to address the specificities of such interventions for particular national communities and nation states." This concept allows us to explore processes of negotiation, contestation, power production and reproduction, and identity construction, as well as notions of belonging emanating from engagements between diaspora communities and their states of origin. It also provides insights into how diasporas are appropriating and applying discourses of transnational civil society (such as democracy, human rights, and the rule of law) to the specific realities of their territorialized homelands.

Whilst African-Canadians may be spatially removed from the discursive tensions that characterize their societies of origin, they are not immune from its manifestations in spite of the centripetal tendencies that their *otherness* and mutual experiences might engender. What happens, then, is a carry-over into Canada of ethnic tensions and suspicions, as well as political divisions that attend inter-group relations in the home countries. Rwandan Tsutsis in Canada were, for example, outraged at the decision by a Quebec court in April 2001 (later upheld by a federal court of appeal in September 2003) against the deportation of Leon Mugesera, who had been accused of giving a speech that incited genocide against Tsutsis. They considered the judge's ruling that Mugesera should not be charged with crimes against humanity a travesty of justice. In response to the verdict of the federal court, members of PAGE-Rwanda (Parents and Friends of Victims of the Genocide in Rwanda) appealed to the federal government to contest the decision of the court by taking the case to the Supreme Court of Canada. Together with other Rwandese associations in Canada, the group organized a demonstration in front of Parliament Hill to register its protest and to submit a petition to the Minister of Citizenship and Immigration demanding that the case be pursued at the Supreme Court (see PAGE-Rwanda 2003). It should be pointed out that, whilst this response was ostensibly supported by Pan-Rwandese associations in Canada, it appears to represent mostly Tsutsi voices. This is not surprising, since they were the ones who suffered the most from the genocidal actions of the Hutu majority. The literature points to the importance of memory as a crucial element of identity and ethnic mobilization. Esman (1994, 14), for example, contends that "[e]thnicity cannot be politicized unless an underlying core of memories, experience, or meaning moves people to collective action". It is worth mentioning that in November 2003, the Minister of Citizenship and Immigration announced that he will appeal the federal court's decision at the Supreme Court.

In similar instances of transnationalization of domestic politics, some members of the Sudanese community have been accused of being agents of the government in Khartoum (South Sudanese Community Association 2003). They are alleged to have engaged in a campaign designed to sow seeds of discord among their compatriots in Canada in order to stymie any coordinated opposition to the interests of the ruling regime. These *agents* are also perceived to be spies who report on the activities of political exiles.

The insertion of home country politics also tends to threaten national mobilization in the context of the diaspora and has implications for the viability of national associations there. Political conflicts are based, not only on differences in vision and policy regarding how social capital should be mobilized for home and diaspora purposes, they also flow from questions regarding who the beneficiaries of such activities would be vis-à-vis the politics of ethnicity and distribution that define the home country. As Hepner correctly observes, actors and beneficiaries are seen "as representatives of political positions, ethno-regional communities, social classes, or kin groups ... [e]mpowering individuals implied empowering specific collective identities over others" (Hepner 2003, 276). What is at play here is the retention of tensions and perceptions of hierarchy and power that attend relations among different groups in the countries of origin. The consequence is a weakening of national associations through internal strife (see Leblanc 2002).

Transnationalization of national politics and the diasporization of civil society provide a means whereby the African diaspora participates in, and influences, the domestic politics of their countries of origin. There are overseas branches of political parties, and African politicians make stop-overs in Canada to confer with, and solicit support from, members of their political parties or groups. Even though most Africans in Canada are not allowed to vote in national elections, they nonetheless serve as an attractive cohort for politicians who can count on their financial support to pursue their agendas. The following provides an illustration of how the diaspora inserts itself into the political processes and institutions of their homelands:

> The Network for Patriotism & Progress, the Montreal-Canada Chapter of the ruling New Patriotic Party has celebrated Three Years of the NPP administration with a Dinner/Dance in Montreal, Canada. The Community Center at 451 Ogilvy in Montreal's Parc Extension was festooned with the NPP slogans, party colors and a large portrait of President John Agyekum Kufour for the occasion ... Local Chapter Chairman, Nana Asumadu Duah recounted ... "that our government has delivered on all fronts and in fact it has over-delivered in just three years in power ... We have so far made steady progress but more needs to be done. We need to recruit more members for the task ahead of winning a second term next December and beyond in 2008." (Ghanaweb 2004)

Political contestation and negotiation sometimes involve diaspora communities demanding participation in political processes of their home countries and recognition of their status as bona fide citizens, even though they may be domiciled elsewhere. Itzigsohn (2000, 1141), for example, describes how Dominican, Salvadoran, and Haitian diasporas have demanded an extension in political space so that they can engage politically with their countries of origin. He argues that diaspora communities usually constitute "a third sector able to monitor and influence the activities of the state and private sector" (Itzigsohn 2000, 1136). Political interest groups within the African diaspora have lobbied host governments to support their causes.

> In some countries such as Canada the pro-democracy movements have worked with other organizations under an umbrella known as the Working Group on Nigeria. The groups bring together a diverse community of activists to strategize their work on Nigeria, and also relate with the Canadian government ... Canada more than any country has made more public comments against the military junta of General Abacha. (Shettima 1999)

As noted above, ethnicity is not just a means for primordial appeals of common origin. It can also serve instrumental purposes, whereby it can be used for different types of competitive mobilization, as well as be constructed for particular causes (see Paul 2000). Consequently, diaspora communities have appealed to ethnicity or nationalism as a means of mobilizing financial, political, and diplomatic support for causes in their homelands. Kurien (1999), for example, notes the massive contributions made by Hindus abroad to Hindu nationalism under the rubric of an intense Hindutva discourse. In Canada, Southern Sudanese groups have organized events and forums aimed at drawing the attention of the larger Canadian society to political developments in their home country. This is meant to galvanize pressure that can be brought to bear on the Canadian government to adopt a strong stance against the Sudanese government. In May 2003, the South Sudanese Community of Ottawa issued a statement condemning the visit of Sudan's Foreign Minister to Canada. It stated, *inter alia*:

1) If Canada wants to play a neutral role in the search for peace in the Sudan conflict as a mediator, it should accord equal chances to both parties; the Government of Sudan and the *SPLA*. We see the visit of the Sudan Foreign Affairs Minister to Ottawa as an *impediment to peace talks.*

2) Canada should clearly *denounce* the double standards applied by the Sudanese government of trying to negotiate peace with the *SPLA*, on one hand, while committing atrocities on the innocent civilians of Darfur Region at the same time. (South Sudanese Community 2003)

It is worth noting that the focus of political actions and protestations is not limited to the governments of the countries of origin. They are, in some cases, directed at the governments of the countries of domicile. This occurs when the latter governments are seen as pursuing policies that do not advance the interests of particular segments of the diaspora community. This was the case in February 2000, when the Federation of Sudanese Canadian Associations (FESCA) organized nationwide protests against the Canadian government's decision not to sanction Talisman Energy for its activities in the Sudan. Drawing from the Harker Report, FESCA argued that, by such an act of omission, the Canadian government was supporting the activities of an oppressive regime. It opined that

[t]he exploitation of oil in Sudan is widely acknowledged to be an important factor in the brutal civil war in Sudan. This was confirmed in the recent Harker mission report! Yet the Canadian government is refusing to use its powers to prevent Calgary-based Talisman Oil from operating in the region. (Federation of Sudanese Canadian Associations 2000)

Diaspora political activists have also targeted non-state actors whose activities bear on the domestic politics of home countries. Project Sudan, for example, credited sustained campaigns by various civil society groups and individuals against Talisman Energy for the decision of the company to stop operations in the Sudan. In a release issued by the group, it contended that

> [t]he impact of human rights activism against Talisman has clearly affected Talisman's share price and Talisman's credibility. Our persistent pressure over the past four years has been recognized by Talisman as a factor in their decision to sell. In Talisman's October 30 press release, Jim Buckee, Talisman CEO, states: "Talisman's shares have continued to be discounted based on perceived political risk in-country and in North America to a degree that was unacceptable for 12 percent of our production," he said in a release. "Shareholders have told me they were tired of continually having to monitor and analyze events relating to Sudan," Buckee said. (Project Sudan n.d.)

Similar activism was visible during the struggle of the Ogoni people of Nigeria against political repression by the government of Sani Abacha and the dangers posed by the exploitation of oil resources in the country's Delta region by multinational corporations. The Movement for the Survival of the Ogoni People (MOSOP) in Canada took a lead role in sensitizing the Canadian public and government about the atrocities being committed against the Ogoni people. It organized public lectures, memorial services, benefit concerts, and protest marches.

HOME AND THE DIASPORA: EXPLORING
THE TENSIONS AND DIALECTICS OF BELONGING

Many African-Canadians tend to think that because of the above-mentioned linkages with their countries of origin, they are as much in tune with the realities and lifestyles of those places as those who remain there. In reality, the situation is different. In fact, the diaspora community has been changed in ways that differentiate them in significant ways from their compatriots at home. It is therefore not surprising that a lot of African-Canadians come back from travels to their home countries with much frustration and trepidation about attitudes and behaviours that they consider unacceptable. There are, for example, complaints about lax attitudes towards work, corruption, absence of the rule of law, etc. The extent of culture shock that these sojourners experience in their countries of origin attests to their location in an *in-between* space and the *double consciousness* (Gilroy 1993) that results from being located in that space. While they feel a strong attachment to their home countries, they realize that they may no longer belong to those places in the sense that they are not really at home in the physical environment that their imagination and antecedent contacts make them think they share a lot in common with.

As pointed out earlier, Africa is undergoing significant socio-cultural changes. These changes can be shocking to African-Canadians, because at the same time as they try to exhibit, and inculcate in their children, *traditional* African values, continental Africans are imbibing Euro-American cultures at an alarming rate. Cultural globalization, or more appropriately, the cultural synchronization that is reflective of the significant influences of Euro-American culture, has led to the emergence of new cultural attitudes, values, and practices. This creates a double alienation for African-Canadians whose cultural preferences seem to be threatened on both sides of the Atlantic. The fact that children on the continent are imitating lifestyles that parents in the diaspora condemn and claim is un-African creates cognitive dissonance for their children when they visit their homelands. It also creates credibility problems for parents back in Canada, because they cannot claim an ideal African lifestyle worthy of emulation by their children.

Another area of cultural disconnect pertains to the excessive formality, in the African setting, of interactions in public institutions and the conspicuous display of status. Many African-Canadians who have adopted some of the informal attitudes of Canadian society find that their attitudes are not appreciated when they go back home. Many have recounted experiences in African organizations where they have not received the necessary attention from, or have been ignored by, officials, presumably because they do not look *important enough*. How they are attired becomes the marker of their status and hence, of the kind of service they get. The diaspora Africans, on the other hand, think it is ridiculous to dress in a suit and tie, for example, in the generally sultry African weather. However, in situations where there is no racial difference between the diaspora and the continental African, other non-verbal markers, such as appearance, are key to determining status, however inaccurate. Interestingly, White persons who dress as casually as the diaspora African are not subjected to the same criteria for determining status, because there is an implicit acknowledgement that their *Whiteness* makes them important and deserving of special treatment. Of course, this discriminatory treatment in their own countries of origin angers returning Africans and creates conflicts with their compatriots. The racialized nature of North American society has made African-Canadians sensitive to an extent that is far more intense than is the case with most people in their countries of origin, with the possible exception of South Africa because of its peculiar racial history. Diaspora Africans, having encountered discrimination and racism in their host society, are therefore critical of the perceived pandering to *White* visitors that is displayed by their compatriots.

African states have realized the contributions of the diaspora to socio-economic development and its potential as a huge asset to be tapped. At the same time, there is a strong desire among Africans domiciled abroad to retain their rights of citizenship vis-à-vis their home countries. These factors have given the issue of dual citizenship and its attendant rights a significant place in the discourse of the contemporary African diaspora, including those in Canada. Africans abroad argue that if they are expected to fulfill certain obligations to their countries of origin, then they must be accorded the rights and privileges that come with those obligations, even if they are not physically resident in those countries. Ghanaians abroad, for example, argued that since their remittances of about US$400 million constitute the fourth largest contribution to the national economy each year (Tettey 2002), they deserved recognition as bona fide legal citizens, even if they held other citizenships. So far, only a handful of countries have ceded to the demands of Africans abroad and allowed dual citizenship. Within this small group, only Ghana, South Africa, and Egypt have passed legislation recognizing such a status. It is worth noting that, even in these cases, beneficiaries of the laws may still be constrained in the kinds of rights they are able to exercise from abroad. For pragmatic and political reasons, these individuals may not be able to vote in national and sub-national elections from their current places of residence.

Despite some movement in the direction of granting dual citizenship on the continent and the fact that "in many countries of settlement a significant proportion of newcomers who get naturalized currently keep their former citizenship as well" (Faist 2000, 210), most African governments are reluctant to do so for a variety of reasons. The *Citizenship of Zimbabwe Act*, for example, prohibits dual citizenship and requires that someone with dual citizenship renounce his/her foreign citizenship in order to retain Zimbabwean citizenship. Even though this act was amended in 2003 to allow for some exceptions, those exemptions only apply in cases related to member countries of the Southern African Development Community. The government embarked on policy changes on the issue in 2001, with the aim of tightening regulations regarding citizenship:

> The official Ziana news agency also said the government was cutting to five years from seven the time in which a citizen could stay out of the country "without lawful excuse" before losing Zimbabwean citizenship. It quoted a government spokesman as saying President Robert Mugabe's ruling Zanu-PF party – which faces an unprecedented challenge sparked by a severe economic crisis – had been forced to tighten the rules to sideline opponents hiding under dual citizenship.
>
> "There are concerns that those with dual citizenship are behind efforts to discredit the government[sic] to use diplomatic and other means to topple the Zanu-PF. Lines of credit, aid, and other forms of assistance have been systematically stopped over the last couple of years to pressure the government," added the state-run *Sunday Mail* newspaper. (Chinaka 2001)

Concerns about the political agenda of citizens abroad are not limited to Zimbabwe, where it might be attributed to the paranoia of a dictator like Robert Mugabe. It is shared by other governments who worry about the potential for nationals with dual citizenship to engage in political destabilization of various sorts, hoping that they could retreat to the safety of their second country of citizenship if things go sour. Furthermore, governments believe that dual citizenship takes away their control over their citizens, because the latter can always avail themselves of the options provided by the other country if they are not satisfied with what their countries of origin provide. Finally, there is the argument to the effect that citizenship comes with certain responsibilities, such as paying taxes, which most Africans in the diaspora do not fulfil. Those who are against dual citizenship argue that diaspora Africans cannot claim rights and privileges, because only those who meet their obligations to the state can claim these.

CONCLUSION

In the preceding discussion, we used the concept of *translocational positionality* to interrogate the engagement that African-Canadians have with their societies of origin. This allowed us to explore linkages that extend beyond the cultural and enabled us to examine other dimensions of the diaspora experience, such as the transnationalization of civil society, the transfer into foreign climes of traditional differences, and the building of social capital for collective purposes. We argue that African-Canadians maintain a significant level of attachment to their countries and communities of origin. These linkages take a variety of forms and occur at differing levels of intensity for particular individuals and groups. The Internet and other communicative tools, such as music CDs and audio-visual broadcasts, also provide a *bridgespace* (Adams and Ghose 2003) that help Africans in the diaspora maintain an affinity to their compatriots and cultures of origin.

Some of the home-diaspora engagement occurs in the public sphere through conspicuous and affective displays of traditions – cultural remittances from the places of origin. As Nurse notes with regard to the Trinidadian Carnival in North America, these celebrations and observances as cultural activities are "not just about merriment, colourful pageantry, revelry, and street theatre. [They] are born out of the struggle of marginalized peoples to shape a cultural identity through resistance, liberation, and catharsis. It is these values that have facilitated [their] replication wherever the … diaspora is found. [They] have acted as a bond between the diasporic community and those at home" (1999, 662). Other linkages derive from a sense of obligation to places of origin that flows from a moral economy framework and the attendant mobilization of social capital for development initiatives at home. These occur at the individual, inter-personal, and group levels in the form of financial remittances and development-focused community initiatives. As Faist (2000, 191) observes, "[t]he concept of transnational spaces covers diverse phenomena such as transnational small groups, transnational circuits, and transnational communities. Each of these is characterized by a primary mechanism of integration: reciprocity in small groups, exchange in circuits, and solidarity in communities."

The evidence also shows that the imaginary home that serves as the basis from which the African-Canadian derives his or her sense of identity, and for which there is a constant longing, may be changing at the same time as it retains *traditional* elements and practices. It is, therefore, not the exact replica of the essentialized ideal on the basis of which the diaspora notion of home is constructed. On the other hand, the diaspora community, while it prides itself on its Africanness, is not identical to its home communities, because it has adopted ways of life that do not dovetail with the expectations or practices of their compatriots. Consequently, at the same time as we see evidence of solidarity and a sense of oneness between these groups, we also acknowledge that there are areas of difference and tension due to the dynamic experiences within these two locales. In recognition of this process of hybridity, Thompson (2002, 417) argues that "we may be entering a new, postmodern epoch in which the idea of a single, nation-state based identity is giving way to a more fragmented and hybridized spectrum of cultural identities."

"Diasporic activities and influence in the homeland, despite their international location, expand the meaning of the term *diaspora politics* to include not only politics inside the state but also inside the people" (Shain and Barth 2003, 451). It is clear that African-Canadians, like other diasporic communities, are engaged with political developments in their home countries. These include involvement in political activity on behalf of home-based political parties or governments, and mobilizing for particular interests vis-à-vis home and host states. While some may be passive or silent, all nevertheless share common interests with regard to issues around dual citizenship and the ramifications of the decisions that their home governments make regarding it. Corporate entities located in host societies, whose activities impinge on the domestic politics of countries of origin, are entangled in diaspora politics, as well. The discussion above about transnational politics and civil society enriches our understanding of "how differentiated transnational social fields become sites for the simultaneous reproduction and contestation of state-produced hegemonies within a deterritorialized civic sphere" (Hepner 2003, 288). The resulting strains have implications for the capacity, or otherwise, of various groups to work together in ways that are beneficial to the diasporic community as a whole and to the countries of origin. Finally, the discussion draws attention to an interesting phenomenon regarding the contestations that surround citizenship. The focus of much of the literature on migration and integration has been on difficulties that immigrants encounter as they seek full citizenship – both cultural and political – in their host countries. But as revealed above, there are many cases where immigrants are locked in conflict with their societies of origin on this same question, as governments, and indeed some compatriots, deny "political and cultural citizenship to the migrant on the grounds that emigration is inevitably accompanied by distancing and degeneration from the culture of origin" (Dirlik 1999, 107).

REFERENCES

Abusharaf, Rogaia M. 2002. *Wanderings: Sudanese Migrants and Exiles in North America.* Ithaca, NY: Cornell University Press.

Adams, Paul C., and Rina Ghose. 2003. India.com: The construction of a space between. *Progress in Human Geography* 27, no. 4: 414–37.

Africa Action. 2001 [online]. *"Disaster" beckons as U.S. cuts lifeline* [cited 5 April 2004]. (www.africaaction.org/docs01/som0111.htm).

Afro Drive. n.d. [online]. [cited 5 April 2004]. Churches and Places of Worship in Canada (www.afrodrive.com/AfricanChurches/default.asp?WCountryID=1).

Anthias, Floya. 2001. New hybridities, old concepts: The limits of "culture." *Ethnic and Racial Studies* 24, no. 4: 619–41.

Apt, Nana. 1996. *Coping with Old Age in a Changing Africa: Social Change and the Elderly Ghanaian.* London: Avebury.

Asanteman Council of North America. n.d. [online]. [cited 5 April 2004]. *An Interview with Nana Owusu-Akyaw Brempong* (www.acona-usacanada.org/news.html).

Bhabha, Homi. 1998. Culture's in between. In *Multicultural States: Rethinking Difference and Identity*, ed. D. Bennett, 29–36. London: Routledge.

British Broadcasting Corporation (BBC) News. 2003 [online]. *Can Africa keep time?* [cited 5 April 2004]. (www.news.bbc.co.uk/2/hi/africa/3211923.stm).

Burman, Jenny. 2001. Masquerading Toronto through Caribana: Transnational carnival meets the sign "Music ends here." *Identity: An International Journal of Theory and Research* 1, no. 3: 273–87.

Charlton, Karen. 1998. Health, health care, and ageing in Africa: Challenges and opportunities. *South African Journal of Gerontology* 7, no. 2: 1–3.

Chinaka, Cris. 2001 [online]. *Zimbabwe tightens ban on dual citizenship* [cited 5 April 2004]. (www.globalpolicy.org/nations/citizen/zimbabwe.htm).

Cusack, Igor. 1999. Being away from "home": The equatorial Guinea diaspora. *Journal of Contemporary African Studies* 17, no. 1: 29–48.

Dabydeen, David. 1988. Man to Pan. *New Statesman and Society* 26, August, 40–1.

Dahan, Michael, and Gabriel Sheffer. 2001. Ethnic groups and distance shrinking communication technologies. *Nationalism and Ethnic Politics* 7, no. 1: 85–107.

Dirlik, Arif. 1999. Bringing history back in: Of diasporas, hybridities, places, and histories. *Review of Education/Pedagogy/Cultural Studies* 21, no. 2: 95–131.

Esman, Milton J. 1994. *Ethnic Politics.* Ithaca, NY: Cornell University Press.

ExpoTimes. 2002 [online]. Voodoo rule (Part 45) *Witchcraft mentality in Toronto* [cited 5 April 2004]. (www.expotimes.net/backissuessept/sept00007.htm).

Faist, Thomas. 2000. Transnationalization in International Migration: Implications for the Study of Citizenship and Culture. *Ethnic and Racial Studies* 23, no. 2:189–222.

Federation of Sudanese Canadian Associations (FESCA). 2000 [online]. *Update: Talisman out of Sudan protests* [cited 5 April 2004]. (www.sandelman.ottawa. on.ca/lists/html/opirg-events/2000/msg00099.html).

Gerloff, Roswith. 2000. An African continuum in variation: The African Christian diaspora in Britain. *BTIB* 4: 84–112.

Ghanaweb. 2003a [online]. *Ghanaian real estate developers to exhibit in Canada* [cited 5 April 2004]. (www.ghanaweb.com/GhanaHomePage/diaspora/artikel. php?ID=38546).

———. 2003b [online]. *Divisions and multiplications in Ghanaian churches in Canada* [cited 5 April 2004]. (www.ghanaweb.com/GhanaHomePage/economy/artikel. php?ID=47078). November 21.

———. 2003c [online]. *Methodist churches in Toronto move towards unity* [cited 5 April 2004]. (www.ghanaweb.com/GhanaHomePage/economy/artikel. php?ID=48387). December 17.

———. 2003d [online]. *Agonas in Canada fund medical bill of boy* [cited 5 April 2004]. (www.ghanaweb.com/GhanaHomePage/NewsArchive/printnews. php?ID=47131). November 22.

———. 2004 [online]. *Montreal NPP celebrates three years of positive change* [cited 5 April 2004]. (www.ghanaweb.com/GhanaHomePage/economy/artikel. php?ID=49690). January 12.

Giddens, Anthony. 1985. *The Nation State and Violence*. Cambridge: Polity.

Gilroy, Paul. 1993. *The Black Atlantic: Modernity and Double Consciousness*. Cambridge, MA: Harvard University Press.

Hall, Edward T. 1994. Monochronic and polychronic time. In *Intercultural Communication: A Reader*, ed. L. A. Samovar and R. E. Porter, 264–71. Belmont, CA: Wadsworth.

Hall, Stuart. 1999. "A Conversation with Stuart Hall." *Journal of the International Institute*. University of Michigan, Ann Arbor. (Fall): 15.

Hepner, Tricia R. 2003. Religion, nationalism, and transnational civil society in the Eritrea diaspora. *Identities: Global Studies in Culture and Power* 10: 269–93.

Itzigsohn, Jose. 2000. Immigration and the boundaries of citizenship: The institution of immigrants' political transnationalism. *International Immigration Review* 34, no. 4: 1127–53.

Kurien, Prema. 1999. Gendered ethnicity: Creating a Hindu Indian identity in the U.S. *American Behavioral Scientist* 42, no. 4: 648-70.

Leblanc, Marie Nathalie. 2002. Processes of identification among French-speaking West African Migrants in Montreal. *Canadian Ethnic Studies/Études ethniques au Canada* 34, no. 3: 121–41.

Manning, Frank. 1990. Overseas Caribbean carnivals: The arts and politics of a transnational celebration. In *Caribbean Popular Culture*, ed. J. Lent, 20–36. Bowling Green, OH: Bowling Green University Popular Press.

Nurse, Keith. 1999. Globalization and Trinidad carnival: Diaspora, hybridity, and identity in global culture. *Cultural Studies* 13, no. 4: 661–90.

PAGE-Rwanda. 2003 [online]. (Parents and Friends of Victims of the Genocide in Rwanda) Communiqué de la Communauté Rwandaise du Canada Mugesera ne devrait pas Avoir Droit de Cité au Canada; OBSERVATOIRE DE L'AFRIQUE CENTRALE 6, no. 39, 22–28 Septembre [cited 4 April 2004]. (www.obsac.com/OBSV6N39-CommRWLtrMugese.html).

Patterson, Orlando. 1994. Ecumenical America: Global culture and the American cosmos. *World Policy Journal* 11, no. 2: 103–17.

Paul, Rachel A. 2000. Grassroots mobilization and diaspora politics: Armenian interest groups and the role of collective memory. *Nationalism and Ethnic Politics* 6, no. 1: 24–47.

Pendakur, Manjunath, and Radha Subramanyam. 1996. Indian cinema beyond national borders. In *New Patterns in Global Television: Peripheral Vision*, ed. J. Sinclair, E. Jacka, and S. C. Cunningham, 67–82. Oxford: Oxford University Press.

Project Sudan. n.d. [online]. *Project Victory! Talisman is out of Sudan* [cited 5 April 2004]. (www.sudan.activist.ca/news/talismanout.html).

Qadeer, Mohammed. 1998. Ethnic Malls and Plazas: Chinese Commercial Developments in Scarborough, Ontario. Working Paper, Joint Centre of Excellence for Research on Immigration and Settlement Series, Toronto.

RainBowNation. n.d [online]. [cited 5 April 2004]. (www.rainbownation.com/polls/votes.asp?PollID=3).

Rapport, Nigel, and Andrew Dawson. 1998. *Migrants of Identity: Perceptions of "Home" in a World of Movement.* Oxford: Berg.

Richmond, Anthony. 2002. Globalization: Implications for immigrants and refugees. *Ethnic and Racial Studies* 25, no. 5: 707–27.

Shain, Yossi, and Aharon Barth. 2003. Diasporas and international relations theory. *International Organization* 57: 449–79.

Shain, Yossi, and Martin Sherman. 2001. Diasporic transnational financial flows and their impact on national identity. *Nationalism and Ethnic Politics* 7, no. 4: 1–36.

Shami, Seteney. 1998. Circassian encounters: The self as other and the production of the homeland in the North Caucasus. *Development and Change* 29: 617–46.

Shettima, Kole A. 1999 [online]. Nigerian Pro-Democracy Movements in the Diaspora. Paper presented at the ISA Conference, February, Washington, DC. [cited 4 April 2004]. (www.webdata.soc.hawaii.edu/fredr/shet.htm).

South Sudanese Community Association of Ottawa-Carleton. 2003 [online]. *On the visit of Sudan National Islamic government Foreign Affairs Minister to Ottawa* [cited 5 April 2004]. (www.gurtong.net/localnews/article_28.html). May 14.

Svasˇek, Marusˇka. 2002. Narratives of "home" and "homeland": The symbolic construction and appropriation of the Sudeten German Heimat. *Identities: Global Studies in Culture and Power* 9: 495–518.

Tettey, Wisdom J. 2001. What does it mean to be African-Canadian? Identity, integration, and community. In *A Passion for Identity: An Introduction to Canadian Studies*, 4th ed., ed. D. Taras and B. Rasporich, 161–82. Toronto: ITP Nelson.

———. 2002 [online]. Africa's brain drain: Networking diaspora communities for socio-economic development. *Mots Pluriels* no. 20, February [cited 5 April 2004]. (www.arts.uwa.edu.au/MotsPluriels/MP2002wjt.html).

———. 2004. Globalization, diasporization and cyber-communities: Exploring African trans-nationalisms. In *Globalization and the Human Factor: Critical Insights*, ed. E. Osei-Prempeh, J. Mensah, and B-S. K. Adjibolosoo, 121-42. London: Ashgate.

Thompson, Kenneth. 2002. Border crossings and diasporic identities: Media use and leisure practices of an ethnic minority. *Qualitative Sociology* 25, no. 3: 409–18.

Tsang, Ka Tat, Howard Irving, Ramona Alaggia, Shirley Chau, and Michael Benjamin. 2003. Negotiating ethnic identity in Canada: The case of "satellite children." *Youth and Society* 34, no. 3: 359–84.

White, Elisa J. 2002. Forging African diaspora places in Dublin's retro-global spaces: Minority making in a new global city. *City* 6, no. 2: 251–70.

Williams, Rhys. 2002. Religion, Community and Place: Locating the Transcendent. *Religion and American Culture* 12, no. 2: 249-63.

9

BETWEEN HOME & EXILE:
Dynamics of Negotiating Be-Longing
among Young Oromos Living in Toronto

Martha K. Kumsa

INTRODUCTION

T HIS CHAPTER PRESENTS an empirical study
examining the experiences of negotiating
be-longing among young Oromo refugees
living in Toronto.[1] I use hyphenated be-longing
to unfreeze the fixity in conventional notions of
predetermined belonging and to emphasize the
often-obscured movement and fluidity inherent in
the longing in belonging (Ilcan 2002; Philip 1992;
Probyn 1996). The study is part of a larger work
in which I explore the experiences of navigating
the shifting territories of identity and cohesion.[2]
I selected a small, community-based sample of
eighteen self-identified, young Oromos of varying
age, class, gender, religion, region of birth, level of
education, routes to Canada, immigration status,
and proficiency in *Afaan Oromo*[3] and English.
Rich qualitative data were generated through
story telling, evocative exercises, one-to-one and
small group conversations, individual and group
reflections, activity participation (participant observation), and a focus group debate. Narrative

activities and exercises were structured around the Lifeline Exercise (Nadeau 1996) divided into weekly themes including childhood memories, experiences of flight/dislocation, life in Canada, dreams and nightmares, and hopes for the future. We met every week in three small groups and in four one-to-one sessions for an average of seven weeks in two rounds. This process built up to a larger focus group debate at the end of the second round of weekly sessions.

Data were generated from February to May 2001, and all sessions were both audio- and video-taped. Six events of ethnographic activity participation were completed intermittently. Throughout those weeks, participants shared sacred stories and precious objects, they sang songs and chanted poems. They cried and laughed as they made sense of their narratives, disputed meanings, and reflected on and co-theorized their personal and collective experiences. For the most part, negotiating meanings and reconstructing narratives happened throughout the multiple sessions of the prolonged engagement as part of my broader strategies of minimizing the effects of power between the researcher and participants (Lather 1991; Smith 1999). But I continued to negotiate my interpretations with participants to enhance trustworthiness as I further analyzed the data. For analysis, I used critically interpretive and reflexive strategies of hermeneutics (Avelsson and Sköldberg 2001; Denzin 2001; Geertz 1973; Mason 1996; Myerhoff and Ruby 1982). To enrich my interpretive repertoire, I used multiple models of narrative analysis from across disciplinary boundaries, including literature, anthropology, psychoanalysis, psychology, and sociology (Cortazzi 1993).

My analysis evidenced that narratives are context-sensitive, collaboratively constructed, edited, and reconstructed stories (Chambon 1995; Chanfrault-Duchet 1991; Gubrium and Holstein 1998; Linde 1993). It showed that stories and narratives constitute the strings by which participants construct a sense of self at the same time as they weave themselves into the fabric of the wider society. Indeed, an overarching finding of the study indicated that the intricate processes of negotiating multiple layers of identity and cohesion are also processes of constructing multiple layers of be-longing simultaneously. For the scope of this chapter, I focus on be-longing and present an analysis of three themes that emerged from the data. I explore competing theoretical perspectives throughout the analysis. But first, background regarding the *glocalizing* processes that brought the young Oromo refugees to Canada is provided.

OROMO GLOBALIZATION

The globalization of Oromo refugees is a unique facet of wider African globalization. By African globalization, I mean the movement of African bodies through global spaces. In this depiction, African globalization is an ancient phenomenon. Some works claim the presence of Africans in Ireland and Britain long before Indo-Europeans arrived in the area (Ali and Ali 1994) and of African travelers in ancient Greece (Miles 1989). But Africans were also forcefully removed from their homelands and brought into the New World during the Atlantic Slave Trade (Rodney 1972). Although Africans are no strangers to forceful mass displacements, I see a dramatic difference between the slave and refugee facets of African movement to the West. In the sixteenth century, Africans were dragged out of their homeland, tied, bound, and brought to the West under torturous duress. Today, coercion has changed in form, content, and direction, thus policing the boundaries and preventing Africans from coming to the West (Chimni 1998; Richmond 1994). While African slaves desperately refused to come then, now many Africans desperately seek to come to the West. They line up at the gates of immigration offices and consulates to acquire immigrant and visitor visas. News headlines seethe with hundreds sinking and perishing in overloaded boats heading for Europe. Many African refugees wait in refugee camps for years and go through the ordeal of humiliating interviews to get resettled in the West.

Historicizing this incredible reversal is crucial for understanding the current realities of the young Oromo refugees in this study. As theorists, such as Fanon (1963) and Foucault (1979), would argue, in the period between the slave and refugee facets of African globalization, the application of disciplinary coercion has moved from the physical body to the soul. This transformation in the technologies of coercion coincides with the emergence, consolidation, and globalization of modernity, with its liberal principles, just as colonialism and imperialism account for the emergence of the nation-state. Just as the nation-state sits at the heart of modernity, the production of refugees sits at the heart of the nation-state. Processes that create and gel together the nation-state also exclude and expel deviants as refugees at one and the same time (Adleman 1999; Keeley 1996). Yet the production and expulsion of refugees is never an isolated internal and local process. It results from the interplay of powerful local and global forces engaged in the project of creating and maintaining nation-states through inclusion and exclusion (Chimni 1998; Ilcan 2002; Moussa 1993). More often than not, regimes that produce refugees are regimes that are put in place by outside forces to serve the interests of external powers (Abdi 1987; Woodward 1987; Zolberg, Shurke, and Aguayo 1989).

African representation in Western imagination has been shifting in congruence with the changes and continuities of the processes by which African bodies move through global spaces. Thus, ancient Greeks and Romans depicted Africans as physically different human beings and as the imagined *Other* – the barbarian beyond the borders – just as they depicted all those who were different from them. Christianity imagined the African as the evil Other, the devil, Satan (Miles 1989). At the dawn of modernity, Western imagination represented the African as the tormented brute savage (Hobbes) and the noble savage (Rousseau), but savage nonetheless (Mama 1995). As skin colour gained *scientific rationality* at the height of modernity and scientific discovery, the inferiority and non-human status of the African became *objective truth*. These representations served to create conditions for, and justify the brutalities of, slavery, colonialism, imperialism, and the *White Man's Burden* of the civilizing mission. Indeed, forces that moved the bodies of African slaves to the West and those that currently move the bodies of African refugees across multiple national boundaries are the same forces using shifting representations and serving different phases of capitalism (Miles 1989; Wallerstein 1997).

The movement of Oromo refugees in the global space is part and parcel of this larger process. Oromos are among the ancient indigenous peoples of the Horn of Africa region, mostly inhabiting present-day Ethiopia, Kenya, and Somalia. Long before Oromo refugee bodies were globalized, ideas about Oromos had migrated to the West mainly through the activities of Western explorers, slave traders, travelers, missionaries, military personnel, anthropologists, and historians. Until recently, extant literature referred to Oromos as Galla, although the people refer to themselves as Oromo (Hassen 1990; Hultin 1996; Jalata 1993; Lata 1998; Melba 1988). Most ethnographic accounts depict the Oromo egalitarian socio-political system of *gadaa* as a powerful instrument of Oromo collective self-identification (Blackhurst 1978; Baxter 1978; Hultin 1996; Kassam 1987; Kassam and Megerssa 1996; Knutsson 1967; Legesse 2000; Van de Loo 1991). While ethnographic works are subtly political, the more overtly political works come from Ethiopianist historiography that constructs Oromos as Gallas and as Others of both ancient and *modern* Ethiopia (Bahrey 1954; Clapham 1990; Haberland 1963; Levine 1974; Ullendorff 1960).

Beyond the racialized imagining of the African Other, then, Oromos stir Western imagination in yet another layer through unique images of Ethiopia. Sorenson (1992) identifies two more othering discourses: anti-communism and Christian mythology. While anti-communist discourses project the image of communist Ethiopia as war-ravaged and a famine-stricken land of poverty and starving children, they have also provided sanctuary for Oromo refugees fleeing from the horrors of communist Ethiopia. In Christian mythology, ancient Ethiopia is constructed as the land of Prester John, the legendary Christian king who triumphed over Islam and whom Europeans sought to locate somewhere in Abyssinia. As the Other of ancient Ethiopia, then, Galla evokes the image of an invading horde of heathens threatening to engulf this Christian island of Abyssinia. As the Other of modern Greater Ethiopia, Galla evokes the image of the uncivilized savage and the inherently *inferior* invading horde bent on destroying modernity and civilization (Hultin 1996; Lata 1998; Melba 1988; Triulzi 1994; Zitelmann 1996). In both cases, the images evoke Western collective unconscious as strong Western identification with, and desire for, Ethiopia, and strong disidentification with, and aversion for, its Oromo Other.

This unfavourable location of Oromos in Western imagination has serious implications for young Oromo refugees, and indeed, for Oromo self-identification in the contemporary glocalizing world dominated by the West and by Western institutional structures. Hence, Melba (1988, 3) laments that Oromo history "is a work [historians] have unjustly treated or unjustifiably ignored in the past," and Lata (1998) warns that Oromos may have cast off the Galla label, but the negative images it evokes persist in the present politicized workings of Western institutions. Legesse (2000) reveals a racialized layer of Western selective identification and disidentification. He glorifies the Oromo *gadaa* as a uniquely African, democratic political system and calls to question Western silence on *gadaa*. Charging the West and Western anthropologists categorically, he specifically takes Fortes and Evans-Pritchard (1940) to task for leaving *gadaa* out of their typology of African political institutions. Asking why (and answering his own question), Legesse writes:

> Was it really because they could find no evidence of democratic institutions in Africa? Did they consider these institutions to be so different from their Western counterparts that they could not possibly be examined under the same intellectual rubric? Was it any more justifiable to compare African and European monarchies, than it was to compare African and European democracies?
>
> I suggest that both types of institutions were equally divergent from, or comparable to, the European prototypes. However, since monarchy was in decline in most of Europe, and the transition to democracy became the epitome of Europe's highest political aspirations, admitting that some varieties of democracy were firmly planted in Africa in the sixteenth century when in fact they were not fully established in Britain, the United States and France until the seventeenth or eighteenth centuries and in some parts of Europe as late as the middle of the twentieth century would have made the ideological premise of the *civilizing mission* somewhat implausible. The idea, further, that African democracies may have some constitutional features that are more advanced than their European counterparts was and still is considered quite heretical. (2000, 29–30)

Such Western identification with Abyssinia and aversion for its Oromo Other sits at the heart of the historical processes that constructed imperial Ethiopia as a modern nation-state and continued to perpetuate the repression of Oromos through years of colonial domination. The massive exodus of refugees is a simultaneous product of the construction of Ethiopia (Holt 1970; Marcus 1975) and the continued maintenance of its hegemony (Abdi 1987; Bulcha 1988, 2002; Clay and Holcomb 1986). An invention of powerful global and local players, Ethiopia was created as a territorial political entity through a unique extension of the infamous western-colonial "Scramble for Africa" (Holcomb and Ibssa 1990). Oromo resistance that later developed into an Oromo national liberation struggle (Hassen 1990; Jalata 1993) was a localizing response to these globalizing processes of colonial expansion. Although they constitute more than half of the Ethiopian population numerically, Oromos were reduced to a politically-dominated, economically-exploited, and culturally-degraded minority. As Western powers continued to consolidate Ethiopian hegemony, their aversion for Oromos crystallized in their violent repression and repeated brutal bombings of Oromo peasants when they rose up against the tyranny of Abyssinian[4] colonialism (Jalata 1993; Melba 1988).

The discursive construction and consolidation of Ethiopia as a hegemony of the Amhara minority ethnic group automatically excluded the Oromo majority, thus forming the crucible in which Oromo national identity was constructed as a counter-hegemonic, discursive practice (Hultin 1996; Megerssa 1996; Lewis 1996; Triulzi 1994). When centuries of oppression exploded into a revolution in 1974 and the pet regime of the West came tumbling down, Western powers lost Ethiopia to the Eastern side of the Cold War divide. This time, even the Oromo national liberation struggle gained some support from the American-led Western nations in fighting against the communist regime. This time the West promised to facilitate the building of true democracy in Ethiopia (Lata 1999). After the 1991 overthrow of the regime, however, they reneged on their promises and instated another Abyssinian minority ethnic domination – this time the Tigre. Thus, as these mutually exclusive, antagonistic identities competed, many Oromos, including the parent(s) of the young Oromos in this study, were jailed, disappeared, executed, exiled, or joined the armed resistance.

Most Western nations continued to actively support the Tigrayan minority group even as they blatantly derailed the fledgling democracy. When the conflict intensified, the West dealt Oromos a bittersweet deal by denying them the necessary support for democratic participation in the affairs of the country but facilitating the *safe departure* of Oromo leaders out of the country into exile (Lata 1998, 1999). When this led to a massive exodus of Oromo refugees, Western NGOs led by the United States made a concerted effort to prioritize the resettlement of Oromo refugees in the West. While it seems humanitarian on the surface, this subtle process resulted in removing the *Oromo roadblock* and facilitating the Tigrayan move to establish a single-ethnic, single-party, minority dictatorship in Ethiopia. The young Oromos in this study came to Canada as part of these complex processes within the nation-state. Some came as children with refugee adults, others as minors reuniting with their refugee parent(s) or as refugees in their own right. And these processes have a deep impact on them, not only because their very dispersal from the homeland is predicated on Western disidentification, but also because this disidentification continues to shape the texture of their mundane, everyday living and sense of be-longing.

UNCERTAIN SPACES OF BE-LONGING

In this section, I theoretically position this paper among the voices in the literature and move on to critically analyze how the different perspectives play out in the empirical data. By analyzing three layers of be-longing: belonging to Canada, be-longing with Blacks, and be-longing with Oromos, I attempt to make visible the need for an alternative framework.

Voices in the Literature

The depiction of be-longing is a hotly disputed territory where two principal, polarized perspectives compete. In nativist discourses, every person belongs to a natural and authentic ethnic or national group rooted in a natural habitat; a homeland. The national substance, the essence that makes one a member of the nation, is transmitted from generation to generation via genealogical continuity (Armstrong 1982; Conner 1994; Van den Berghe 1992). In this sense, "full belonging, the warm sensation that people understand not merely what you say, but what you mean, can only come when you are among your own people in your native land" (Ignatieff 1993, 7). Constructionist discourses dispute this essentialist fixity and argue that be-longing to any categorical identity is created within social relations and through multiple forms of othering and exclusion (Ilcan 2002; Probyn 1996). In nativist discourses, be-longing is given, final, and binding. In constructionist views, it is a constant movement through social distance, neither final nor binding. But how do refugees negotiate these disputed territories of be-longing? And how do these polarized notions of be-longing empirically play out in the experiences of refugees?

Empirical studies of the experiences of refugees abound. Extant literature is steeped with them. Bosnian refugees in Australia (Colic-Peisker and Walker 2003) and the United States (Keyes 2000), Somali refugees in the United Kingdom (Griffiths 1997), Burmese (Hyndman and Walton-Roberts 2000), Ghanaian (Manuh 1998; Opoku-Dapaah 1992), Salvadoran (Jacob 1994; Young 2001), Southeast Asian (Phillion 2001; Beiser 1999), Central American (Hrycak 2001), and Eritrean and Ethiopian women (Moussa 1993) refugees in Canada are only a few examples. Some works localize the problem of settlement and focus on issues of mental health, loss, and victimization (e.g., Beiser 1999; Kamaldeep 2002; Kohli and Mather 2003; Young 2001). Others externalize the focus towards global, structural barriers (Alastair 2003; Leddy 1997; Opoku-Dapaah 1992). While most of these studies do not directly examine identity or be-longing, the issues they do examine sit at the core of identity and be-longing, albeit implicitly. Many studies do examine identity as their core issue (see Camino and Krulfeld 1994; Fantino and Colak 2001; Griffiths 1997; Manuh 1998; Okeke-Ihejirika 2003; Phillion 2001; Saucier et al. 2002). However, they fall short of making the theoretical link between identity and be-longing. Indeed, there are studies that do explore refugee be-longing (see Jodeyr 2003 and Kohn 2002), but they too fall short of making visible the intimate link with identity and cohesion. This intimate link remains invisible even in works that critically interrogate borders and develop transnational frameworks for research (Hyndman and Walton-Roberts 2000) and argue for postnational practice (Alastair 2003).

Zooming in on the experiences of Oromo refugees, studies range from those examining political factors in Oromo refugeeization (Abdi 1987; Bulcha 1988, 2002; Clay and Holcomb 1986) to those exploring issues of identity in Oromo refugees (Gow 2001, 2002; Sorenson 1996). Other works whose main focus is on other groups also discuss experiences of Oromo refugees as asides (Matsuoka and Sorenson 2001; Sorenson 1992, 1993). Reflecting the wider polarization, however, this body of literature is also permeated with a dichotomous depiction of Oromo identity. While some present a strong nativist depiction (Bulcha 1988, 2002), others hotly dispute this and paint a strong constructionist picture instead (Sorenson 1992, 1996). Furthermore, like their cohorts in the wider discourse, these works fail to explore the intimate interwovenness of identity, cohesion, and be-longing. I argue, therefore, that without this crucial link, studies with refugees and other diasporic communities cannot overcome the constraining blindfolds of these dichotomized perspectives.

Coming to Canada as an Oromo refugee myself and subjecting my three teenage children to the refugee life, I find these mutually exclusive binaries severely constraining. They fail to capture the complexities of our experience as we attempt to make sense of our new realities and relate to each other in a new way in a new land. They fail to capture the lived, mundane realities of many Oromo refugees, young and old alike. They foreclose the creative possibilities of the in-between spaces of marginality in which refugee lives are embodied and embedded. Some works do capture these spaces of hybridity by making visible both the shifts and the fixities in the construction of identity among Oromo refugees (Gow 2001, 2002). Beyond overcoming the great nativist-constructionist divide, however, these works hardly make the crucial link between identity and be-longing. It was in an attempt to make sense of our reality and bridge this yawning gap in the production of knowledge that I embarked on the study of identity and cohesion. In this journey, I have discovered the intimate link to be-longing and developed what I call dispersal-affinity as an alternative conceptual framework for both analysis and practice. To elicit and stress the need for dispersal-affinity, therefore, I critically engage competing perspectives in the literature as I construct my analysis of the empirical material in the following subsections.

Be-longing to Canada

For young Oromo refugees, escaping the horrors of Ethiopia and landing in Canada does not automatically mean they be-long to Canada. Canadian belonging is a contested territory they have to negotiate artfully in ways unique to them. As well, Ethiopia is not something they leave behind or escape

(Matsuoka and Sorenson 2001). They continue to wrestle with temporally and spatially dislocated Ethiopia. Encounters with Abyssinians in Toronto mean renegotiating old power relationships in their new home, where old hostilities continue in new ways. The stereotypical question, Where are you from? draws war-ravaged Ethiopia right into the heart of their interaction with Canadians. Television images of starving Ethiopians peer at them through Canadian eyes. Racializing discourses congealing Canada as a White nation greet them the instant they arrive, and they have to make sense of what it means to be Black in Canada. They experience these as exclusionary boundaries of be-longing that they have to negotiate. The discourse of Canadian peacekeeping is constructed against the touchstone of warring Others, thus congealing Canada as a peaceful nation and sending the message: If you are from warring Others, you don't be-long with us. Television images of famine and poverty are constructed against Canadian plenty and wealth, erecting more boundaries of othering and not be-longing. Below are some narrative clips from primary school encounters of those who came to Canada as children.[5]

> EDO: It's little kids stuff … [They say] "I see you guys on TV," blah blah blah and joke around … You know, the poor people thing … malnourished kids come on TV. So they go, "You guys are poor" and stuff like that. And I go, like, "Well, I'm not Ethiopian!" They go, like, "What are you?" I'm, like, "Oh, shut up," or something, you know? … [They say] "You're Ethiopian! You look Ethiopian!" … I go, "That's a different part of that country, I'm not from that part that you see on TV!"… I don't wanna be known as Ethiopian, but I have to say Ethiopian because nobody knows our problem …

> WARTU: Yeah! Is it true that in Ethiopia you drink dirty water? I'm, like, "No! Like, what part of Ethiopia? Like, I've never even seen that part! I never seen dirty water back home!"

> IBSITU: And it makes you, like, it makes you feel, like, bad inside, like, you know, did I really come from there? But I get mad, and I get really defensive.

Yet Ethiopia is shrouded in ambiguity, and sometimes identifying Oromo kids as Ethiopians is not to exclude, but to include them as those different from the different Other – to distinguish them from *bad* Blacks and Africans. Here, Western identification with Ethiopia is at work:

> IBSITU: And sometimes they think it is a complement, too. They go, "No, you're not African, you look different, you're not Black."

> WARTU: You don't look African …

KUWEE: You're Brown, not Black?

IBSITU: Yeah, my friend's, like, she hates Africans, OK? She goes, "I think African girls are so rude." I'm, like, "Excuse me! I'm African!" She goes, "No, you're not. You're not African, you're like, you know, you're, you're ..." "I'm African!" (people laugh) She goes, "You're not!" I go, "I'm Black!" And "You know, Ethiopians are so different!" I go, "But we're African, though." She goes, "You are?" I'm just, so stupid!

Thus, even after the rupture with Ethiopia and escape to Canada, Ethiopia maintains its symbolic grip through its discursive continuity in Canadian imagination. Be-longing to Canada requires negotiating these formidable boundaries of exclusion and becoming Canadians. Throughout the sessions, including the larger focus group, participants shared experiences and discussed various layers of becoming Canadians and be-longing to Canada. Below are some excerpts.

WALANA GROUP

WARTU: Those kind of things make you feel, like, "You know what? I don't belong here!" Even if you're a citizen, you know you don't belong there ... It doesn't make any difference if you are a citizen. It doesn't change you to say, "You know what, I'm Canadian because I'm a citizen."

ADDOOYYEE GROUP

JALANE: Do you consider yourself, ... like, do you feel like a Canadian citizen?

DINSIRI: There is always the back home for me. So I don't feel Canada is, like, you know, my country. But at the same time, I feel that I am, I pay my taxes; I do any other thing other Canadians do. So I'm as much a Canadian as they are ...

JALANE: But is that sort of a *head* knowledge ... or do you really, really feel that? Like, do you really feel you're a Canadian? (people laugh)

AYANE: I mean, how do you feel like a Canadian? ... I do feel like a Canadian, I feel like an Oromo and a Canadian ... Whether I like it or not, I have a lot of Canada in my life ... a lot of Canadian culture ... a lot of Canadian things are a part of who I am ...

JALANE: What does it mean to be Canadian?

AYANE: You can be a Canadian and, for example, if your family was Chinese, and you were born here, you can be a Canadian. But you will still have something else, but as long as you don't have that other level, like, your identity and culture, you don't have anything else. That's a Canadian!

KUWEE: So who is a Canadian?

AYANE: You have to have European ancestry [if] you're a Canadian ... a very volatile definition, but still, if you are European, you're Canadian.

JALANE: If you are European, you're Canadian?

AYANE: That's the same for me ... you have to be White to be Canadian.

JALANE: How can you feel Canadian, then, if you're not White?

FOCUS GROUP

F: But there's a difference! ... I am an Oromo by identity and a Canadian by citizenship. But, like, I'm not, like, Canadian by identity and culture and ...

M: Hold on! Hold on! Hold on!

F: No! There's a difference! No! No! No! Citizenship and identity are different!

M: Whose culture are you living in?! (laughs)

M: Sure, everybody can be Canadian! But say if I become a Canadian, and let's say I rob a bank, then I'm no more a Canadian. Everybody is gonna say, he's an immigrant from Ethiopia, or something. (people laugh)

F: That's true! You're not Canadian.

M: That's right!

M: But if you do, like, if I play football or basketball good, then they're gonna say I'm Canadian. (people laugh)

GAMMEE GROUP

EDO: I don't wanna forget my background and say I'm Canadian. I do wanna be called Oromo-Canadian, because I do live here and ... because I did grow up here, too, so ... I don't wanna just exclude Canada ...

Y. B.: Canada is not like Africa to me. I like it still … No, I don't feel like I belong, but I still feel home, if I go for a different place to move, whatever, I still miss Canada … I still feel home. That's the only town I like. I stayed here longer …

YOM: I feel like I'm an Oromo. I don't feel like I'm a Canadian at all! I wish I could …

LATIFA: I'm a Canadian citizen … but I don't know; I don't consider myself to be Canadian. Like, I consider myself Oromo-Canadian, I don't know … OK. Like, when I went to Australia, I felt homesick … and I wanted to come back to Canada. Yeah. Even when I went to the States, I couldn't wait to come back to Canada, to Toronto … This is where I always come back.

GEE: Me, I just got my citizen! (people laugh) … Proud? … No. I feel that little bit happy because I can leave and come back. Even if I could go home, back home, and come back anytime I want. They can't say no to me, you know. I am Canadian! … I think, me, I'm Oromo, period! … people in this country could call me Canadian-Oromo. If they prefer, they could call me Oromo. I don't care!

What comes out loud and clear from these narratives is the tension between citizenship and nationality (dubbed identity) – citizenship associated with contingency, and nationality with essence. Nationality is tangled up with a deeper sense of home, ancestry, and origin (Armstrong 1982; Conner 1994; Geertz 1973; Van den Berghe 1992). The thicker the blood and the farther back it goes into genealogy and history, the deeper the sense of be-longing it evokes. Participants experience this end as a site of exclusion with no space to become Canadians and be-long to Canada. Oromos are and will always be Oromos, and Canadians always Canadians. At the other end of the tension, however, most participants experience citizenship as a site of inclusion, as something malleable and instrumental, something they can weave into their Oromo souls, become Canadians, and be-long to Canada. Yet they know that Oromos cannot *really, really feel* Canadian and be-long to Canada, as they find be-longing to be layered. They can attain some dimensions of it, but true Canadianness is something unreachable, something that remains beyond acquiring culture, paying taxes, and gaining citizenship. Navigating this tension between the exclusion and inclusion of essence and contingency, participants seek solace in the hybridity of becoming Oromo-Canadian and flutter between Oromoness and Canadianness. This fluttering varies from participant to participant and, for a participant, from moment to moment.

This tension also makes visible another tension between the routes (mobility) of exile and the roots (anchorage) of home in the discourses of globalization and diasporization (Clifford 1997; Ilcan 2002; Malkki 1997). Participants experience home and be-longing as both fixed and mobile, depending on which discourses they slip in and out of. In the nativist discourses, home is fixed and tangled up with homeland, as Wartu laments, "those kind of things makes you feel like, 'You know what? I don't belong here!'," with or without Canadian citizenship. She can only be-long to one, and only one, authentic nation rooted in its true homeland, and that is where she is born. Constructionist discourses challenge such deep territoriality of the nation and one-to-one correspondence between peoples and places (Gupta and Ferguson 2001; Malkki 1997). Speaking from within these discourses, Y. B. and Latifa long for Toronto when they long for home, and a male focus group participant defines his Canadian be-longing situationally, depending on whether he robs a bank or plays basketball "well." Thus, beyond the instrumentality of Canadian citizenship and the exclusivity of its nationality, participants challenge the notions of both fixity and eternal mobility. They create a fluid space between home and exile where they perform their unique sense of home and be-longing (Bhabha 1994; Gow 2002; Ilcan 2002; Probyn 1996). In this space, be-longing is experienced and performed as layered and multifaceted.

Be-longing with Blacks

Just because racializing discourses that congeal Canada as a White nation mark them as Blacks and leave them out, it does not mean that Blackness is up for grabs for young Oromos. As a form of categorical identity, Blackness has to be negotiated and earned. Participants encounter immense conflicts, both within their families and in the communities among their Black peers. On the one hand, Oromo families and community elders cope with the colour-coded exclusion by splitting Blackness into good and bad, thus triangulating the Black/White, bad/good dichotomies in order to be different from the different (Cole, 2003). They attempt to control and *save* their children from dressing like, talking like, and walking like, *bad* Blacks. They strive to save them from Jamaicans who they assume epitomize bad Blackness. On the other hand, some of their Black peers challenge young Oromos for not being Black enough and for being nerdish and acting White (Dei et al. 1997). It is in the context of these forces tearing them apart that young Oromos negotiate the hotly contested territories of Blackness – away from the White world, yet so deeply immersed and soaked in it.

Y. B.: Once you're Black, you're Black! … They treat you the same.

GEE: They don't care if you are African.

LATIFA: You know what? That Jamaican thing, I think that's in the African culture.

Y. B. That's within Africans. Basically, to White people, Black is Black. There's no such thing as Jamaican to them. Just, once you're Black, you're Black …

LATIFA: No! It's just, like, to the Ethiopians, like, Jamaicans are the bad guys, and then, to the other White culture, it's just Black in general … Like the Oromo and Ethiopian culture, they use Jamaican as a negative.

To White people, "Once you're Black, you're Black," says Y. B., speaking from homogenizing discourses of racialization. It is only Oromos and other Africans that label Jamaicans as bad Blacks. And group members agree on this. Thus, as the young Oromos hold adults responsible for badmouthing and portraying Jamaicans in a negative light, divisive schemes of racialization and their project of lateralizing conflict slip by unnoticed. Despite discourses of homogeneity, however, Blackness proves to be a deeply contested territory where boundaries are moved and re-moved, displaced and re-placed. This discursive multiplicity and fluidity affirms the claim that Blackness is a historical category rather than a skin colour (Hall 1996). It is a space of multilocality where young Oromos have to bend, transform, and relocalize it into their unique singularities. As an uneven site of difference and struggle, Blackness has to be negotiated and earned. Who is Black and who is not is disputed and constantly contested. Fully embracing and longing to be-long in Blackness is not good enough to be accepted into the space of those who identify as Black. This is evidenced in the clip below:

GEE: He just say, "Fake nigger!" (people laugh) … Some Jamaican guy, he's just saying that because … "Fake nigger, fake nigger!" I looked at him. I'm sending message, he just don't. I looked at him, I shook my head and turned around, and he's still talking. I meant it, if he understanding me, I mean, like, you're nigger, too! What the hell, you're cursing yourself, too! And I'm talking.

KUWEE: Maybe he meant, fake means, like, you're not a real nigger, he is the real nigger?

GEE: No! Not even just that. It's just that, I don't know. Some niggers just don't have a line to talk to girls.

LATIFA: No, fake nigger, there is no definition behind it. Not just …

EDO: May be, like, it means, like … What he said is, like, I'm a nigger, you know, it shows how, like, I don't know, man! (people talk)

GEE: You weak, you not, you can't stand out for yourself …

LATIFA: Weak, like a wannabe.

GEE: Weak, like you wanna be Black.

Y. B.: Yeah, fake, weak.

Latifa says, "Fake nigger, there's no definition behind it," but Gee interprets it as, "You weak," and "You can't stand out for yourself," and "You wanna be Black." To me, this suggests that Gee's Blackness is not real enough for his Jamaican friend. At best, it is an aspiration, and Gee is a *wannabe Black*. At worst, it is bogus Blackness, and Gee is a *fake nigger* who does not deserve the appellation. This puts Gee in an ambiguous position in the eyes of his friend. He is Black, just like himself. Yet he is not Black, in that his Blackness does not quite contrast with the White Other. Here, neither Blackness nor Whiteness signifies a skin colour. If the fake Blackness in the above clip is shrouded in vague terms, below it is crystallized in the name of Ethiopia:

KUWEE: So [your White friends] recognize you as different from other Blacks. And how about other Blacks?

EDO: Yeah. They kind of segregate you, too. Not if you, like, it depends how you act with them …

YOM: Yeah. I know, like, when I first came, I used to have this Jamaican friend. He thinks, like, we Ethiopians, we don't act like we're Black. So he told me that he doesn't like Ethiopian people … Yeah, like, he told me they act like Whites. He thinks, like, we say we're White, and we're not Black and stuff.

KUWEE: And we kind of look down on them, on other Black people, right?

YOM: Yeah, that's why they don't like us.

EDO: But we mix! I mean, my school is, like, Black. They are usually, like, Jamaicans. Like, I don't hang around with them, but we say, like, always, hi, whatever. So.

KUWEE: But you don't get really closer and become friends?

EDO: Because of my mom, you know. (giggles) She's, like, making me hate them … I don't know. It's the way they [Oromo parents] talk about them. It's the way they hate and, I don't know. They hate everybody, man! (laughs)

They don't like Jamaicans, or ... They don't like the way they dress, you know. So as soon as you do something, they think you are a part of that, you know. That's not true. But it does put something on you, like ...

Here, the hating of Ethiopians is ironic, in that Ethiopia constituted the very symbol of Blackness. The love of Ethiopia was first crystallized into the movement of "Ethiopianism" in Jamaica (Cohen 1997). But some Jamaicans don't like Ethiopians and, by extension, Oromos. And the sentiment of hostility is constructed as mutual, thus, yet again, obscuring the racializing processes that pit them against each other in the first place. Thus, to some Jamaicans, Oromos evoke the African, and Africa spells multiple ghostly returns of the repressed from the collective unconscious of enslaved Africans. As Cohen argues, "To many, *Africa* signified enslavement, poverty, denigration, exploitation, White superiority, the loss of language, and the loss of self-respect" (1997, 40). Africans from the continent also signify Africans that collaborated with White slave raiders and sold their ancestors into slavery. Seen in this light, some Jamaicans experience this as a deep-seated aversion in their encounters with Ethiopians and Africans.

Sometimes these hostilities erupt into confrontations, even for Gee, who believes he be-longs with Jamaicans fully. Sometimes Oromoness and Blackness are mutually exclusive, and Gee faces a deadly situation where he has to choose between his Oromo and Jamaican be-longing:

He's, like, half Oromo, and he used to go to my school ... I saw him getting beat up by Jamaican people. Like, ten people and him alone, like, beating him up ... These guys are my friends, and the guy, I know him too. I just don't know him too well, but I know him as Oromo, period. But I know the Jamaican people more. I chill with them ... Cool friend with me, you know. Sometimes we hang around. But this guy, Oromo guy, we don't talk a lot. I just know him. So I went in and stop, "Yo, leave him, leave him, leave him!" There is this other guy, the same Jamaican people, don't like me, you know, we don't get along. He's kind of, like ... "So, Yo, what? You got any problem? Yo, what up, what up, are you gonna help us or what?!" And I told them, "Leave the kid alone, he just wanna get out of here, you can't even fight one on one? Just leave him alone, I know the kid, leave him alone!" So this guy say, "You wanna stick up with that nigger now? What up? What up?" He start pushing me. I say, "Yo, cool yourself down, man, you know me, cool yourself down!"

And he went around, and after two day, three day, he came in the washroom. I was in the washroom. He came behind me, and he said, "What up, man?" I look back and I say, "What up, what's goin' on?" I swear to God, he put a gun on my head! He told me, "Yo, I will shoot you down and leave here. And don't you ever, ever step to me!" ... And he's shaking, too, the same time. I knew he's scared. But it's just that, you know, he's trying to be, you know, powerful. And he's pulling that gun. I swear to God, this kid scare me! I was scared, I be honest … "Yo!" I said, "Nigger! Stop poking me up!" I say, "Yo! Get out of my face!" And the kid's, like, "You wanna deal one deal?" And I tell him, "Yo, I have nothing to do with you, you now. I didn't even say nothing to you. What you put a gun on me for?" And the kid say, "You shut up!" You know how kids get powerful, you know? You know how it is when you carry a weapon behind … I cut that kid up, and I went to the other niggers we chilling with, and I say, "Yo, what's wrong with this guy? You know, he's acting stupid … the young thug, you know, the young blood …." And after, the same kid came up to me and say, "Sorry, you know; I'm your friend."

Gee's simultaneous be-longing in Oromoness and Blackness came to logger-heads dangerously and physically. He be-longs with both warring identities, but the in-between space could not contain him safely. His deadliest confrontation was when Black gangs attacked him and knocked out his four upper front teeth. At other times, Gee navigates comfortably in his be-longing with both Blacks and Oromos. Though perhaps not as deadly as Gee's experience, other participants also experience Blackness as an uneven terrain of multiple definitions they have to tread, sometimes in harmony and solidarity and other times in discord and conflict. They find that *their* Blackness wears other shades of yet other colours when reflected back from the eyes of their Black peers who define Blackness in their own unique ways. For some participants, their Blackness gets reflected back tainted with colours of backward, uncivilized Africans. For others, it is smeared with *Fresh off the Boat* (FOB). "They don't like us; to them we are FOB refugees," laments Qoricha about her Black peers. "Even the streets have the toughest rules and skills; I was so green I couldn't fit in," moans Jaba, longing to be-long with his Black peers who define Blackness differently and defend its boundaries with passion.

Other times, the young Oromos find other Black peers with whom they redefine their unique Blackness in ways that make be-longing comfortable. For example, finding that being a serious student is stigmatized as *acting White* and being a *nerd* (Dei et al. 1997), Edo, Jaba, and Yom befriend other Blacks who rename excelling in education as *acting Black*, and they embrace it like other Blacks before them (Willie 2003). Thus, young Oromos continue to bend and localize the boundaries around Blackness to fit their realities and their deepest needs of be-longing. They continue to further contest and dispute the territory of Blackness. And they find that they cannot fully and wholly be-long with Blacks despite their deepest yearnings. Even Gee, who gains a sort of be-longing by doing *nigger talk* and *nigger walk* and by being *bad* and being *cool*, learns the hard way that be-longing is neither final nor complete (Ilcan 2002). And when the Blackness of their peers could not wholly contain *their* Oromo

Blackness, participants long back to wholly be-long with their Oromo peers. Would their Oromo be-longing be final and binding?

Be-longing with Oromos

Away from colour-coded be-longing, even the most taken-for-granted turf of Oromoness, where the young Oromos automatically and naturally long to be-long, presents a hotly disputed terrain. Who is authentic Oromo and who is not is fiercely contested, and participants are torn apart by yet other forces shaping their be-longing. On the one hand, young Oromos embrace Oromoness and passionately defend its boundaries against encroaching Others. Now there is no boundary among them and they be-long with each other. On the other hand, the moment the external boundary dissolves and the young Oromos face each other, old internal boundaries reincarnate and new ones emerge. And now participants define and redefine the boundaries of their unique Oromoness and defend them against their own Oromo peers.

Thus, in the context of negotiating Canadianness where Canada threatens to swallow their Oromoness, participants hold on to Oromoness and adopt the Oromo-Canadian hyphenation. They actively background the Canadian end and foreground the Oromo. In their encounters with threatening Oromos from the United States, however, they reverse this dynamic in an interesting twist. In this movement, Canada surges into the foreground as Oromo recedes. They embrace the Canadian end of the hyphen closely and defend it against Oromo-Americans, thus endearing Canada, be-longing to it, and reversing the hyphenation as Canadian-Oromos. Usually, even the hyphenation is discarded, and they refer to themselves as Canadians. Thus Oromos seek each other out at the same time as they shy away from each other into their Canadian and American be-longing. This finding makes visible the ways in which young Oromos weave together the same strands of geographically designated identification differently to construct different longings of be-longing in different contexts (Ilcan 2002). This is evidenced in the clip below:

> TICK: They [American Oromos] actually do treat us different way when we went for our tournaments there. You Canadians, eh? … We went there, and then, you know how the White Canadians, when they go to the U.S., they use that word, Eh? Eh? Eh? (people laugh). They're like, you Canadians, eh, like, you know. And then, how is it up there? You guys play hockey, too, you guys do that? How is it freezing, na na na? And go back to your ice! When they come here, we kind of feel different about them, too, like they're gangsters! … When we … Odaa and Oromia [Toronto Oromo soccer teams] go to the U.S., we cheer for each other, and the Americans cheer for their own. Beat those Canadians, la, la, la …

JABA: Oromo in Canada, the poor guys, the one's taking the welfare, right? And who will live in Metro housing and the Oromo in America who work in gas stations ... When the Atlanta people came and played against Toronto, they were saying, "*Deemnee dhukkee irraa kaafna!* [Let's go beat the shit out of] those people on welfare!"

IBSITU: You know those Atlanta guys, they're crazy, OK? ... they party a lot, whatever, eh? So, I guess they were asking us, let's go home ... We go, "No!" You know, you don't get that much excited, right? Then they go, "What's wrong with you? See American girls back home."

WARTU: Back home in America! (people laugh)

IBSITU: Yeah! "See, they're chill, they're chill ... Like, you guys, you're so stush!"

WARTU: They have this mentality, like ... Canadian girls are, like, more cheap; they love Americans. They think that we love them, they think we love Americans!

All of these non-hyphenated references to Americans and Canadians are all references to young Oromos in the United States and in Canada, respectively. The boundaries within Oromoness are constructed and consolidated just when the boundaries around it are dissolved. The territoriality of Oromoness and its attendant be-longing is localized and firmly re-inscribed in geography just at the point where Oromoness itself is actively deterritorialized and globalized (Clifford 1997; Gupta and Ferguson 2001; Malkki 1997). While the soccer tournaments bond young Oromos together, their local geographical identities interrupt this bonding and fragment Oromoness. This further demonstrates that be-longing can never be final or complete (Ilcan 2002). *Us* and *them* are reterritorialized, and who longs to be-long where is geographically determined, thus simultaneously and paradoxically freezing and unfreezing Oromoness.

As Wartu and Ibsitu's narratives in the above clip suggest, young Oromos also seek each other out for intimacy. They long to be-long together intimately. Indeed, Ayane's narrative affirms this. Yearning for intimacy, young Oromos have actively created and maintained Oromo youth spaces on the Internet. By so doing, they further de-territorialize and create digital Oromoness in the virtual space. As an active participant in this process, Ayane says,

That was after Atlanta soccer tournament ... so we came back, and it was all sorts of different connections ... People came from everywhere from the U.S. and then us from Canada. And it's people we knew from back home, you know … but you met new people, too, so after that, we tried to keep everybody together. But it was really such a nice thing to be among Oromo young people. It was such a positive experience, and we wanted it to continue, so that's how the virtual community was started … for a lot of people, this was a way to meet others, not only friends, but also meet potential mates, partners, boyfriends, girlfriends, whatever.

Scattered all over the globe, young Oromos seek each other out as they long to be-long with each other. Like other dispersed peoples in the lands of others (Bhabha 1994), the young Oromos find themselves alienated from the familiar and desperately seek solace in cyberspace (Herbst 2001). They use the Oromo *gadaa* as a symbolic anchor (Gupta and Ferguson 2001) of community and be-longing. Herbst names this anchor *GadaaNet* to signify this seeking of solace in the ideal of the ancient Oromo *gadaa*. Speaking out of such deep longing to be-long, Ayane says, "It was really such a nice thing to be among Oromo young people." Yet there was no shortage of young Oromos in Toronto. But these were Oromos either from a different region of Oromia or they are from a different religion, and Ayane felt left out. Ayane's longing for digital Oromia comes from this place of Oromo exclusion. In an ironic reversal, however, she looks back on this space of be-longing and detests the very Internet youth group she helped create:

> Those Americans are weird. I ended up hating that group … They think they have reached *there*, you know! They show off, like, This is us! This is the life! We are living it! They're *there*, you know, no more growth. No, no, no! Excuse me! I call this rotting! … They say they love intelligent, hard working, independent Oromo girls. But they lie! They're liars, honestly! … That's a very closed group! When it comes to the real stuff, they choose ornamental girls, decorative girls, you know.

Ayane's narrative indicates the gelling together of an exclusive young Oromo elite group in digital Oromia, and how the face-to-face spaces of inequity extend into the virtual space. In the first place, those who go online are those who have the physical, instrumental, and technical access to the Internet. Far beyond the digital divide, class, gender, language, region, and religion interplay in the inclusion/exclusion of constructing longing and be-longing in digital Oromia. The fierce exchanges in chat rooms reveal that be-longing is not only deterritorialized but also stratified within digital Oromia. Indeed, side by side with its provision of solace, *GadaaNet* (Herbst 2001) also creates hotly contested spaces of longing to be-long.

Globalized Oromoness is further fragmented and relocalized in many more ways. When the boundary between Canadian and American Oromos dissolves, others are raised among Canadian Oromos. And they split Oromos into *olders* and *young bloods*, embracing the young, othering the old. When the boundary of age dissolves and the young bloods face each other, they split into FOB (freshies) or old timers, from this or that religion, and from this or that Ethiopian province. Boundaries are moved and re-moved, vanish and reemerge, creating new longings to be-long. Oromoness gets so illusive that young Oromos start asking who, then, is an Oromo? Now the boundaries move elsewhere to separate those who are pure and those who are mixed, those who speak *Afaan Oromo* and those who do not. Oromoness is localized again by ancestry and by language. But those who come from mixed ancestry and those who do not speak a word of *Afaan Oromo* fiercely claim Oromoness. Disrupting yet another undisputed territory of racialized Oromoness, they discover blond, blue-eyed, White Oromos. Constantly moving between settlement and unsettlement (Ilcan 2002), they unsettle even their most settled beliefs in the purity of genealogical be-longing and ideas of blood and ancestry. Be-longing to Oromoness proves as deeply contested as other identities; it cannot be taken for granted.

TOWARDS AN ALTERNATIVE FRAMEWORK

The findings from the above analysis both validate and unsettle extant notions of be-longing. The essentialist view constructing authentic be-longing as a warm sensation that comes from being among one's own people who understand, not what one says, but what one means is untenable. Findings do validate this position, in that the young persons feel intense affinity for Oromos back home and that they essentialize their own be-longing. But this does not mean that this intense longing to be-long is inherent. Nor does it mean that warm understanding comes only from other Oromos. Participants have enjoyed warm understanding in their interaction with others and bitter misunderstanding in their interaction with Oromos. In its emphasis on continuity, however, the essentialist view overlooks the discontinuities of meaning and understanding. Its fixity forecloses the fertile possibility of young Oromos be-longing in the here and now of life in Canada. In this, the findings validate the constructionist notion of constantly negotiated and fluid be-longing. They validate the constant longing in be-longing and the constant desire and yearning for the Other. In its emphasis on movement, however, this position overlooks the continuities and fixities also inherent in the longing in be-longing. Moreover, emphasizing desire and longing to be-long, this position overlooks the aversion, the longing not to be-long. Yet the findings strongly indicate both desire and aversion in be-longing, thus affirming the flight and search in dispersal-affinity.

The findings emerging from the analysis also indicate that dispersal-affinity is layered. Taking into account both movements and fixities, dispersal-affinity responds to the simultaneous flight and search in the young Oromos' simultaneous seeking and shying away. In congruence with these realities, dispersal-affinity interweaves four paradoxical spaces into a meaningful whole. First, the temporal space signifies the paradox of continuities/discontinuities. Here the past is deeply ingrained in the rolling present and anticipated future. Not only the discontinuities of the refugee facet, but also the continuities of the slave facet of African globalization, shape their negotiation of be-longing. Secondly, the glocal space signifies the paradox of global/local. Here, intertwined processes of global homogenization and local fragmentation shape their deepest sense of be-longing as they negotiate be-longing in the interface of diasporization and globalization, territorialization and deterritorialization, placement and displacement. Thirdly, the reflexive space signifies the paradox of conscious/unconscious. Here, be-longing is negotiated in the conscious-unconscious blur of both the individual and the collective. This accounts for the ghostly return of the slave in the everyday racialization of their be-longing. Fourthly, the relational space signifies the paradox of singularities/multiplicities. In this space, be-longing is negotiated in the dialogue between the unique singularities of individual participants and the ordinary multiplicities of the social. Here, be-longing is a relational process of Self and Other, signifying myriad creative possibilities of dispersal/affinity.

CONCLUSION

In summary, then, for young Oromos, the notion of be-longing is tangled up with ever-increasing uncertainty. Fully be-longing to Ethiopia is impossible, because it leaves out their Oromoness. Landing in Canada does not mean they automatically be-long to Canada. Despite homogenizing discourses of racialization, fully be-longing with Blacks is not possible either. Nor is fully be-longing with Oromos possible, despite their intense affinities. Every turf of be-longing has to be contested and its boundaries negotiated, as nobody can be "simultaneously in all, or wholly in any" categorical identity (Haraway 1991, 193). In this sense, I view be-longing as a living space of poetics, thus affirming the notion of movements in and through social relations in the longing in be-longing (Ilcan 2002; Probyn 1996). However, these are not just movements of Self towards Other. These are fiercely directional movements in that the young Oromos long away from spaces of perceived exclusion and oppression towards spaces of perceived inclusion and freedom. This has important implications for social justice. If justice is defined as freedom from oppression (Young 1990), I see the longing in be-longing as a longing for justice. If be-longing is a Self/Other relational process and thus requires demarcation of boundaries to make sense of the world, then the question, for me, has little to do with erasing boundaries. As the findings indicate, boundaries seem to be a fact of life. It seems impossible to think of a world without boundaries (Lamont and Molnar 2002). Nor is this necessarily desirable in my view. For me, the question is how can we make the crossing of these boundaries easy and equitable? How can we make multiple layers and forms of be-longing readily available? How can young

Oromos be-long with Oromos, with Blacks, with Whites, and with other groups in Canada, elsewhere in the world, and back home in Africa?

REFERENCES

Abdi, Taha. 1987. The plight of Oromo refugees in the horn of Africa. *Refuge* 6, no. 4: 7.

Adleman, Howard 1999. Modernity, globalization, refugees and displacement. In *Refugees: Perspectives on the Experience of Forced Migration*, ed. A. Ager, 1–23. New York: Pinter.

Alastair, Christie 2003. Unsettling the "social" in social work: Response to asylum seeking children in Ireland. *Child & Family Social Work* 8, no. 3: 223–31.

Ali, Ahmed, and Ibrahim Ali. 1994. *The Black Celts: An Ancient African Civilization in Ireland and Britain.* Wales: Punite.

Alvesson, Mats, and Kaj Sköldberg. 2001. *Reflexive Methodology: New Vistas for Qualitative Research.* London: Sage.

Armstrong, John. 1982. *Nations before Nationalism.* Chapel Hill: University of North Carolina Press.

Bahrey, Abba. 1954. The history of the Galla. In *Some Records of Ethiopia, 1593–1646*, ed. C. F. Beckingham and G. W. Huntingford, 111–29. London: Hakluyt Society.

Baxter, Paul T. W., and Uri Almagor, eds. 1978. *Age, Generation and Time: Some Features of East African Age Organizations.* London: C. Hurst.

Beiser, Morton. 1999. *Strangers at the Gate: The Boat People's First Ten Years in Canada.* Toronto/Buffalo/London: University of Toronto Press.

Bhabha, Homi. 1994. *The Location of Culture.* London: Routledge.

Blackhurst, Hector. 1978. Continuity and change in the Shoa Galla Gada system. In *Age, Generation and Time: Some Features of East African Age Organizations,* ed. P. T. W. Baxter and U. Almagor, 245-67. London: C. Hurst.

Bulcha, Mekuria. 1988. *Flight and Integration: Causes of Mass Exodus from Ethiopia and Problems of Integration in the Sudan.* Upssala: Scandinavian Institute for African Studies.

———.2002. *The Making of an Oromo Diaspora.* Upssala: Scandinavian Institute for African Studies.

Camino, Linda A., and Ruth M. Krulfeld, eds. 1994. *Reconstructing Lives, Recapturing Meaning: Refugee Identity, Gender, and Culture Change.* New York: Routledge.

Chambon, Adrienne S. 1995. Life history as dialogical activity: "If you ask me the right questions, I could tell you." *Current Sociology* 43, nos. 2–3: 125–35.

Chanfrault-Duchet, Marie-Françoise. 1991. Narrative structures, social models, and symbolic representation in the life story. In *Women's Words: The Feminist Practice of Oral History,* ed. S. B. Gluck and D. Patai, 72-92. New York: Routledge.

Chimni, B. S. 1998. The geopolitics of refugee studies: A view from the South. *Journal of Refugee Studies* 11, no. 4: 350–74.

Clapham, Christopher S. 1990. *Transformation and Continuity in Revolutionary Ethiopia.* Cambridge: Cambridge University Press.

Clay, Jason W., and Bonnie K. Holcomb. 1986. *Politics and the Ethiopian Famine, 1984–1985*. Cambridge: Cultural Survival.

Clifford, James. 1997. *Routes: Travel and Translation in the Late-Twentieth Century*. Cambridge, MA: Harvard University Press.

Cohen, Robin. 1997. *Global Diasporas*. London: University College of London Press.

Cole, Alyson. 2003. Triangulating the Black/White Divide: The Case of Julius Lester. Paper presented at the thirty-first annual conference of the National Association for Ethnic Studies, 3–5 April 2003, Phoenix, AZ.

Colic-Peisker, Val, and Iain Walker. 2003. Bosnian refugees in Australia. *Journal of Community & Applied Social Psychology* 13, no. 5: 337–60.

Connor, Walker. 1994. *Ethnonationalism: The Quest for Understanding*. Princeton: Princeton University Press.

Cortazzi, Martin. 1993. *Narrative Analysis*. London/Washington: Flamer.

Dei, George S., Josephine Mazzuca, Elizabeth McIsaac, and Jasmine Zine. 1997. *Reconstructing "Drop-Out:" A Critical Ethnography of the Dynamics of Black Students' Disengagement from School*. Toronto/Buffalo/London: University of Toronto Press.

Denzin, Norman K. 2001. *Interpretive Interactionism*. 2nd ed. Thousand Oaks: Sage.

Fanon, Frantz. 1963. *The Wretched of the Earth*. New York: Grove.

Fantino, Ana Marie, and Alice Colak. 2001. Refugee children in Canada searching for identity. *Child Welfare* 80, no. 5: 587–96.

Fortes, Meyer, and E. E. Evans-Pritchard, eds. 1940. *African Political Systems*. London: Oxford University Press.

Foucault, Michel. 1979. *Discipline and Punish: The Birth of the Prison*. Translated by A. Sheridan. New York: Vantage.

Geertz, Clifford. 1973. *The Interpretation of Cultures*. New York: Basic.

Gow, Greg. 2001. Viewing "Mother Oromia." *Communal/Plural* 9, no. 2: 203–22.

———. 2002. *The Oromo in Exile: From the Horn of Africa to the Suburbs of Australia*. Melbourne: Melbourne University Press.

Griffiths, David. 1997. Somali refugees in tower hamlets: Clanship and new identities. *New Community* 23, no. 1: 5–24.

Gubrium, Jaber F., and James A. Holstein. 1998. Narrative practice and the coherence of personal stories. *Sociological Quarterly* 39, no. 1: 163–87.

Gupta, Akhil, and James Ferguson. 2001. Beyond "culture": Space, identity, and the politics of difference. In *Culture, Power, Place: Explorations in Critical Anthropology*, ed. A. Gupta and J. Ferguson, 33–51. Durham/London: Duke University Press.

Haberland, Eike V. 1963. *Galla Sud-Aethiopiens*. Stuttgart: Kohlhammer.

Hall, Stuart. 1996. Ethnicity: Identity and difference. In *Becoming National: A Reader*, ed. G. Eley and G. Suny, 339–49. New York: Oxford University Press.

Haraway, Donna. 1991. *Simians, Cyborgs, and Women*. New York: Routledge.

Hassen, Mohammed. 1990. *The Oromo of Ethiopia*. Cambridge: Cambridge University Press.

Herbst, L. E. 2001. *Globalgadaa: Oromo Democracy in Diaspora and on the Internet.* Paper presented at the forty-fourth annual African Studies Association meetings, Houston, TX.

Holcomb, Bonnie K., and Sisai Ibssa. 1990. *The Invention of Ethiopia: The Making of a Dependent Colonial State in Northeast Africa.* Lawrenceville, NJ/Asmara, Eritrea: Red Sea.

Holt, Peter M. 1970. *The Mahdist State in the Sudan, 1881–1898: A Study of Its Origins, Development, and Overthrow.* Oxford: Clarendon Press.

Hrycak, N. R. 2001. Central American Refugee Women: A Help-Seeking Model. Ph.D. diss., University of Calgary, Calgary, AB.

Hultin, Jan. 1996. Perceiving Oromo: "Galla" in the great narratives of Ethiopia. In *Being and Becoming Oromo: Historical and Anthropological Enquiries,* ed. P. T. W. Baxter, J. Hultin, and A. Triulzi, 81–91. Lawrenceville, NJ/Asmara, Eritrea: Red Sea.

Hyndman, Jennifer, and Margaret Walton-Roberts. 2000. Interrogating borders: A transnational approach to refugee research in Vancouver. *Canadian Geographer* 44, no. 3: 244–58.

Ignatieff, Michael. 1993. *Blood and Belonging: Journeys into the New Nationalism.* Toronto: Viking/Penguin.

Ilcan, Suzan. 2002. *Longing in Belonging: The Cultural Politics of Settlement.* Westport, CT/London: Praeger.

Jacob, André G. 1994. Social integration of Salvadoran refugees. *Social Work* 39, no. 3: 307–12.

Jalata, Asafa. 1993. *Oromia and Ethiopia.* Boulder: Lynne Reinner.

Jodeyr, Simin. 2003. Where do I belong?: The experiences of second generation Iranian immigrants and refugees. *Psychodynamic Practice: Individuals, Groups, & Organizations* 9, no. 2: 205–14.

Kamaldeep, Bhui, ed. 2002. *Racism and Mental Health: Prejudice and Suffering.* Philadelphia: Jessica Kingsley.

Kassam, Aneesa. 1987. The process of becoming: Gabra Oromo transition rites (Jilla). *Azania* 22: 55–75.

Kassam, Aneesa, and Gemetchu Megerssa. 1996. Sticks, self, and society in Booran Oromo: A symbolic interpretation. In *African Material Culture,* ed. M. J. Arnoldi, C. M. Geary, and K. L. Hardin, 145–66. Bloomington: Indiana University Press.

Keeley, C. B. 1996. How nation-states create and respond to refugee flows. *International Migration Review* 30, no. 4: 1046–66.

Keyes, E. F. 2000. *The Experience of Bosnian Refugees Living in the United States.* Ph.D. diss., University of Virginia.

Knutsson, Karl E. 1967. *Authority and Change: A Study of the Kallu Institution among the Matcha Galla of Ethiopia.* Gothenburg: Museum of Ethnography.

Kohli, Ravi, and Rosie Mather. 2003. Promoting psychosocial well-being in unaccompanied asylum seeking young people in the United Kingdom. *Child & Family Social Work* 8, no. 3: 201–12.

Kohn, R. 2002. Belonging to two worlds: The experience of migration: Commentary. *Journal of South African Psychiatry Review* 5, no. 4: 6–8.

Kumsa, Martha K. 2004. *Sieves and Reeds: Identity, Cohesion, and Be-longing in a Globalizing Space. Young Oromos in Toronto*. Unpublished Ph.D. diss., University of Toronto.

Lamont, Michele, and Virag Molnar. 2002. The study of boundaries in the social sciences. *Annual Review of Sociology* 28: 167–95.

Lata, Leenco. 1973. *Gada: Three Approaches to the Study of African Society*. New York: Free Press.

———. 1998. Peculiar challenges to Oromo nationalism. In *Oromo Nationalism and the Ethiopian Discourse: The Search for Freedom and Democracy*, ed. A. Jalata, 123–52. Lawrenceville, NJ/Asmara, Eritrea: Red Sea.

———. 1999. *The Ethiopian State at the Crossroads. Decolonization and Democratization or Disintegration?* Lawrenceville, NJ/Asmara, Eritrea: Red Sea.

Lather, Patti. 1991. *Getting Smart: Feminist Research and Pedagogy*. New York: Routledge.

Leddy, Mary Jo. 1997. *At the Border Called Hope Where Refugees Are Neighbours*. Toronto: Phyllis Bruce Book, HarperCollins.

Legesse, Asmarom. 2000. *Oromo Democracy. An Indigenous African Political System*. Lawrenceville, NJ/Asmara, Eritrea: Red Sea.

Levine, Donald N. 1974. *Greater Ethiopia*. Chicago: University of Chicago Press.

Lewis, Herbert S. 1996. The development of Oromo political consciousness from 1958–1994. In *Being and Becoming Oromo: Historical and Anthropological Enquiries*, ed. P. T. W. Baxter, J. Hultin, and A. Triulzi, 37–47. Lawrenceville, NJ/Asmara, Eritrea: Red Sea.

Linde, Charlotte. 1993. *Life Stories: The Creation of Coherence*. Oxford: Oxford University Press.

Malkki, Liisa. 1997. National Geographic: The rooting of peoples and the territorialization of national identity among scholars and refugees. In *Culture, Power, Place: Explorations in Critical Anthropology*, ed. A. Gupta and J. Ferguson, 52–74. Durham/London: Duke University Press.

Mama, Amina. 1995. *Beyond the Mask: Race, Gender, and Subjectivity*. London: Routledge.

Manuh, Takyiwaa. 1998. Ghanaians, Ghanaian Canadians, and Asantes: Citizenship and identity among migrants in Toronto. *Africa Today* 45, nos. 3–4: 481–94.

Marcus, Harold G. 1975. *The Life and Times of Menelik II*. Oxford: Clarendon.

Mason, Jennifer. 1996. *Qualitative Researching*. London: Sage.

Matsuoka, Atsuko, and John Sorenson. 2001. *Ghosts and Shadows: The Construction of Identity and Community in an African Diaspora*. Toronto: University of Toronto Press.

Megerssa, Gemetchu. 1996. Oromumma: Tradition, consciousness and identity. In *Being and Becoming Oromo: Historical and Anthropological Enquiries*, ed. P. T. W. Baxter, J. Hultin, and A. Triulzi, 92–102. Lawrenceville, NJ/Asmara, Eritrea: Red Sea.

Melba, Gada. 1988. *Oromia: An Introduction*. Khartoum, Sudan: Gada Melba.

Miles, Robert. 1989. *Racism*. New York: Routledge.

Moussa, Helene. 1993. *Storm and Sanctuary: Ethiopian and Eritrean Women Refugees*. Dundas, Ont.: Artemis Enterprises.

Myerhoff, Barbara, and Jay Ruby. 1982. Introduction. In *A Crack in the Mirror: Reflexive Perspectives in Anthropology*, ed. R. Ruby, 1–35. Philadelphia: University of Pennsylvania Press.

Nadeau, Denise. 1996. *Counting Our Victories. Popular Education and Organizing*. Canada: Repeal the Deal Productions Media Resources for Mobilization.

Okeke-Ihejirika, Philomena. 2003. *Homeland vs. Identity: The Experiences of First Generation African Youth in Multicultural Canada*. Paper presented at the forty-sixth annual meeting of the African Studies Association, 30 October – 2 November, Boston.

Opoku-Dapaah, Edward. 1992. Barriers to the educational pursuits of refugee claimants in Canada: The case of Ghanaians. *Refuge* 12, no. 3: 27–31.

Philip, Nourbese M. 1992. *Frontiers: Essays and Writings on Racism and Culture*. Stratford, Canada: The Mercury Press.

Phillion, R. N. 2001. Culture, Identity and Change: The Experience of Southeast Asian Refugee Adolescents in Canada. Ph.D. diss., York University, Toronto.

Probyn, Elspeth. 1996. *Outside Belongings*. New York/London: Routledge.

Richmond, Anthony. 1994. *Global Apartheid: Refugees, Racism, and the New World Order*. Toronto/New York/Oxford: Oxford University Press.

Rodney, Walter. 1972. *How Europe Underdeveloped Africa*. Dar Es Salaam: Tanzania Publishing House.

Saucier, J. S. R., H. Doucet, J. Lambert, J. Frappier, L. Charbonneau, and M. Malus. 2002. Cultural identity and adaptation to adolescence in Montreal. In *Immigrant and Refugee Children and Their Families: Clinical, Research and Training Issues*, ed. F. Azima and J. Cramer, 133–54. Madison, CT: International Universities Press.

Smith, Linda T. 1999. *Decolonizing Methodologies: Research and Indigenous Peoples*. London/New York: Zed.

Sorenson, John. 1992. Essence and contingency in the construction of nationhood: Transformations of identity in Ethiopia and its diasporas. *Diaspora* 2, no. 2: 201–28.

———. 1993. *Imagining Ethiopia: Struggles for History and Identity in the Horn of Africa*. New Brunswick, NJ: Rutgers University Press.

———. 1996. Learning to be Oromo. Nationalist discourse in the diaspora. *Social Identities* 2, no. 3: 439–67.

Triulzi, A. 1994. Ethiopia: The making of a frontier society. In *Inventions and Boundaries: Historical and Anthropological Approaches to the Study of Ethnicity and Nationalism*, ed. P. Kaarsholm and J. Hultin, 235–45. Roskilde: Roskilde University Press.

Ullendorff, Edward. 1960. *The Ethiopians*. London: Oxford University Press.

Van de Loo, Joseph. 1991. *Guji Oromo Culture in Southern Ethiopia: Religious Capabilities in Rituals and Songs*. Berlin: Dietrich Reimer.

Van den Berghe, Pierre. 1992. The modern nation-state: Nation builder or nation killer? *International Journal of Group Tensions* 22, no. 3: 191–208.

Wallerstein, Immanuel. 1997. The insurmountable contradictions of liberalism: Human rights and the rights of peoples in the geoculture of the modern world system. In *Nations, Identities, Cultures*, ed. V. Y. Mudimbe, 181–98. Durham: Duke University Press.

Wille, Sara S. 2003. *Acting Black: College, Identity, and the Performance of Race*. New York/London: Routledge.

Woodward, Peter. 1987. Political factors contributing to the generation of refugees in the horn of Africa. *Refuge* 6, no. 4: 4–6.

Young, Iris M. 1990. *Justice and the Politics of Difference*. Princeton: Princeton University Press.

Young, Marta Y. 2001. Moderators of stress in Salvadoran refugees: The role of social and personal resources. *International Migration Review* 35, no. 3: 840–69.

Zitelmann, Thomas. 1996. Reexamining the Galla/Oromo relationship. The stranger as a structural topic. In *Being and Becoming Oromo: Historical and Anthropological Enquiries*, ed. P. T. W. Baxter, J. Hultin, and A. Triulzi, 103–13. Lawrenceville, NJ/Asmara, Eritrea: Red Sea.

Zolberg, Aristide R., Astri Shurke, and Sergio Aguayo. 1989. *Escape from Violence. Conflict and the Refugee Crisis in the Developing World*. Oxford: Oxford University Press.

NOTES

1   An early draft of this paper was presented at the 46th annual meeting of the African Studies Association, 30 October to 4 November, 2003, Boston, Massachusetts.

2   This larger work is my interdisciplinary doctoral dissertation entitled: Sieves and Reeds: Identity, Cohesion, and Be-longing in a Glocalizing Space. Young Oromos in Toronto, Faculty of Social Work, University of Toronto, 2004.

3   *Afaan Oromo* means the Oromo language. Literally, it translates as the Oromo mouth.

4   Many works use Ethiopia and Abyssinia interchangeably, while some make a distinction. I follow the later in depicting Abyssinia as the land of Abyssinians and Ethiopia as the geopolitical entity created by the interplay of powerful global forces at the time of the European colonization of Africa. While Abyssinians evolved into two distinct ethnic groups (Amhara and Tigre), there is no ethnic group called Ethiopian. The name *Ethiopia* came from ancient Greeks who referred to all Black Africa as Ethiopia, and by Ethiopia, they meant burnt-faced people (Melba 1988).

5   Here some notes on notation and quotation are in order. The quotes in this paper are all excerpted from the transcripts of one-to-one and small group conversation as well as the larger focus group debate. To protect the anonymity of participants, I have used the research names they coined for themselves in the conversations. For quotations from the larger focus group, there is only the *M* (male) and *F* (female) distinction between voices, as we withheld both real names and the research names of participants, again to protect anonymity. My name remains Kuwee throughout the conversations and is indicated by a *K* in the focus group debate. Quotations that appear in one segment are from the same small

group or one-to-one session. There were three small groups in the study: the *Addooyyee*, the *Gammee*, and the *Walana*. At the orientation sessions, participants self-selected and formed their own small groups. Those who were not comfortable sharing in groups chose one-to-one sessions. There are some demographic differences among the groups. One female and four males constitute the *Gammees*, the youngest group (three 17s, one 19, one 21). At the time of the conversations, they were all in high school, except for one in college. Two females and three males constitute the *Walanas* (two 17s, one 19, one 24), of which three were in high school, one in college, and one in university. The *Addooyyees* are the most homogeneous group in that they were all female and all were in graduate school, except for one in university. They were also the oldest as a group (21, 23, 25, 28). The focus group is a larger debate where willing participants from all the small groups and one-to-one sessions participated.

10

IN SEARCH OF IDENTITY:
Intergenerational Experiences of
African Youth in a Canadian Context

Philomina Okeke-Ihejirika and Denise L. Spitzer

INTRODUCTION

T HIS CHAPTER IS BASED on a three-year research project that examines the experiences
of African women in Alberta, one of the ten
Canadian provinces. Although our research targets
African women in general, this chapter focuses
specifically on a sample of the youth population
within this larger group. In contrast to the United
States, the majority of Blacks in Canada have immigrated to this country in the twentieth century.
Even in the province of Alberta, where a number
of Black communities were established in the nineteenth century, most Blacks are either of Caribbean
or continental African descent (Okeke et al. 2000).
Economic downturns and political unrest across
the African continent have encouraged a continuously rising trend of immigration to North
America (Mkandawire 1997).

Research on African immigration often focuses
on men's experiences, especially with respect to the
brain drain (Das 1974; McDonald and Crush 2002;
Pascal 2003). Women's experiences of migration

have often been regarded as ancillary to the movement of men (Boyle and Halfacree 1999). In recent years, however, greater attention has been paid to the unique experiences of female immigrants and refugees (Buijs 1993; Wilson and Frederiksen 1995) who usually bear the responsibility of not only caring for family members, but also reinforcing the boundaries of ethnocultural communities in their new homeland (Spitzer et al. 2003). Research on immigrant women in Canada has tended to focus on the intersections of gender, ethnicity, and class in the context of work, health, and citizenship (Elabor-Idemudia 2000; Kinnon 1999; Mulvihill, Mailloux, and Atkin 2001; Stasiulis and Bakan 1997). With some notable exceptions (Elabor-Idemudia 2000; Musisi 1999), however, the experiences of African immigrant women in Canada remain understudied. Our earlier research clearly shows that African women's experiences tend to be homogenized within a "Black pool" of Caribbean and/or older diasporic communities that appeared to bury the peculiarities of African women's experiences (Okeke et al. 2000).

To begin to address this gap in our understandings, our project, entitled *In Search of Identity, Longing for Homelands: African Women in Alberta*, seeks to illuminate the experiences of African women in the context of transnational and flexible identities and allegiances. Preliminary findings from our research thus far suggest that these women have not completely left Africa; they serve as the bridge between African and diasporic communities. The majority of African immigrant women in Alberta followed their husbands to Canada in search of better employment; others found themselves in Canada as refugees who left their homeland unprepared in order to escape war and conflict. Very few of these women made a conscious decision to immigrate, for instance, to pursue tertiary training. Their social backgrounds and the circumstances surrounding their arrival in, and adjustment to, a new homeland have placed two formidable sets of challenges before them: their struggle to establish themselves in a new homeland, and their efforts to nurture social ties with the homeland they left behind, ties they consider crucial to their survival as a people. This chapter poses the question: 'What impact do these challenges African women face have on their children here in Canada?'

Canada is a nation that prides itself on its multicultural heritage. Unlike the United States that is often considered a melting pot, Canada purports to nurture the *Canadian mosaic* – a conglomerate of cultures under one flag (Taylor 1983). Given the transnational aspirations of their parents and the multicultural principles around which their lives are shaped in Canada, the younger generation are caught between two major forces: Canadian immigration policy that targets economically viable professionals that could blend into multicultural Canada with little or no socio-ethnic chaos, and parents who are bent on establishing a new homeland with a proud African identity and strong linkages to the continent.

The imagining of home and homeland is an important anchor, particularly for diasporic peoples (Gupta and Ferguson 1997b; Cohen 1997). As identities become increasingly transnational and deterritorialized, however, the issue of how these concepts are formed demands attention. Furthermore, the presumption that persons can draw upon a *natural* identity grounded in a particular locale must be disrupted by an interrogation of the contested and imagined claims to place and community (Gupta and Ferguson 1997a). Immigrants and refugees engage in multiple identities that allow them to ally with or resist various values and meanings as they emerge in shifting and disparate contexts (Glick-Schiller, Basch, and Blanc-Szanton 1992). This flexibility is also challenged by the demands, especially in a pluralist society, to situate cultural identity around attachments that render others outside these boundaries (Hall 1996). These issues of identity formation are particularly intriguing for women whose responsibility to enculturate children requires them to model what they deem as culturally-appropriate behaviour as a means of shoring up the borders between us – in this instance an *African identity* – and the Other, represented as *Canadian society* (Spitzer et al. 2003; Wilson and Frederikson 1995). We are interested in learning about the ways in which women not only occupy different subject locations at different moments (Ong 1995), but how women choose to present themselves and structure these identities.

This chapter unveils the voices of African youth in the diaspora and their struggles to understand their place as dual citizens of, at minimum, two homelands. The population of immigrant youth in Western countries, including Canada, is increasing, and like other immigrants, how African parents and their children adjust and adapt in order to advance in Canada will also contribute, in no minimal terms, to the reshaping of the Canadian mosaic (Bacon 1999; Mackey 1999; Sims and Omaji 1999). Immigration is, in a sense, a new beginning that entails a reconstructing of cultural practice, notions of self, and attachment to the larger society, the success of which is greatly predicated on the immigrant's sense of the personal and social resources at his/her disposal (Espiritus 1992; Sayad 2000; Suarez-Orozco 2001). Global migration is creating individuals and communities whose social locations now raise serious questions about the taken-for-granted notion of citizenship. This notion, which tended to anchor individual's rights and freedoms in relation to specific nation-states, is now seriously contested, because "migration requires individuals and groups to develop multiple loyalties and identities ... [and] calls into question the idea of citizenship as having a unique focus of loyalty to a particular nation-state" (Osler and Starkey 2003, 243). How immigrant African youth confront the process of building Canadian citizenship (given the peculiarities of their social origin, the barriers they face, and their coping strategies) calls for further investigation and debate. As Anderson (1991) points out, any multicultural society embodies sites of citizenship where its members are socialized into "imagined communities." How well youth of different origins understand, and are represented by, models of citizenship would significantly mediate the process, as well as the results. Regardless of the reasons that brought them into a new environment, immigrants carry their experiences, values, and predictable patterns and contexts into the struggle to make *a home away from home*. We loosely employ the notion of citizenship in this paper, intending to highlight, rather than blur, its inter-connectedness with identity as an equally contested ground. In forging identities within a larger society, immigrant youths, we argue, bear the mark of the migration experience (Sayad 2000). Their views embody a characteristic element of migration; a historical experience of domination, in transnational terms, by the mainstream culture that the immigrant lives out in both the symbolic expressions of identity, as well as in the struggle to attain a certain material status. Bearing in mind that the fluidity of social relations African youth experience is embedded, their identities cannot be theorized in terms of

> a coherent, monolithic, and enduring construct [but more as a probe into the manner in which the diversity of constructs] are implicated in the ability to transverse increasingly discontinuous social, symbolic, and political spheres. The children of immigrants must construct identities that will, if successful, enable them to thrive in incommensurable social settings such as home, schools, the world of peers, and the world of work (Suarez-Orozco 2001, 137).

We are ultimately concerned with how well these young women are able to juggle or recreate hybrids of African and Canadian cultures that enable them to find a comfortable ground.

In addition to the common challenges a mainstream culture presents to any immigrant community outside the home, parents and children also struggle with family tensions that come with shifts in gender roles and a reshaping of home, both as an institution and in terms of the status of family members. Hence, parental assertions of the *old ways* could be seen as both mechanisms for sustaining tradition, but also as desperate moves to stabilize the *structured whole* in a new world. We argue, however, that regardless of the tensions associated with resisting the dilution of a *traditional* way of life, emerging diasporas often expect that women recreate the home left behind in their values, choices, and practices (Espin 1999; Morck 2000; Prieur 2002). Thus, these young African women, in their behaviour, see themselves and are seen by others as carriers of traits of a specific culture. What they articulate as their parents' expectations for them imply not only the presumption of a culture away from home competing with an immediately present culture, but also an older and more conservative culture compared to the global model – the *Western culture*. This characteristic dissociation, a common feature of immigrant youth perceptions of self and society, often places the Western culture as one stripped of these old traits and now professing a modern contrast (Wakil, Siddique, and Wakil 1981).

Focusing on the responses of the African youth we interviewed, we also explore, in a broader sense, the implications of transnational immigration and citizenship for establishing a solid base and identity for new African communities in the diaspora. We focus, in particular, on perceptions of fluid allegiances, imagined homelands, and intergenerational tensions within this group. We must emphasize at the onset that the following analysis does not aim to generalize the experience of African youth in Canada based on the experiences of those sampled. We recognize that even within this purposively qualitative sample, we are dealing with experiences mediated by immigrant origin, gender, age, religion, and so on (Prieur 2002). Africa is a continent of over fifty countries, diversely oriented in social, economic, and political terms. It is safe, therefore, to argue that the experiences of Africa's youth in the diaspora present their own complexities that research has yet to capture. We are also clearly aware that current trends and social relations in the country of immigration impact on, or overlap with, these young women's views, making it difficult to rigidly locate any trait or situation.

METHODOLOGY

This work is guided by principles of feminist research that demand attention to questions of voice and the needs of informants and communities involved in explorations (Reinharz 1992). Feminist scholarship recognizes the fact of women's subordinate status in society and the low priority it has commanded in mainstream, traditional disciplines. The main objective of feminist research is to uncover the specificities of women's oppression as a basis for exploring possible avenues of bringing fundamental improvements to their lives. The appropriate methods of achieving this main objective may be debated, but most feminist researchers would agree that women's voices and viewpoints constitute their primary data base (Shields and Dervin 1993, 66).

Feminist scholarship attempts to identify and analyze the relations of power embedded in women's lives. As Smith (1986) argues, women's everyday experiences tell the stories of their oppression. According to her, it is from the basic aspects of their lives that one can begin to trace the impacts of larger, oppressive social forces. Smith points out that beginning from the experiences of women does not imply a myopic view of social reality, but offers insights into the ways in which female subjects experience social, cultural, and economic contexts (1986, 7–9). In other words, a feminist perspective does not imply a narrow focus on women's lives, but rather, allows the researcher to begin a systematic inquiry into where women are located socially, economically, and politically.

In placing women's experiences within a broad social context, feminist scholarship confronts, not only the relations of gender, but those of class, race, ethnicity, and other social categorizations that define women's conditions of existence. As Morgan (1988, 91) notes, gender "is not something unchanging that is brought into every encounter, but is often shaped and patterned in different interactional contexts." Thus, gender relations "must also be seen holistically and in context, and as socially and culturally complex" (Shields and Dervin 1993, 66). The feminist standpoint certainly finds significant resonance in mainstream approaches, such as critical ethnography and grounded theory, that stress the need to build our knowledge of human experiences from the point of view of those who live these experiences, allowing their voices to guide our explorations (Baker, Wuest, and Stern 1992; Field and Morse 1985; Smith 1986).

The diversity of experiences – personal, political, religious, and linguistic – contained under the rubric of African women also demand the use of diverse methods to triangulate information and provide rich insights into women's lives (Neufeld et al. 2001). To this end, we employed multiple methods: a literature review, focus groups, interviews with community leaders, and a province-wide survey. The primary research team is comprised of the two co-authors and a community partner, the Edmonton Immigrant Services Association. The authors of this article come from different disciplinary backgrounds (economics and anthropology) and possess complementary expertise working with African women within the continent and in Canada. A community advisory committee was established that includes representatives from immigrant service agencies, ethno-cultural associations, and women's organizations. The purpose of the community advisory committee was to provide input into research instruments, identify potential participants, and facilitate the dissemination of results. The work of the committee was particularly important with regards to participant recruitment in members' community networks, as gaining entry into communities where discrimination is a problem can be quite challenging (Arcury and Quandt 1999).

Research assistants affiliated with disparate religions (Moslem and Christian), national origins (Somali/Kenyan, Niger/Nigerian), and community animators from Mauritius, Zimbabwe, and South Africa also assisted with the recruitment and facilitation of focus group discussions. They provided varied points of entry into a wide range of African-Canadian communities, points which are necessary when working with diverse populations (Neufeld et al. 2001). The multiple positions of research team members in terms of origins (Nigeria, Malawi, and the United States), socioeconomic class backgrounds, and religion (Christian and Jewish), provide a diversity of insights and variable insider/outsider statuses vis-à-vis informants (Wolf 1996). It is still important, however, to recognize powerful differentials between researchers and informants and necessary, as well, to acknowledge the agency of informants to participate in research (Ong 1995).

For the purposes of this chapter, we concentrate on focus group findings. Focus groups or group interviews are not identical to conversations. They resonate, instead, with everyday gatherings of women and are therefore appropriate methods for enlivened and enlightening discussion (Kelly 1978; Reinharz 1992). Five focus groups were hosted between December 2002 and July 2003 with women from various geographical and linguistic regions, including the Horn of Africa and Central, West, Southern, and Eastern Africa. In addition, a focus group was conducted with young African women to explore their unique experiences maturing in a diasporic community. This chapter focuses on the findings from the latter. Participants ranged in age from eighteen to twenty-five and included young women from Eritrea, Ghana, Nigeria, Sierra Leone, the Sudan, and Ethiopia. Two informants, Zahra[1] and Rachel, were born in Canada to Eritrean and Ethiopian parents, respectively, who came to Canada as refugees. Rose and Teresa arrived as children of independent immigrants, eight months and ten years old, respectively. The former is from Ghana, the latter from Nigeria. Mary and Surya came to Canada as adolescents. Mary was about thirteen years old when she came from Nigeria with her mother, an independent immigrant. Surya was fifteen years old when she came with her family as a refugee from Sierra Leone. Myriam, from Sudan, is also a refugee and the only member of the study group who came alone to Canada. She was about twenty-four years old when she arrived. We interviewed them about their experiences in Canada and their visions of the future. In order to address the questions raised earlier, this paper examines four major themes from these interviews: family roles, community life, social values and dating, and identity.

Context

In order to situate the experiences of African women in Alberta, we must provide a brief overview of their status and some of the issues that pertain to youth. Nearly 80 percent of foreign-born women are employed full-time; however, they occupy the lowest rungs of the labour market and are often overqualified for their level of employment (Statistics Canada 2000). While 58.5 percent of African immigrants in Alberta have completed post-secondary education, this has not translated into commensurate professional or economic status in Canada (Lamba, Mulder, and Wilkinson 2000). Over 41 percent of African women in Alberta are employed in the service sector, 18.5 percent occupy business, finance, or administrative positions, while more than 9 percent work in processing and manufacturing. An additional 8.3 percent are found in the health sector (Lamba, Mulder, and Wilkinson 2000). Professional gate-keeping and demands for Canadian experience produce significant barriers to the employment of newcomers in their previous fields of endeavour.

Furthermore, women are more likely than men to secure employment upon arrival, regardless of wage status, and may therefore remain in these "survival jobs" while their partners pursue education or more suitable employment opportunities. It is important to note that, while most newcomers to Canada experience a decline in socioeconomic status, visible minority immigrants and refugees are less likely to become upwardly mobile in the subsequent generation than migrants from European source countries (Basavarajappa and Jones 1999; Kazemipur and Halli 2000). This suggests that racism plays a significant role in depressing socioeconomic status. Thus, overt and more subtle forms of racism can undermine personal interactions, and institutionalized forms may constrain access to power (Fleras and Elliott 1999; Jones 2000). These phenomena contribute to experiences of everyday racism and the reasons organizations cite to account for the failure of ethnic minorities to attain the values of the dominant society, thereby discounting the existence and persistence of inequality (Essed 1991).

Despite social and economic disappointments that often result in thwarted ambitions, many immigrant and refugee parents see their children's education as a means of ensuring upward mobility (Bauder 2001). Indeed, immigrant youth are employed at lower rates than their Canadian-born counterparts, because the former are often more invested in education. For instance, over 28 percent of Canadian-born women between fifteen and eighteen are employed, compared to 14.2 percent of recent young immigrant women and 24.4 percent of women from established immigrant families. Bauder (2001) asserts that education is a crucial means of ascending the socioeconomic hierarchy within immigrant communities. Education, however, is also a major socializing agent that inculcates students with particular sets of values and aspirations that could conflict with parental ideals, potentially contributing to intergenerational tensions.

Intergenerational conflict is often regarded as an artifact of adolescent individuation and is presumed to be particularly charged among immigrant parents and their children. Both the length of residence in Canada and the number of years of schooling in a Western system appear to be related to the desire of immigrant youth to assume the dominant values, desires, and expectations of Euro-Canadian youth (Merali and Violato 2002). Parental expectations of their adolescent children's behaviour, however, are not uniform and may be related to family size and parental education. Compared to the average, for instance, parents with higher education and fewer children tend to be supportive of their children's desire to adopt values and behaviours of the dominant Canadian youth culture (Merali and Violato 2002). Other factors are also salient. In a survey of adolescents in Alberta, speaking a language other than English or French at home was associated with attendance at a place of worship and more conservative attitudes towards social and sexual behaviour (Bagley, Bolitho, and Bertrand 2001). Youth in our focus group reflect on the dynamics of these desires and expectations from family, community, and friends as they make their way into adulthood as young African women in Alberta.

RESULTS

Family Roles

According to these young women, the structure of family roles are somewhat less rigid than what might still be the case back in African countries. They admit that many of the tasks are shared among siblings, but point out that because of their age and primary focus on schooling, at the moment, a good deal of the household work shifted to their mother. Most of them are speaking from a fairly long period of living at home. Even though a good number of these young women are well over eighteen years of age and would therefore officially be considered adults, they all reside with their parents. Mary is from Nigeria and is the oldest in her family. She was well over ten years old when she arrived in Canada with her family "in search of a better life." As the eldest sibling with a much younger brother, Mary helps her mother to run the house, "making sure things are in order ... [taking] responsib[ility] for different household duties and chores ... making sure things run properly." She seems to accept these domestic duties as responsibilities she can be depended upon to embrace, having spent her formative years back home. Most of the informants point out, however, that they spend a good deal of time outside the home and so end up merely helping their mothers around the house rather than assuming substantial responsibility for duties. Zahra, the daughter of Eritrean refugees, was born in Canada. When she is at home, she can be counted upon to help out with "like, washing the dishes, or shoveling the snow, or things like that," but "mostly, I am considered a child and a student." Rose came as a child to Canada and has little or no memory of life in Ghana. She insists that "there are no really defined rules" in her family. But the rest of the young women believe that the division of tasks at home is gendered.

Those who came to Canada as children or were born in Canada seem to use their parents as the benchmark for assessing whatever they define as the *African* model of familial behaviour and gender roles. Whatever their impressions of the gendered division of domestic work, which they agree exists, their responses clearly show that they feel their parents' expectations differ from what they perceive to be the *Canadian* model. According to Zahra, "as a girl I would not want to be [stuck in the kitchen] ... but between my parents I feel, though, that there are still some gender roles that they brought back here to Canada from Eritrea ... such as my mom mostly doing the cooking and the cleaning ... and my dad mostly doing the more manly roles around the house."

Many Canadian families may not consider these descriptions of household distribution of duties among parents and children unusual or unique to immigrants, in particular; however, respondents appear to presume that most Canadian households enact a more equitable domestic division of labour. In their responses, these young women imply a transfer of cultural elements that are not necessarily in tune with the Canadian way of life. As noted earlier, such a stance is very common with immigrant children who perceive the mainstream culture not only as a modern alternative, but the model that the *older* one has yet to catch up with. Rachel was born in Canada to Ethiopian refugees and notes, for instance, "My dad would not ever be seen cleaning the bathroom and doing stuff like that. He cooks sometimes … but the majority of it, my mom and I will do, like, stuff, and my dad would be more of, like, doing fixing the car, if it's something wrong in the house than everything else." Surya agrees and states that "I have my own roles, and my brother has his own roles." As she further explains, "no, he is not cooking … Sometimes he is cleaning the parlour and I clean the kitchen, he is not doing anything, because it is our roles, or types." Interestingly, all of them accept this gendered division – as long as they live at home. With the exception of Surya, who accepts the gender bias as the natural order of things, all of the participants have serious doubts about their maintenance of what they as see as *the African way* at home in their own generation as parents. They do not think their parents can transfer these *ways* to this younger generation.

All of the respondents brought a very clear awareness of the different worlds they lived in: life outside and life at home, often with both parents. For Zahra, the situation works well, but only for now. She remarks, "It doesn't bring any … er … much conflict, because my brother does the exact amount of work that I do. But I feel that if I were to get married … I would not want to be stuck in the role of female, doing all the female things. I would expect my husband to do the same."

Community Life

Besides their schooling, community life for these young women revolves around their families, the local church, Black students' groups, the youth wing of Black associations, and country of origin organizations. Most of the young women are involved in Black organizations, in some cases with minimal or no tangible pressure from their families. In contrast, their involvement in ethnic organizations is often grounded in the need to satisfy their parents who are often active in these associations. Only one of the informants was involved with an organization that extended beyond Black/African communities.

The young women ascribe to multiple definitions of, and identifications with, community. Every one of them, including those born in Canada, seem to have some idea that their parents' own vision of community carried from Africa was different, in many ways, from what obtains in Canada. Thus, when they describe community life, they account for their parents' allegiances, as well as their own. In Rose's view, "my community would be Edmonton, because on my day-to-day basis, I don't run into many African or Caribbean or Black people. It is only when I make an active effort to, outside of school."

These young women's definition of community also overlaps, in various degrees, with their sources of social support. Most of the young women obtain support from their parents, friends they grew up with, and religious institutions. To them, life in Canada is more like highly dispersed sets of social groupings, many of which have no communal hold but only interconnect at various points. As Mary remarks, "[It's a] social network. There's no community ..." She further explains that "[t]here's no community, because we don't interact with [many people around us]. We don't go out to the community [around]. So I'm in a community, but I'm not part of that community." Beyond their immediate family surroundings, they see something of a community life in country-of-origin organizations, although most of them are still far from being firmly established and are struggling to mobilize transnationals as a distinct population.[2] Myriam, the Sudanese refugee who came alone to Canada only a few years ago, also notes that

> the Sudanese ... help [newcomers] a lot, first, to understand the life here ... We have women's group ... those women need a lot of help. Whenever they have problems, they turn to the community. So they find what they need from the community, in terms of language and problems with kids at school. A lot of things like that, they cannot go direct. They do not know where to turn. So the first thing, they will go to the community.

The issue of racism came up during our discussions, but individual women related this concept more in terms of what happens in a specific context. Those who grew up in Canada admit to a few hurtful moments in their childhood when they had to confront racism head-on, but they easily shrugged off their experiences of name calling (such as *browntoast*) and racist innuendos from classmates at school. Most feel that they suffered little and that racism directed at them was usually subtle. As Rachel notes, for instance, classmates could engage in name calling, "But from teachers ... [it] is always, like, you don't know ... what they are thinking, and I think they can easily think that you are Black, you do not know the stuff ... sometimes I wonder [if] they are just ... not too sure ... [when] I observe how they treat me [differently from] ... other people in class." Surya feels that her own situation has a lot to do with coming to Canada at an older age. According to her, "When I first got to school, I don't have friends, a lot of friends, because I don't know why, and I'm not allowed to talk in class ..." Myriam could relate to Surya's experience. Unlike Surya, who was fifteen years old when she arrived in Canada with her parents, Myriam was well over twenty, by herself, and struggling with Canadian English. As she explains, "The problem I found was ... with my accent ... Even [when] other people, they say it … like the Chinese women in the class … I know that their pronunciations are not right, but she will say, is OK. And then, when it comes to me … she will say, Could you repeat it? … I get so upset in the class." In response to Myriam's comments, Rachel explains that racism in Canada is very subtle. There is just no way of knowing whether it is racism or not. In her view, the teachers either do not really understand Myriam, or they are "asking you purposely to, like, make you [look] dumber …"

It seems, however, that for these young women, racism has not presented an insurmountable obstacle on their path. Their responses suggest some understanding of the challenges they face in a society whose relationship with those outside the mainstream population is mired in ignorance. Even in their perceptions of racism, as well as responses to what they consider racist attacks, there is hardly any impression of frustration that could get in the way of everyday life or goals for the future.

On the whole, these young women's descriptions of community life, what they know as community, and their experiences of racism suggest an emerging, albeit tentative, pattern. They are taking hold of a new form of community life as Black Canadian youth to which their parents cannot relate. But they also covet that taste of what community life should be in the country-of-origin associations that their parents are struggling to build. Although they fluidly move between these two perceptions, they are clearly aware that, however dispersed they may be, family and friends are their best options for support and therefore comprise their "community" in Canada.

Social Values and Dating

Again, the *double life* these young women live is succinctly portrayed in their perceptions of the values that guide their actions and decisions. Zahra tries to capture the two paths African youth struggle to merge:

> Being raised in Canada … I've been surrounded by Canadian values, like going to Canadian schools, even though you're taught Canadian values, but when you come home, is a different lesson from your parents, who have been raised in Africa and spent all … most of their life in Africa. So one … in my home … I have to live up to the expectations of my parents, and those expectations are mostly things they will expect. They will expect … things I will expect from them back home in Africa. So some of them are achievable, but some you just don't want to live up to that because [of] being surrounded by Canadians … growing-up in Canada. There's something different outside of your house.

Part of the struggle is to find a definition of the *good girl* agreeable to both parent and daughter. Rose feels that there is a difference between Canadian and

African norms, but admits that she is not exactly sure of what that difference is. As she puts it, "I don't think I have a strong sense of the African good girl since I was ... raised here," but feels that her parents would agree with the idea of "someone who works hard, has values and morals." Zahra said: "Because I spent most of my life in Canada and I've only been back home to Eritrea once ... I am surrounded most of the time by Canadian values." Teresa thinks it "would probably be someone who is responsible and respectful and also has self respect for herself and someone whose goal is really focused, and like she said, like, she is educated also, and loyal, and what else."

Obviously, these young women are aware of the cultural duality they live out on a daily basis and are already making choices. They know their limits at this point and are reserving the freedom to make further choices when they leave home. They tell us, for instance, that their parents have their own expectations for them as good girls. In their view, however, their parents' ideas of a good girl come with values from an older generation, some of which do not have much currency for them. As one of them pointed out, their parents expect obedience and good behaviour, defined as refraining from drinking alcohol and smoking and staying away from boys. The respondents, however, would like to relax the rules a little. These perceptions of good traits do not really indicate a real difference between Canadian and African cultural expectations. The emphasis, it seems, is on the *manner* these traits are expressed in each culture rather than their essential content as social values.

Rachel, who was born in Canada, feels that while her parents may not associate being a good girl with drinking and smoking, she will settle for something a little less stringent. In her view, "Well obviously, she cannot be drinking everyday and getting drunk and stuff. But if she drinks, like, on special occasions, like, you know, when she goes out ... social drinking ... I don't think that's bad at all. Like everybody in the world does that, you know. I know so many people do that, you know." Surya supports this view, insisting that many young African women would avoid the extremes. According to her, "You don't have to be, like, bad girl in school, a bad girl in the street, you don't have to say bad language in your mouth. You have to follow all the rules ... [at home]." Mary picks up the emphasis and asks, "Who is a good girl? ... [T]here are lot of things that I do being a good girl [that] were passed on by my parents ... Like, just being respectful, ... doing well in school, books, ... knowing what is expected of you [at] home and then presenting yourself well in public ... just being a nice person, whatever that means."

There is certainly some confusion about values, which tend to shift between perceptions of African and Canadian features. The definition of a good girl, for example, embeds values, such as obedience, respect, and self-comportment, as well as having a high regard placed on education by both parents and children. These values are not necessarily peculiar to African cultures. The focus on pursuing educational aspirations is evidently shared by most cultures. These young women consistently emphasize the importance of their training, both to themselves and their parents. Reflecting on her childhood, Mary recalls, "I think for me the main focus was always on school, so as far as dating and relationships go, it was school first. They always made an issue of it." For Rose, "My parents always … ehm, I think I've motivated myself well; they have wanted me to do well in school, but … nothing specific – you have to do what you have to do. I think I take that upon myself, for the most part." Teresa also points to her parents' influence on her education. "My family has always focused mainly on education first, and then everything else came … after it." For Rachel, too, education was the key emphasis. According to her, "My parents always said, 'Do good in school … and then go ahead and date …' because they think boys can quickly change your mind about school."

Most of them agree, however, that despite the points of agreement with their parents, their lives remain wedged somewhere between African and Canadian values. Zahra thinks that, for now, her parents will influence her values more than society: "Right now, I will lean more towards the African values, because I am still living with my parents. And they feed me and clothe me, and they provide me with the bed that I sleep in, so I think, if I want to stay there, I have to listen to them. But when I become more independent, I'll probably lean more over to Canadian values." As a parent, Zahra points out, "I'll probably lean more towards Canadian values in raising [my children] … but I will select and teach them [about] … where they came [from] and things like that." It is Mary, perhaps, who came to Canada as a teenager, who succinctly articulated the complex duality in which African youth experiences are immersed. As she puts it, "I guess it really depends on what the issue is, because there are Canadian values that are on … the African side. So I will not say that I have acquired too much … [or] … one more than the other. But more so what my mom has instilled in me is not specific to Nigerian. But just being a well-rounded, good person."

Dating, however, is a potential site of intergenerational conflict and remains a topic these focus group participants tend to avoid in discussions with their parents. African parents, they feel, will never understand dating because of their background. These young women, however, opened up and told us about some of the challenges they have with dating. Zahra points out that

> [my parents cannot relate to] most of the [ads] that come up in the TV about dating and things like that … because I think, with my parents, their first relationship was each other. But being in Canada and kids are dating younger. I haven't been involved in any relationships. But I'm not blaming it on my parents and what they did because of that, but I think, if I were to tell them, like, I am dating, or if I'm planning to do anything with that person, they might get kind of edgy.

One concern participants shared was the apparent *shortage* of eligible Black men who, in apparent agreement with their parents, were regarded as the only appropriate potential partners. Their parents, these women explain, would want them to marry a Black man, preferably one who was born in Africa or grew up with his parents in Canada. Their parents are not so sure about Blacks with social origins outside the continent. The girls, however, lament the fact that there are very few suitable candidates, even within the larger pool of Black men.

The young women agree that their educational ambitions could, however, make the problem of finding a good mate even harder. Rose explains, "I think in Edmonton, and perhaps spreading towards the rest of Canada now, there seems to be a greater portion of ... Black females with higher degrees of education compared to males." Black young men, according to them, are not as keen to achieve in academics and the professions. All of them concurred with Rose, who insists: "I would like to be in a relationship with someone who has the same degree of education as me." They believe that there are a lot more females than males in the total population of Black youth. There are even still fewer men within the tiny group of high achievers, they claim. Even though the respondents were not concerned about the ethnicity of a potential spouse, they expressed a strong preference to marry Black men of African origins. Currently, these young women anticipate facing potential problems in the future with regards to finding a suitable mate.

Identity and Homeland

All of the informants employed a fluid assortment of identities that were rendered meaningful by their context. While the ordering of these intersecting associations could be construed as ranging from local (ethnicity, country of origin) to global (pan-Black, woman), they are not necessarily arranged in a hierarchy. As Rose observed, "I consider myself both [Black/African], but it depends on whom I am surrounded with. Like, if I am in Ghana, then I am called Canadian. If I am surrounded by Black people from here, I am considered an African or Black person." Rachel, who was born in Canada, and Myriam, who moved to this country from the Sudan, identify themselves first, but not exclusively, with their ancestral country of origin. Myriam explains, "even though I am in Canada, I am still seeing myself as a Sudanese woman from Africa. Even if I get Canadian citizenship, it's going to be on paper. So, I love to be African woman. I am African woman."

In contrast to responses from adult focus group respondents, attachment to imagined African homelands is often troubled by lack of competency in their familial language. Older family members often provide a bridge between the younger generation and other kin. Zahra, for instance, has very little contact with this homeland she talks about. According to her, "Only my dad's family

... is back home, and the kids do not speak English well. And, er ... I depend on my dad to keep me in touch with his family back home and with Eritrea." When relatives call from Africa, one of the respondents said, "I don't hear what they are saying ... I hand the phone over to mother." Sustaining native skills in the next generation is difficult. As school-age children, the much younger women like Zahra spend very little time at home. The young women identify the loss of native language as widening the generation gap between parents and children. As students, the younger generation spends most of the day with English speakers. Often, their parents, and in some cases, older siblings, are the only people they could practice these skills on. This makes even more difficult the task of parents who are determined to *Africanize* their children. With mainly parental presence and meetings with people of the country of origin, the idea of homeland is more imagined than real, and the fluid ordering of identity is only practical.

CONCLUSION

This brief overview of the responses from young, female African-Albertans represents the first step in our exploration of the process of identity formation among African immigrant and refugee women in Alberta. Our conclusions, therefore, are grounded solely in these data and are contingent upon further analyses.

As Hall (1996) notes, identities are multiple, intersecting, and at times, antagonistic. Our informants seem to be aware of these possibilities as they move through various identity contexts accompanied by networks of family, classmates, friends, co-religionists, and community members. For instance, these young women enact the sexual division of labour deemed culturally appropriate within their household and hold to the values, behaviours, and desires that will earn them the appellation of "good girls" while they reside with their parents. These perceptions not only solidify bonds with their parents and what they perceive to be their "traditional African values," but they help to demarcate the boundaries between their desire to shore up an African identity and the potential onslaught of threats to that identity posed by Canadian society. However, they further express desires to make those borders more porous, to contaminate the in-between spaces they occupy – spaces that constitute the fertile ground for cultural hybridization (Bhabha 1996).

Similar to their mothers who came here as African nationals struggling to construct an African identity, these children must strive to find their place in multicultural Canada. Given the diversity of groups that fuel this continental immigration, the scope and population for a national identity is simply not there for adjustment, adaptation, and advancement. When these young women came together to discuss their experience, they differentiated between Canadian and African features. The difficulty they have in definitively identifying African features could also be a reflection of the unstable nature of a diaspora still in formation. But it certainly indicates a weaker access, compared to their parents, to the specificities of national, ethnic, and even smaller cultural groupings for reasons of identity. As noted earlier, the African population is vastly diverse, and the values these young women associate with being African are elucidated from their relationship with parents – individuals and couples from various parts of Africa. Many of these parents grew up in specific cultural settings. They had little need to explore the larger African identity and never knew they were Black until they came to Canada. Even as they rally around people of similar cultural values and traditions, they also recognize the need to go beyond these smaller groupings for wider and more effective support networks. As these young women clearly indicate, their own generation is likely to thrive more on the larger African and Black identities than in the country-specific ones their parents work on.

The foregoing raises a number of crucial questions regarding the balance between African and Canadian values, allegiances between African and pan-Black identities, and the relationship between language and identity. Like their parents, they see education and marriage to other Africans as essential to carrying on the dual purposes of maintaining cultural linkages to parents and ethnic origins and to fulfilling aspirations for upward mobility for themselves and their families. Whether in their parents' homes or outside in the *community*, young, first generation African women appear to be negotiating multiple identities as they make their way through Canadian society. As they establish their own households, their desires and abilities to forge hybrid identities and practices will undoubtedly become more evident. For now, they must fluidly meander through the *homeland* identity they occupy with their parents, the multicultural identity that is still under construction, and the racist (and sometimes ignorant) perceptions of Euro-Canadian society they must continually reject.

REFERENCES

Anderson, Benedict. 1991. *Imagined Communities*. London: Verso.

Arcury, Thomas A., and Sarah A. Quandt. 1999. Participant recruitment for qualitative research: A site-based approach to community research in complex societies. *Human Organization* 58, no. 2: 128–41.

Bacon, Jean. 1999. Constructing collective ethnic identities: The case of second generation Asian Indians. *Qualitative Sociology* 22, no. 2: 141–60.

Bagley, Christopher, Floyd Bolitho, and Lorne Bertrand. 2001. Ethnicities and social adjustment in Canadian adolescents. *Journal of Immigration and Integration* 2, no. 1: 55–76.

Baker, Cynthia, Judith Wuest, and Phyllis Stern. 1992. Method slurring: The grounded theory/phenomenology example. *Journal of Advanced Nursing* 17: 1355–60.

Basavarajappa, K. G., and Frank Jones. 1999. Visible minority income differences. In *Immigrant Canada: Demographic, Economic and Social Challenges,* ed. S. S. Halli and L. Driedger, 230–60. Toronto: University of Toronto Press.

Bauder, Harald. 2001. Employment, ethnicity, and metropolitan context: The case of young Canadian immigrants. *Journal of Immigration and Integration* 2, no. 3: 315–41.

Bhabha, Homi. 1996. Culture's in-between. In *Questions of Cultural Identity,* ed. S. Hall and P. du Gay, 53–60. London: Sage.

Boyle, Paul, and Keith Halfacree, eds. 1999. *Migration and Gender in the Developed World.* New York: Routledge.

Buijs, Gina, ed. 1993. *Migrant Women: Crossing Boundaries and Changing Identities.* Oxford: Berg.

Cohen, Robin. 1997. *Global Diasporas: An Introduction.* Seattle: University of Washington Press.

Das, Man Singh. 1974. Brain drain controversy and African scholars. *Studies in Comparative International Development* 9, no. 1: 74–83.

Elabor-Idemudia, Patience. 2000. Challenges confronting African immigrant women in the Canadian workforce. In *Anti-Racist Feminism: Critical Race and Gender Studies,* ed. A. Calliste and G. S. Dei, 91–110. Halifax: Fernwood.

Espin, Olivia. 1999. *Women Crossing Boundaries: A Psychology of Immigration and Transformations of Sexuality.* London: Routledge Press.

Espiritus, Yen Lee. 1992. *Asian American Pan-Ethnicity: Bridging Institutions and Identities.* Philadelphia: Temple University Press.

Essed, Philomina. 1991. *Understanding Everyday Racism: An Interdisciplinary Theory.* Newbury Park, CA: Sage.

Field, Peggy A., and Janice Morse. 1985. *Nursing Research: Application of Qualitative Approaches.* Rockville, MD: Aspen Systems.

Fleras, Augie, and Jean L. Elliott. 1999. *Unequal Relations: An Introduction to Race, Ethnic and Aboriginal Dynamics in Canada.* Scarborough: Prentice Hall/Allyn and Bacon Canada.

Glick-Schiller, Nina, Linda Basch, and Cristina Blanc-Szanton. 1992. Transnationalism: A new analytic framework for understanding migration. In *Towards a Transnational Perspective on Migration: Race, Class, Ethnicity and Nationalism Reconsidered,* ed. N. Glick-Schiller, L. Basch, and C. Blanc-Szanton, 1–24. New York: New York Academy of Sciences.

Gupta, Ahkil, and James Ferguson. 1997a. Culture, power, place: Ethnography at the end of an era. In *Culture, Power, Place: Explorations in Critical Anthropology,* ed. A. Gupta and J. Ferguson, 1–29. Durham: Duke University Press.

———. 1997b. Beyond "culture": Space, identity, and the politics of difference. In *Culture, Power, Place: Explorations in Critical Anthropology,* ed. A. Gupta and J. Ferguson, 33–51. Durham: Duke University Press.

Hall, Stuart. 1996. Introduction: Who needs identity? In *Questions of Cultural Identity,* ed. S. Hall and P. du Gay, 1–17. London: Sage.

Jones, Carmara. 2000. Levels of racism: A theoretical framework and a gardener's tale. *American Journal of Public Health* 90: 1212–15.

Kazemipur, Abdolmohammad, and Shiva S. Halli. 2000. *The New Poverty in Canada: Ethnic Groups and Ghetto Neighbourhoods*. Toronto: Thompson Educational.

Kelly, Jane H. 1978. *Yaqui Women: Contemporary Life Histories*. Omaha: University of Nebraska Press.

Kinnon, Dianne. 1999. *Canadian Research on Immigration and Health*. Ottawa: Minister of Public Works and Government Services Canada.

Lamba, Navjot, Marlene Mulder, and Lori Wilkinson. 2000. *Immigrants and Ethnic Minorities on the Prairies: Statistical Compendium*. Edmonton: Prairie Centre of Excellence for Research on Immigration and Integration (PCERII).

Mackey, Eva. 1999. *The House of Difference: Cultural Politics and National Identity in Canada*. London: Routledge.

McDonald, David A., and Jonathan Crush, eds. 2002. *Destinations Unknown: Perspectives on the Brain Drain in Southern Africa*. Pretoria: African Institute of South Africa.

Merali, Noorfarah, and Claudio Violato. 2002. Relationships between demographic variables and immigrant parents' perceptions of assimilative adolescent behaviors. *Journal of Immigration and Integration* 3, no. 1: 65–81.

Mkandawire, Thandika. 1997. The social sciences in Africa: Breaking local barriers and negotiating international presence. The Bashorun M. K. O. Abiola distinguished lecture presented to the 1996 African Studies Association annual meeting. *African Studies Review* 40, no. 2: 15–36.

Morck, Yvonne. 2000. Hyphenated Danes: Contested fields of gender, generation and ethnicity. *Young* 8, no. 3: 2–16.

Morgan, Nicole. 1988. *The Equality Game: Women in the Federal Service, 1908–1987*. Ottawa: Canadian Council for the Status of Women.

Mulvihill, Mary Ann, Louise Mailloux, and Wendy Atkin. 2001. *Advancing Policy and Research Responses to Immigrant and Refugee Women's Health in Canada*. Ottawa: Centres of Excellence for Women's Health.

Muisisi, Nakanyike. 1999. Catalyst, nature, and vitality of African-Canadian feminism: A panorama of an émigré feminist. In *Émigré Feminism: Transnational Perspectives*, ed. A. Heitlinger, 131–48. Toronto: University of Toronto Press.

Neufeld, Anne, Margaret Harrison, Karen Hughes, Denise L. Spitzer, and Miriam Stewart. 2001. Participation of immigrant women caregivers in qualitative research. *Western Journal of Nursing Research* 23, no. 6: 575–91.

Okeke, Philomina, Chrstina Nsaliwa, Mary Ebinu, Jenny Kelly, Adenike Yesufu, and Malinda Smith. 2000. *Black Women and Economic Autonomy in Edmonton, Alberta: Barriers to Accessing Equal Opportunities*. Report prepared for the Status of Women Canada.

Ong, Aiwha. 1995. Women out of China: Traveling tales and traveling theories in postcolonial feminism. In *Women Writing Culture*, ed. R. Behar and D. Gordon, 350–72. Berkeley: University of California Press.

Osler, Audrey, and Hugh Starkey. 2003. Learning for cosmopolitan citizenship: Theoretical debates and young people's experiences. *Educational Review* 55, no. 3: 243–54.

Pascal, Zachary G. 2003. A program for Africa's computer people. *Issues in Science and Technology* 19, no. 3: 79–85.

Prieur, Annick. 2002. Gender remix: On gender constructions among children of immigrants in Norway. *Ethnicities* 2, no. 1: 53–77.

Reinharz, Shulamit. 1992. *Feminist Methods in Social Research*. New York: Oxford University Press.

Sayad, Abdelmalek. 2000. El Ghorba: From original sin to collective lie. *Ethnography* 1, no. 2: 147–73.

Shields, Vickie R., and Brenda Dervin. 1993. Sense-making in feminist social science research: A call to enlarge the methodological options of feminist studies. *Women's Studies International Forum* 16, no. 1: 65–81.

Sims, Margaret R., and Alice Omaji. 1999. Migration and parenting: A pilot study. *Journal of Family Studies* 5, no. 1: 84–96.

Smith, Dorothy E. 1986. Institutional ethnography: A feminist method. *Resources for Feminist Research* 15, no. 1: 6–13.

Spitzer, Denise, Anne Neufeld, Margaret Harrison, Karen Hughes, and Miriam Stewart. 2003. Caregiving in transnational context: "My wings have been cut: Where can I fly?" *Gender & Society* 17, no. 2: 267–86.

Stasiulis, Daiva, and Abigail Bakan. 1997. Negotiating citizenship: The case of foreign domestic workers in Canada. *Feminist Review* 57: 112–39.

Statistics Canada. 2000. *Women in Canada 2000: A Gender-Based Statistical Report*. Ottawa: Minister of Industry.

Suarez-Orozco, Carola. 2001. Immigrant families and their children: Adaptation and identity formation. In *Blackwell Companion to Sociology*, ed. J. R. Blau, 128–39. Oxford: Blackwell.

Taylor, Rupert J. 1983. *Canadian Mosaic*. Toronto: MacLean Hunter.

Wakil, Parvez., S. Siddique, and F. A. Wakil. 1981. Between two cultures: A study in socialization of children of immigrants. *Journal of Marriage and the Family*, November: 929–40.

Wilson, Fiona, and Bodil Frederiksen. 1995. Introduction: Studies in ethnicity, gender and the subversion of nationalism. In *Ethnicity, Gender and the Subversion of Nationalism*, ed. F. Wilson and B. Frederiksen, 1–6. London: Frank Cass.

Wolf, Diane. 1996. Situating feminist dilemmas in fieldwork. In *Feminist Dilemmas in Fieldwork*, ed. D. Wolf, 1–55. Boulder, CO: Westview.

NOTES

1   All names are pseudonyms.
2   As noted earlier, Alberta has one of the highest populations of immigrant Blacks. The African population is especially young, and although a significant number of adults were born in Canada, the majority left Africa after the mid-1980s.

Index

A

Abdi, Ali A., x, 14

Abolition Act (1793), 51

Aboriginal people, 26–27, 54, 77. *See also*
  First Nations
  civilizing mission, 98
  racism against, 97

Abyssinia, 178–79, 202n4

Abyssinians in Toronto, 183

academic freedom, 106
  and academic responsibility, 104
  at the expense of minorities, 105

academy, 15, 103
  Black scholars, 15
  Euro-Canadian/American dominance
    of, 103
  minority faculty and students, 103,
    106–7
  race, class, and gender in, 15, 96
  Western Canon, 67, 73, 75

*Act for the Preservation and Enhancement
  of Multiculturalism in Canada,* 25,
  100, 135, 143

Adler, Mortimer, 75

Afaan Oromo, 175, 195

Africa
  democracy, 179
  deteriorating economic and political
    factors, 55, 114, 130n3
  disease assumption, 35
  signifying enslavement, 190
  socio-cultural changes, 167

Africadey, 155

African-born immigrants, 6, 26, 50, 117.
    See also African-Canadians
  average earnings, 116, 119
  Canadian labour market, 115
  contrast with North American Blacks, 7
  earnings compared to Canadian born,
    16, 126–27
  education level, 8, 16, 116, 126, 211
  increasing numbers of, 4, 113
  lack of research on, 5
  low return on education, 101, 115,
    126–27, 153
  medical examinations, 35–36
  professionals seeking better conditions,
    55
  varying motives for emigration, 4

African-born immigrants (men)
  earnings, 115, 119
  estimated returns to university degrees,
    124
  in high-skilled occupations, 117
  in low-skilled occupations, 118
  probability of high-skilled
    employment, 125

African-born immigrants (women). *See
    also* African-Canadians (women)
  average earnings, 115
  bridge between African and diasporic
    communities, 206
  estimated returns to university degrees,
    124
  following husbands, 206
  in high-skilled occupations, 118
  information about life in Canada, 143
  in low-skilled occupations, 118, 143
  marginalization, 144
  probability of high-skilled
    employment, 126
  refugees, 206

African-Canadian, 7, 9, 70
  authors' definition of term, 12
  complex and contested concept, 6
  identity, 10, 33

African-Canadians, 27. *See also* African-
    born immigrants; Black-
    Canadians
  citizenship, 13
  clashes with state institution, 40
  connections with societies of origin
      (*See* diaspora communities)
  creolization, 153
  econometric analysis, 16
  entitlement to Canadian citizenship, 96

points system, 16, 33, 36, 114
   unstated assumptions, 35
Canadian multiculturalism policies, 13,
      26–27, 100, 134, 206
   Multicultural Act, 25, 100, 135, 143
Canadian reality, 58
Canadian schools, 40, 63–83. *See also*
      curricula; education
   dropouts, 102
   failure to address needs of African
      students, 66
Canadian work experience, 128, 136, 211
canon debate, 67, 83
Caribana, 58
Caribbean Blacks, 7, 50, 55, 98–99
   students, 102
Caribbean/Latin Americans
   average earnings, 115
   educational levels, 116
   probability of high-skilled
      occupations, 127
Carifête, 58
Cariwest, 58
"Casualties" (Clarke), 59
celebrations, 156
   festivals, 58, 155
Charter of Rights and Freedoms, 25, 38,
      100, 143
Chautauquan, 52
chieftaincy, 156
child rearing
   African strategies, 40
   suppositions of abuse, 40
childcare subsidies, 142
Christianity, 178
   African as the evil Other, 177
citizenship, 6, 13, 96, 187, 207
   authentic, 41
   formal *vs.* informal, 32
   interconnected with identity, 208
   tension with nationality, 186
   vis-à-vis home countries, 168
Citizenship of Zimbabwe Act, 168
civil rights movement, 55
Clarke, George E., "Casualties," 59
Co-operative Commonwealth Federation
      (CCF), 52
Codjoe, Henry M., x, 14

colonialism, 179
Commons, John R., 52
communism, 180
   anti-communism, 178
community attachment, 32
community life
   African women in Alberta, 214–16
"Confronting a History of Exclusion"
      (Kong), 84
consciousness raising, 96
constructionist discourse, 187
   on be-longing, 181–82
continental African immigration. *See*
      African-born immigrants
countries of origin. *See* home countries
criminal justice, 57, 99
critical and postmodern theorists, 71
critical ethnography, 210
critical feminist scholarship, 19
cross-national civil society, 162
culture, 96. *See also* language and culture
   African cultural products in Canada,
      156
   Anthias' three dimensions of, 152
   backward cultures, 39–40
   Black American, 8
   chieftaincy, 156
   cultural disconnect, 166–67
   cultural globalization, 167
   cultural institutions, 31
   cultural remittance, 152
   ethno-specific cultural establishments,
      156
   Eurocentric culture as the tacit norm,
      100
   formality, 167
   home-cultural expectations, 69
   hybrids of African and Canadian, 17,
      150, 186, 208
   link to ancestors, 153
   simplification of, 42
   sovereign power of African culture, 11
   Western culture, 208
culture wars, 67
curricula, 63–83, 104
   absence of African studies, 79
   absence of Black knowledge, 65, 79
   bias, 67

Blacks as slaves, not as accomplished
people, 80
democratization and diversity in, 84
eurocentrism, 76–77
exclusion of Black students, 66
exclusionary history, 82–83
First Nations in, 104
hegemony of the dominant classes,
14–15, 64, 66, 80–81
hidden, 83
institutional racism, 14–15
marginal, 103
monocultural content, 82
push for reform, 73–74
racism, 76, 83
"sin of omission," 77–78, 80, 82

D

Da Costa, Matthew, 50
daycare. *See* child rearing
"Deadly Ebola Virus May Be in Canada,"
35
Dei, George S., x, 15
democratic political systems
Oromo *gadaa*, 178–79
diaspora
contemporary meaning, 4
diaspora communities
contribution to socio-economic
development in home
countries, 167
home-diaspora links, 18, 151, 157–58,
162–63, 169, 189
lobbying of host governments, 164, 166
mobilizing for causes in homeland,
164–65
remittances to home countries, 159
diaspora politics, 170
diasporization of civil society, 164
discrimination, 14, 16, 33, 57, 119, 139
anti-discrimination legislation, 143
labour market discrimination, 16–17, 37
workplace, 15–16, 98, 126, 143
disidentification, 180
dispersal-affinity, 19, 182, 195–96
distance shrinking technology, 162
domestic politics
deterritorialization, 18–19

double consciousness, 166
Douglas, James, 54
*Draft Report on the Education of Black
Students in Toronto Schools,* 81
dual citizenship, 168–69
DuBois, W.E.B., 75
Dunbar, Paul Laurence, 58

E

e-mail. *See* Internet
Economy and Society (Weber), 28
Edmonton, 58, 68
banning of Blacks, 53
Edmonton Immigrant Services
Association, 210
education, 43, 54–55, 115, 211. *See also*
academy; curricula
African-born immigrants, 8, 16, 116,
126
African-Canadian students, 63–83
barriers, 135, 137
Canadian education and training, 138
correlation with employment, 135,
137
Euro-centred approaches to learning,
95, 104
foreign credentials, 126–28, 134, 137,
143
instructors of colour, 103
racism in, 94
returns in socioeconomic status, 101,
115, 127, 153
upward mobility, 212
value of, 16, 69
elderly people
African views on, 153
Employment Equity Act, 143
Encyclopedia Britannica, 75
Enlightenment, 85
as source of modern racism, 74
equalizing the playing field, 39
essentialist view (of Africans), 67
essentialized ideal of home, 18
Ethiopia, 18, 178–79, 182–83, 202n4
communism, 180
discursive continuity in Canadian
imagination, 184
ethnic associations, 160

essentialized ideal of, 18
  identity and homeland, 219–20
  imagined homelands, 209
home countries, 150–51
home country politics, 163
home diaspora links. *See under* diaspora
  communities
homeland identity, 20
Hoo Kong, 81–82
  "Confronting a History of Exclusion,"
  84
host society, 150, 152
How Jews Became White Folks (Brodkin), 9
human capital, 116
human capital theory, 16, 125, 127
human rights, 98–99
Hume, David, 75
Hutus, 163

I

identity, 8, 28–29, 32, 150, 157, 181, 207
  Black American, 8
  citizenship and, 208
  government policies and, 33
  and homeland, 219–20
  hybrid, 17, 150, 186, 208
  hyphenated, 40, 42
  impact of power on, 32
  and knowledge production, 101
  link to be-longing, 182
  racial, 9
  theoretical political basis of, 13
"imagined communities," 207
Immigration Act (1953), 113
Immigration Act (1967), 25
Immigration Act of 1978, 114
immigration as source of skills and
  knowledge, 10, 114. *See also*
  points system
Immigration Authorities approach to
  Africanness, 6
Imperial Order of the Daughters of the
  Empire, 54
in-between spaces, 166
in-between status, 150, 154
*In Search of Identity, Longing for
  Homelands,* 206

Independence Day celebrations, 154–55
independent-class immigrants, 16, 141
Indigenous populations. *See also*
  Aboriginal people; First Nations
  land and resources, 97
individual freedom, 105
institutional multiculturalism, 38–39
institutionalized racism, 49, 56, 97, 99
  obstacles to educational and
    professional goals, 97
intergenerational tensions, 19, 209, 211–
  12, 217–18
  parental influence, 69, 207
International Day for the Elimination of
  Racial Discrimination, 80
international labour market, 149
International Qualifications Assessment
  Services, 137
Internet, 160–62, 169
  connection to home cultures, 157
  Oromo youth spaces on, 193–94
invisibilization of Africans, 15, 82

J

Jamaicans, 190
  as *bad* Blacks, 187–88
James, Carl, 66
Japanese Canadians, 98
job satisfaction, 125
Johnson, Ben, 41

K

Kenya, 178
King, Martin Luther, 78
kinship affiliation, 29–31
knowledge, 37, 67, 69–70
  Black, 65
  as both subjective and objective, 71
  counter and oppositional forms of, 104
  devaluation of African knowledge and
    skills, 14
  Euro-Canadian/American dominance
    of, 103
  hegemonic, 70, 95
  hierarchization of, 36
  high-status knowledge, 83
  identity and knowledge production,
  101

AFRICA: MISSING VOICES SERIES

Donald I. Ray and Peter Shinnie, general editors issn 1703-1826

University of Calgary Press has a long history of publishing academic works on Africa. Africa: Missing Voices illuminates issues and topics concerning Africa that have been ignored or are missing from current global debates. This series will fill a gap in African scholarship by addressing concerns that have been long overlooked in political, social, and historical discussions about this continent.

Grassroots Governance?: Chiefs in Africa and the Afro-Caribbean
Edited by D.I. Ray and P.S. Reddy · Copublished with the International Association of Schools and Institutes of Administration (IASIA) · No. 1

The African Diaspora in Canada: Negotiating Identity and Belonging
Edited by Wisdom Tettey and Korbla Puplampu · No. 2

A Common Hunger: Land Rights in Canada and South Africa
Written by Joan G. Fairweather · No. 3